Polish-Soviet Relations, 1932-1939

EAST CENTRAL EUROPEAN STUDIES

OF COLUMBIA UNIVERSITY

Polish-Soviet Relations
1932-1939

BY BOHDAN B. BUDUROWYCZ

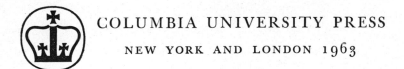

COLUMBIA UNIVERSITY PRESS
NEW YORK AND LONDON 1963

East Central European Studies of Columbia University

The East Central European Studies, a companion series to the Studies of the Russian Institute, comprise scholarly books prepared under the auspices of the Program on East Central Europe of Columbia University or through other divisions of the University. The publication of these studies is designed to enlarge our understanding of an important region of the world, which, because of its relative inaccessibility in recent years as well as because of the linguistic problems it presents, has been somewhat neglected in serious academic study. The faculty of the Program on East Central Europe, without necessarily endorsing the conclusions reached by the authors, believe that these studies contribute substantially to knowledge of the area and should serve to stimulate further inquiry and research.

East Central European Studies

TO MY PARENTS

Preface

The purpose of the present study is to trace the course of Polish-Soviet relations from the conclusion of the nonaggression pact between the two nations in July, 1932, until the fourth partition of Poland in September, 1939, and to assess the nature of that relationship. Poland's dealings with countries other than the Soviet Union have been treated only in so far as they affected her relations with the USSR. References to the domestic policies of either country have been omitted unless they had an immediate bearing upon the subject implied in the title; consequently, no attempt has been made to discuss in any detail the problem of the non-Polish national groups in eastern Poland or the activities of the Communist Party of Poland, but the reader is referred in the footnotes and in the bibliography to the copious literature on these subjects.

The book is based mostly on contemporary sources, including official documents, memoirs, news dispatches, and articles in periodicals of various shades of opinion published in Polish, Russian, and the chief Western European languages. Special attention has been paid to the materials scattered in various Polish émigré publications and to the files of Soviet and Polish newspapers which appeared during the period under investigation. My bibliography is largely selective; it can be supplemented by many articles and pamphlets of lesser significance listed in the *Bibliographie zur Aussenpolitik der Republik Polen, 1919-1939, und zum Feldzug in Polen, 1939* (Bibliographische Vierteljahreshefte der Weltkriegsbücherei, Heft 33; 2d ed., Stuttgart, 1943), as well as by numerous items in the *Bibliography of Books in Polish or*

Relating to Poland Published Outside Poland since September 1st, 1939 (2 vols., London, 1954-59), compiled by Janina Zabielska. The system of transliteration follows that of the Library of Congress, with some minor modifications: diacritical marks have been omitted, and established English usage has been observed in the spelling of well-known Russian proper names.

I am happy to acknowledge my indebtedness to Professor Henry L. Roberts, Director of the Program on East Central Europe, Columbia University, who supervised the work on the original dissertation, gave freely of his time in reading, amending, and commenting on the manuscript, and was chiefly responsible for making possible its publication in book form. Professor Oscar Halecki, of Fordham and Columbia universities, also proved most helpful in his thoughtful criticism and encouragement. I am grateful to Professor Alexander Dallin, Director of the Russian Institute, Columbia University, Professor Zygmunt J. Gąsiorowski, of the University of California at Berkeley, and Professor John H. Wuorinen, of Columbia University, for their careful reading of the manuscript and for numerous constructive suggestions. Among the former diplomats in the service of the Polish Republic who responded to my inquiries and volunteered to furnish useful information on many important issues, I should like to mention the late Ambassador Wacław Grzybowski, Professor Tadeusz Romer, of McGill University, and Ambassador Michał Sokolnicki, of Ankara, Turkey. I owe a debt of gratitude to Miss Louise E. Luke, of the Russian Institute, Columbia University, for her invaluable assistance in the preparation of the final version of this volume and for her kindness and patience in answering my numerous queries. My editor, Mr. William F. Bernhardt, was always ready to help me with his competent advice and guidance. Dr. Victor Turek, Director of the Polish Research Institute in Canada, facilitated my work by providing me with important bibliographical data. My special word of thanks goes to the staffs of the libraries and institutions from whom I received assistance in the task of research and writing, notably to the librarians and archivists of the Columbia University Libraries, the Slavonic Division of the New York Public Library, the Library of Congress, the National Archives, the Harry Elkins Widener Memorial Library, the University of Toronto Library, the Polish Institute of Arts and Sciences in America, the Józef Piłsudski Institute of America, and the Kościuszko Foundation. I am much obliged to Professor Ludwik Krzyżanowski, the editor of *The Polish Review*, as well as to Professor G. S. N. Luckyj and the University of Toronto Press, the editor and the publishers of *Canadian Slavonic Papers*, for their permission to use some material from my articles which appeared in those two periodicals. I would like to thank Oxford University Press for permission to reproduce the map of the Polish partition from *The War in Maps* by Francis Brown and Emil Herlin (copyright 1942 by Oxford University Press). I also extend my sincere appreciation and thanks to the Ford Foundation, under whose auspices I began the work on the present study, and to the Program on East Central Europe, Columbia University, whose generous financial assistance enabled me to complete my research and made possible the publication of this book; obviously, neither of them is responsible for the author's views, opinions, and errors of judgment.

Toronto, Canada   BOHDAN B. BUDUROWYCZ
June, 1962

Contents

Map

Polish-Soviet Relations, 1932-1939

Key to Abbreviations

DBFP	Great Britain. Foreign Office. Documents on British Foreign Policy, 1919-1939.
DGFP	Germany. Auswärtiges Amt. Documents on German Foreign Policy, 1918-1945.
Polish White Book	Poland. Ministerstwo Spraw Zagranicznych. Official Documents Concerning Polish-German and Polish-Soviet Relations, 1933-1939.
USFR	United States. Department of State. Foreign Relations of the United States.

I. The Nonaggression Pact

The Polish-Soviet conflict of 1919-20 ended in a stalemate. Both the ambitious plans for a world revolution cherished by fanatic Communist doctrinaires and the visionary projects of Polish federalists were replaced by realistic bargaining at a conference table. The Soviet attempt to make Poland a bridge to Western Europe was blocked, and Moscow's dreams about the collapse of the entire system of Versailles proved premature. While both sides regarded the Riga Treaty as a provisional arrangement, it undoubtedly brought a certain degree of stability to the whole war-torn area of Eastern and East Central Europe. Now, in the words of Churchill, "the 'Sanitary Cordon' which protected Europe from the Bolshevik infection was formed by living national organisms vigorous in themselves, hostile to the disease and immune through experience to its ravages."[1]

The years immediately following the signature of the peace treaty were marked by a continuous state of tension between Poland and Russia. War scares flared up periodically on both sides of the frontier and seemed to indicate that an armed clash might occur at any moment;[2] often, however, the rumors about an impending conflict were used as a means of diverting attention from the internal troubles of the two countries. Measures initiated by both governments to improve this explosive situation eventually led to the establishment of formal diplomatic relations between Moscow and Warsaw and to the signature of the protocol of Octo-

---

[1] Churchill, *The Aftermath*, p. 276.

[2] See *Survey of International Affairs*, 1920-23, pp. 227-29. The state of insecurity was sustained by frequent raids of armed bands across the Polish-Soviet frontier. These incursions came to an end only after both Poland and the USSR created special military formations with the specific purpose of protecting their boundaries.

ber 7, 1921, which contained a mutually acceptable timetable for carrying out the provisions of the Riga settlement.[3] At the same time, the requirements of everyday contacts between the two neighbors hastened the conclusion of several technical agreements and conventions.

This brief pacific interval was interrupted by another period of strife, during which Polish efforts to forge a solid bloc of the border states were effectively countered by Russian moves to deprive Poland of her desired role as leader and protector of the Baltic republics. The Treaty of Rapallo, which paved the way for cooperation between Germany and Russia, Poland's two inveterate enemies, showed that Moscow had no intention of abandoning its attitude of hostility toward Warsaw.[4] Nevertheless, attempts to normalize the situation along the *cordon sanitaire* continued. In the spring of 1922 the representatives of Estonia, Latvia, Poland, and the RSFSR met informally at Riga to discuss a project of limitation of armaments, and declared in favor of a scheme which envisaged the formation of demilitarized zones along their mutal frontiers. At the Moscow Disarmament Conference in December of the same year, the delegations of the border states announced their readiness to negotiate about arms reduction on the condition that the Soviet government sign a multilateral nonaggression convention with its Baltic neighbors and Poland. The conference ended in a failure, chiefly owing to Russia's insistence that the disarmament scheme should be discussed simultaneously with a nonaggression declaration. The situation became even more strained when the RSFSR and the Ukrainian SSR renewed their protests against the anti-Soviet activities of the Russian and Ukrainian émigrés in Poland and challenged the impending decision of the Conference of Ambassadors to recognize Poland's eastern frontiers.[5]

[3] See USSR, Ministerstvo Inostrannykh Del, *Dokumenty vneshnei politiki SSSR*, IV, 394-96. In spite of this arrangement, the stipulations of the peace treaty were executed only partially and with considerable delay.

[4] The interests of Berlin and Moscow in the Polish question did not always coincide. As Z. J. Gąsiorowski observes, the revision of the frontier with Poland was a vital issue for Germany, but only of secondary importance for the USSR; consequently, Russia's Polish policy "could and did show a flexibility which time and again disturbed and vexed the Germans." "Stresemann and Poland after Locarno," *Journal of Central European Affairs*, XVIII, No. 3 (Oct., 1958), 296.

[5] For the text of the Soviet notes see Kliuchnikov and Sabanin, eds., Part III, Vol.

In the summer of 1923, when the Ruhr crisis was becoming increasingly threatening, Moscow made an unsuccessful attempt at persuading Poland and the Baltic states to sign a pledge with the USSR to maintain a neutral attitude toward Germany. Although Warsaw showed some interest in coming to terms with Russia, its project of a general East European guarantee treaty was regarded by the Kremlin as a scheme to establish Poland's hegemony over Latvia, Estonia, and Finland.[6] The Soviet government made, therefore, several overtures to Berlin and suggested that joint German-Russian pressure be brought to bear upon Warsaw with the purpose of pushing Poland back to her ethnic frontiers. At first, these negotiations seemed to progress satisfactorily, but Russia's hopes were frustrated by Stresemann's cautious approach and by the developing rapprochement between Germany and the Western powers. Moscow tried to save the situation by directing its energies toward the creation of a system of neutrality and nonaggression pacts as a "counterattraction" to the arbitration and security treaties negotiated at Locarno. In a sudden display of "good will" toward Poland, Foreign Commissar Chicherin visited Warsaw on the very eve of the Locarno Conference. The timing of this visit emphasized its importance in the general European situation, and Chicherin was quick to point out that the conclusion of a lasting agreement between Poland and the USSR would have a profound influence upon the whole international complex of forces and relations.[7] However, while Moscow was willing to agree not to violate the status quo in Eastern

---

I, pp. 235-38; English translation in Degras, ed., I, 458. It should be noted that, by the Treaty of Riga, the RSFSR and the Ukrainian SSR abandoned "all rights and claims" to the territories ceded to Poland. In December, 1923, and in November, 1926, Moscow reaffirmed that it had no intention of placing in doubt the provisions of the peace treaty with regard to the frontier between Poland and the USSR; at the same time, however, the Kremlin insisted that it could not accept as final the situation established as a result of the decisions of third powers and specifically claimed that the issue of Eastern Galicia continued to be an unsettled international problem.

[6] See USSR, Tsentral'nyi Ispolnitel'nyi Komitet, *Sozyv III, Sessiia II, Stenograficheskii otchët* [Third Convocation, Second Session, Stenographic Minutes] (Moscow, 1926), p. 1060; English text in Degras, II, 112. For Polish reaction see Zaleski, pp. 25-26.

[7] USSR, *III S"ezd Sovetov, Stenograficheskii otchët* [Third Congress of Soviets, Stenographic Minutes] (Moscow, 1925), p. 89; English translation in Degras, II, 37.

Europe, it refused to modify its position with regard to the Baltic problem and to give up its claim to Bessarabia.

This gradual process of pacification was disrupted temporarily as a result of Piłsudski's coup d'état in May, 1926, but widespread apprehensions that the Marshal would at once adopt a defiant and hostile policy toward Russia failed to materialize.[8] The new helmsman steered Poland's course in a cautious way, warily watching for dangers and risks ahead. The European situation had radically changed since 1920, international relations were stabilized, and Poland was evidently too weak, both militarily and economically, to challenge the growing power of the Soviet Union, even though Piłsudski regarded with some uneasiness the German-Russian agreement of April 24, 1926, which represented a further strengthening of the Rapallo connection. No less objectionable was the exchange of notes between Moscow and Kaunas, in which the USSR once more gave its full support to Lithuania in the Wilno (Vilnius) dispute.[9]

In August, 1926, a draft Polish-Russian nonaggression treaty was submitted to Foreign Minister Zaleski by Soviet envoy Voikov. Its main ideas were a mutual obligation to refrain from any aggressive action, a reciprocal guarantee of neutrality in case of an attack against either of the signatories by a third power, a pledge to enter into no political and economic agreements directed against the other party, and an arrangement to have all disputes settled by a mixed conciliation court.[10] In October of the same year the Polish government agreed to open negotiations, but the proposed draft met with a cool reception in Warsaw.[11]

[8] According to *Kommunisticheskii Internatsional*, Piłsudski's seizure of power signalized the danger of an adventurous policy on Poland's part and could lead to a state of undeclared war between Moscow and Warsaw (VIII, No. 8 [Aug., 1926], 15). See also Laroche, p. 36.

[9] In Litvinov's words, the real objective of the USSR was to "deter Lithuania from coming to an understanding with Poland." See the files of the Auswärtiges Amt in the National Archives, Washington, container 2317, serial 4562H, frames 157794-98.

[10] *Izvestiia*, Aug. 28, 1926. At the same time Moscow hastened to assure the Germans that, since Poland was certain to reject the Soviet overtures, she would be "unmasked" and isolated in the eyes of public opinion. Auswärtiges Amt, frames E157810-13.

[11] As Zaleski put it, Russia was offering Poland "a Rapallo, a bilateral agreement . . . excluding the application of the Covenant of the League of Nations"; what Poland wanted, however, was "a Locarno," inspired by loyalty toward the League. *Osteuropa*, II (1926-27), 119. According to the Polish deputy foreign minister, the Soviet offer "was all bluff and an expression of Russian two-facedness." Auswärtiges Amt, frame E157836.

While Piłsudski was quite prepared to eliminate "trifling everyday frictions" and to settle at least some of the outstanding "practical problems" affecting Polish-Soviet relations, he did not
believe in the possibility of a large-scale *détente* with Russia at
that time.[12] Moscow's insistence on signing separate treaties with
the Poles and with the Baltic states was interpreted in the Polish
press as an attempt to isolate Poland; on the other hand, Soviet
propaganda continued to accuse the old Marshal of harboring
ambitions to "create an unbroken chain of states from Rumania
to Finland" which would negotiate with the USSR "through Poland and with Poland's help."[13]

The conversations between Moscow and Warsaw came to an
abrupt end as a result of Voikov's assassination in June, 1927,
which was alleged by the Soviet government to be part of a world-
wide international plot aimed at provoking foreign intervention
against Russia.[14] This incident cast long shadows on Polish-Soviet
relations. The Kremlin's remedy was simple, though far from
adequate. In December, 1928, Maksim Litvinov, then deputy
foreign commissar of the USSR, proposed to Poland the signing
of a protocol which would bring into force the Kellogg-Briand
Pact for the renunciation of war between the Soviet Union, Poland, and Lithuania without waiting for the completion of the
process of its ratification by other states. The Polish government
expressed its desire to extend the protocol by the inclusion of all
Baltic states and Rumania, and Russia accepted this condition.[15]
On February 9, 1929, the so-called Litvinov Protocol was signed
in Moscow by the representatives of Estonia, Latvia, Poland, Rumania, and the USSR; it was open for the accession of other countries, but only Danzig, Lithuania, Persia, and Turkey decided to
join the original five signatories. This accord formed a useful
political device for securing the western frontiers of the Soviet
Union, but the absence of any sanctions made its enforcement
problematic.[16]

The signing of the protocol had no perceptible effect on Polish-

[12] Beck, *Final Report*, p. 3.
[13] USSR, *IV S"ezd Sovetov, Stenograficheskii otchët* (Moscow, 1927), p. 26; English
translation in Degras, II, 190.
[14] Kliuchnikov and Sabanin, p. 385.
[15] See Sabanin, ed., pp. 3-10.
[16] See Hartlieb, pp. 51-52.

Soviet relations, and each side blamed the other for "departing" from the spirit of the agreement.[17] During the fall of 1929 the "cold war" between Moscow and Warsaw was intensified, and Litvinov's pessimistic speech before the Central Executive Committee of the USSR in December of that year tried to shift the blame to the Polish side.[18] Apprehensions that the persistent state of tension might eventually develop into open conflict were aggravated during the spring and summer of 1930, when rumors of an impending Polish-Russian war assumed such dimensions that Foreign Minister Zaleski was forced to deny them in an official statement. At the same time he stressed that a consistent effort to expand and deepen Warsaw's political and economic contacts with Moscow constituted one of the most important elements of Polish foreign policy.[19] This declaration of good will was later amplified by additional assurances that the Poles would try to maintain the best possible relations with their eastern neighbor;[20] however, the skeptical stand taken by Poland with regard to the Russian proposals submitted to the preparatory commission on disarmament incurred the Kremlin's disapproval and prompted Molotov to make some critical remarks concerning Warsaw's general attitude toward the Soviet Union.[21]

It was only the beginning of the Franco-Russian negotiations in May, 1931, that led to a gradual improvement of Polish-Soviet relations. There was, as yet, no visible reversal of Moscow's foreign policy, but some signs of change could be already detected in the decline of the partnership between Russia and the Weimar Republic and in a certain lessening of the Kremlin's hostility toward the Western powers. The Japanese aggression in Manchuria necessitated a radical change in the deployment of the Red Army and prompted the USSR to mend its fences in Europe.

[17] USSR, *V S"ezd Sovetov, Stenograficheskii otchët* (Moscow, 1929), Biulleten' No. 1, p. 28; English translation in Degras, II, 377.

[18] USSR, Tsentral'nyi Ispolnitel'nyi Komitet, *Sozyv V, Sessiia II, Stenograficheskii otchët* (Moscow, 1929), Biulleten' No. 14, p. 17; English translation in Degras, II, 383.

[19] *Izvestiia*, Jan. 11 and 16, 1931.

[20] *Ibid.*, Feb. 14, 1931.

[21] USSR, *VI S"ezd Sovetov, Stenograficheskii otchët* (Moscow, 1931), Biulleten' No. 1, p. 35; English translation in Degras, II, 478.

Besides, the tension which developed during the forced collecti-
vization and the struggle for the fulfillment of the goals of the
First Five-Year Plan compelled the Soviet rulers to concentrate
their attention on internal affairs and required, whenever possible, a relaxation in the field of foreign relations. On their part
the Poles, disturbed by an increase of revisionist tendencies in Germany[22] and afraid of Russo-German collusion, were now prepared to meet Moscow halfway and to assure themselves a free
hand in the west, the more so since their Baltic neighbors were
becoming increasingly clamorous in their demands for a nonaggression pact with the USSR. Poland was already beginning to
feel the full effect of the depression, with its overwhelming sense
of bewilderment, confusion, and loss of direction, and this economic impasse forced Piłsudski to avoid any risks in the game of
international politics.[23] Moreover, the period of French ascendancy in Europe was coming to an end, and the Poles could no
longer expect that their alliance with the Third Republic would
guarantee their security. The situation called for a reappraisal of
Warsaw's attitude toward its two powerful neighbors. While no
strong hopes could be entertained for an immediate settlement
of Poland's differences with Germany, the old Marshal, who had
been trying unsuccessfully for years to reach an understanding

[22] On the growth of German revisionist propaganda after 1930 see Breyer, pp. 28-
30; the increase of tension in German-Polish relations in 1931-32 is discussed in detail
by H. Roos in his *Polen und Europa*, pp. 37-44. In this connection see Colonel
Miedziński's account of his conversation with Beck, held shortly after Hitler's bel-
ligerent speech in Beuthen on April 18, 1932, where the future Polish Foreign Minister is quoted as saying: "As far as the events in Germany are concerned, we have to
take into account the possibility of a serious encounter there. Our *détente* with
Russia is the necessary prelude. Besides, the Western world thinks that we are
squeezed between two hostile powers like between the arms of a pair of pincers. . . .
We must demonstrate that we are able to pry those pincers open." B. Miedziński,
"Popioły są jeszcze gorące" [The Ashes Are Still Hot], *Wiadomości* (London), Oct.
26, 1952.
[23] Poland was hit by the depression harder than any of her neighbors. The economic crisis affected both industry and agriculture. Unemployment almost doubled
between the end of 1928 and the end of 1933, while the output of industrial production
declined from 136.2 in December, 1928 (1927 = 100), to 92.3 in February, 1931. See
Dziewanowski, *The Communist Party of Poland*, pp. 133, 334. The plight of the
village, where unemployment was rampant even during the postwar prosperity, became all but desperate, mainly because of a rapid decline in the prices of agricultural
products.

with Berlin, could now strengthen his bargaining position by playing the Russian card.[24]

Formal steps to renew the discussions between Poland and the USSR were taken on August 23, 1931, when the Polish minister to Moscow delivered to the Narkomindel a new draft of the nonaggression treaty which again envisaged the participation of the Baltic states and Rumania.[25] The Russians questioned, however, Warsaw's sincerity, and described this offer as an attempt to strengthen Poland's international position "by assertions of a *détente* in Polish-Soviet relations"; therefore, as Litvinov confided to the Lithuanian envoy, the Soviet government was "not at present inclined to embark on negotiations."[26] The official answer of the Kremlin to the Polish proposal was contained in the Tass communiqué of August 27, which regretted the failure of the Poles to abandon their "unacceptable and irrelevant" conditions and stated bluntly that there was no reason for the resumption of talks.[27]

Despite this declaration, as well as the Narkomindel's assertions that Moscow had no incentive for a renewal of negotiations, efforts to reach an understanding were continued. A statement made by Foreign Minister Zaleski intimated that the Polish government was ready to sign a nonaggression pact with Russia "at any time."[28] It was answered, in turn, by Molotov's assurances that the USSR "desired to live in peace and friendship with all countries," and

[24] According to B. Jaworznicki, the Polish government was insincere in concluding the nonaggression pact with the USSR and intended to use its "sham rapprochement" with Russia as a bargaining point in future negotiations with Germany. "Polsko-radziecki pakt o nieagresji z r. 1932," *Sprawy Międzynarodowe,* V, No. 5 (Sept.-Oct., 1952), 76. A similar opinion has been expressed by G. Jaszuński in his commentary to the Polish edition of Beck's memoirs (*Pamiętniki Józefa Becka,* p. 41) and by A. Ia. Manusevich in the chapter on the Polish-Soviet nonaggression pact in Akademiia Nauk SSSR, Institut Slavianovedeniia, *Istoriia Pol'shi,* III, 348-49.

[25] *Kurjer Warszawski,* Aug. 25, 1931. It seems that this offer had been preceded by certain feelers put forth by Western diplomats who wished to mediate between Poland and the USSR. These offers were rejected by the Russians, who indicated that they were capable of conducting their relations with Warsaw "directly and without the intervention of a third power"; they also refused to negotiate with Poland "as a member of a group." *DBFP,* 2d Series, VII (London, 1958), 217.

[26] *DBFP,* 2d Series, VII, 219.

[27] See *Izvestiia,* Aug. 27, 1931.

[28] *Kurjer Warszawski,* Oct. 30, 1931.

only wished that the deeds of the Polish leaders would match their words.[29] Meanwhile preliminary talks in Moscow were slowly gathering momentum. On October 14 Litvinov proposed to the Polish government that the wording of the pact to be concluded between the two countries should follow the draft of the Franco-Russian treaty which had been initialed on August 21, 1931. This proposal was repeated by the Soviet Foreign Commissar during his meeting with Polish Minister Patek early in November, but the Poles maintained that the Riga Treaty and the Moscow Protocol of 1929, as well as the "conditions of direct neighborhood," required a different basis for negotiating a pact between Poland and Russia.[30] At the same time, however, the Polish government agreed that the old Soviet draft, presented by Voikov to Zaleski in 1926, should serve as a basis for the negotiations.[31]

The Soviet sources were at first rather pessimistic and freely expressed their opinion that the talks were not likely to bear fruit in the near future. It seemed, indeed, very significant that *Pravda* chose this time to publish, without any comment, a manifesto of the Central Committee of the Communist Party of Poland to "the working people of the world," which openly charged the Polish government with bad faith:

The events in Manchuria have revived the anti-Soviet policy of Polish fascism and its preparation for war. Mr. Zaleski is uttering from the tribune of the Sejm and the League of Nations hypocritical words about Poland's peaceful intentions toward the USSR, with which she allegedly wishes to sign a nonaggression pact. Not a word is being said, however, about the fact that immediately after Japan's invasion of

[29] *Izvestiia*, Nov. 12, 1931.

[30] *Kurjer Warszawski*, Nov. 23, 1931. The main stumbling block seems to have been Article V of the draft Franco-Soviet treaty which obliged each of the contracting parties to "abstain . . . from action of any kind calculated to promote or encourage agitation, propaganda or attempted intervention" directed against the other signatory; both parties also undertook not to "create, protect, equip, subsidize or admit" in their respective territories "military organizations for the purpose of armed combat with the other party" or groups "assuming the role of government or representing all or part of its territories." League of Nations, *Treaty Series*, CLVII, 419. This provision was unacceptable to Poland, which wanted to avoid constant Soviet interference in her internal affairs and was reluctant to curb the activities of such émigré bodies as the "government-in-exile" of the Ukrainian People's Republic.

[31] *Izvestiia*, Nov. 22, 1931; *Kurjer Warszawski*, Nov. 23, 1931.

Manchuria Piłsudski left for Bucharest in order to define more precisely, together with the Rumanian General Staff, the plans for their joint attack against the USSR.[32]

The official Soviet attitude toward the negotiations with Poland was curtly defined by Stalin in his interview with Emil Ludwig on December 13, 1931, in which the Russian dictator tried to appease the fears of German revisionists and to allay their suspicions that Moscow was prepared to guarantee Poland's territorial integrity:

I know that a certain dissatisfaction and alarm may be noticed among some German statesmen on the grounds that the Soviet Union . . . may take some step that would imply on the part of the Soviet Union a sanction, a guarantee, for Poland's possessions and frontiers. In my opinion such fears are mistaken. We have always declared our readiness to conclude a nonaggression pact with any state. . . . We have openly declared our readiness to sign such a pact with Poland, too. . . . As soon as the Poles declared that they were ready to negotiate . . . we naturally agreed and opened negotiations. . . . We, exactly like the Poles, must declare in the pact that we will not use force or resort to aggression in order to change the frontiers of Poland or the USSR, or violate their independence. Just as we make such a promise to the Poles, so they make the same promise to us. Without such a clause, namely, that we do not intend to go to war for the purpose of violating the independence or integrity of the frontiers of our respective states, no pact can be concluded. . . . Is this the recognition of the Versailles system? No. Or is it, perhaps, a guaranteeing of frontiers? No. We never have been guarantors of Poland and never shall become such, just as Poland has not been and will not be a guarantor of our frontiers.[33]

During the Moscow parleys Poland was represented by her minister to the USSR, Stanisław Patek, and by Tadeusz Schaetzel, the chief of the Eastern Department of the Foreign Ministry; the Soviet delegation was headed by Litvinov or, in his absence, by N. N. Krestinskii, acting people's commissar for foreign affairs. Both sides agreed to a compromise on the question of the participation of the Baltic states and Rumania, and accepted the principle of parallel, simultaneous, but separate negotiations, which

[32] *Pravda,* Dec. 5, 1931.   [33] Stalin, *Works,* XIII, 118-19.

were to lead eventually to the conclusion of "a chain of parallel and basically analogous treaties."[34] While Marshal Piłsudski showed little enthusiasm for the whole project and ridiculed "all those useless pacts, short-lived and worthless,"[35] his instructions to the Polish representatives in Moscow were sober and realistic. He regarded the proposed pact as an important political declaration rather than a simple legal document;[36] consequently, he was interested chiefly in its fundamental principles and paid less attention to the details. The Marshal wanted to avoid any possible contradiction between the provisions of the treaty and the obligations earlier assumed by Poland; he also did everything in his power to protect the interests of Russia's small neighbors by refusing to accept any vague definition of aggression. As a result of Piłsudski's insistence, the violation of the territory or the frontiers of one of the contracting parties was to become the key factor in determining the aggressor.

The hammering out of the provisions of the treaty took some time, not only because an agreement of this kind "required long negotiations and close consideration,"[37] but mostly owing to the excessive wariness of the Soviet representatives; besides, the talks were slowed down at the very beginning to allow the Baltic states to "keep in line" and to avail themselves of the precedents established in the negotiations between Poland and Russia.[38] Both sides tried hard to settle their differences while refusing at the same time to yield an inch on any of the issues involving the thorny points of national prestige. Finally, after all essential questions had been agreed upon, the Polish Foreign Office instructed its delegates "to cut short the talks even at the expense of abandoning some trifling point of law or some detail of wording."[39]

The text of the pact was initialed by Patek and Litvinov on January 25, 1932. While the negotiations had been in progress, the Polish press gradually modulated its sharply anti-Soviet tone. References to the possibility of closer political and economic ties with the USSR were slowly replacing acrimonious attacks, and the parliamentary opposition expressed itself with increasing effectiveness in favor of a Polish-Soviet rapprochement. Now pub-

[34] Beck, *Final Report*, p. 8.   [35] Laroche, p. 106.   [36] Beck, *Final Report*, p. 9.
[37] *Ibid.*, p. 7.   [38] *Ibid.*, p. 9.   [39] *Ibid.*, p. 10.

lic opinion in Poland was unanimous in welcoming the initialing of the treaty, hailing it as an important event in the pacification of Eastern Europe and as an outward sign of the community of Polish-Russian interests. As *Kurjer Warszawski* put it,

It would be pointless to conceal the fact that we are sincerely gratified. . . . There had been enough time to think things over and to digest thoroughly the whole problem. If today . . . the project is being realized, this must be regarded as a sign of persistent good will on both sides. It is, for the moment, of no interest to us what considerations prompted the Moscow government to this step. As far as Poland is concerned, the essence of the whole issue consists in the fact that Moscow desires peace on its western frontiers. Is it compelled by economic reasons to seek an agreement with France, or is it simply safeguarding its position in Europe because of its preoccupation with the Far East? Has it some plans to submit to the disarmament conference at Geneva, or is it afraid that the advance of Hitlerism might jeopardize the fruits of Rapallo? One can indulge in the most diversified speculations concerning this vast topic, but the fact remains the same: Soviet policy in Europe desires peace. Since Poland, too, wants peace and must wage a policy of peace, since she has no aggressive designs against Soviet Russia, the nonaggression pact recently initialed has all the features of a really valuable agreement.[40]

These sentiments were not entirely shared by Moscow, as was shown by the wary, noncommittal tone of Litvinov's official statement of January 25 and by the restrained reaction of the Soviet press which took pains to stress that the USSR had no intention of "making fetish of these pacts" and that political agreement of any kind could contribute to a relaxation of international tension only if the contracting parties "feared no peaceful obligations" and pursued "no indirect aims."[41] The Kremlin was obviously annoyed by the fact that the Polish-Soviet treaty was to remain in abeyance until the successful completion of the Russo-Rumanian negotiations, conducted since early January in Riga.[42] Nonaggression pacts had been concluded by the USSR with

[40] *Kurjer Warszawski,* Jan. 27, 1932.
[41] *Izvestiia,* Jan. 24 and 26, 1932. For a discussion of Moscow's attitude toward the issue of nonaggression pacts see "Soviet Treaties of Neutrality and Non-Aggression, 1931-1932," *Bulletin of International News,* VIII, No. 20 (March 31, 1932), 543-48.
[42] See Hartlieb, pp. 91-93.

Finland, Latvia, and Estonia, but no progress whatever had been registered on the way to a rapprochement between Moscow and Bucharest, owing chiefly to Russia's reluctance to recognize, even by implication, Rumania's annexation of Bessarabia. Rumanian Foreign Minister Ghica visited Warsaw in January to give the Polish leaders a firsthand account of his government's point of view, and his hosts apparently tried to persuade him that their two countries should show more independence in settling their mutual affairs and pay less attention to the wishes of Paris, where a violent campaign against the policy of rapprochement with the USSR was being conducted at that time by the conservative circles.[43] Shortly after this visit Polish Deputy Foreign Minister Beck intervened personally in the negotiations and arranged a meeting betwen Litvinov and Rumanian Minister to Warsaw Cadere.[44]

The Polish government was obviously interested in the prompt conclusion of a Russo-Rumanian pact; at that time, however, even the future of the Polish-Soviet treaty appeared dark as a result of the arrest and trial of two suspects charged with the attempted murder of a counselor of the German Embassy in Moscow. The Soviet press claimed that a person allegedly employed by the Polish Foreign Ministry was responsible for the "conspiracy" and accused "individuals hiding in Polish diplomatic uniforms" of directing terroristic plots on Russian territory.[45] This outburst of indignation proved short-lived and was not followed by any further action, but it convinced the Poles that it was advisable to lose no time in regulating their relations with the Soviet Union. Now it was becoming increasingly clear that Poland would sign her pact with the USSR despite the fact that this independent action was likely to weaken the ties of friendship between Bucharest and Warsaw. Another attempt to help the Russians and the Rumanians in patching up their differences by offering them the services of a Polish mediator ended in failure, and diplomatic pressure exercised with great skill and patience by Beck and

[43] Beck, *Dernier rapport*, pp. 282-83 (this edition contains important appendixes and other materials not included in the English translation quoted above).

[44] Beck, *Final Report*, p. 9.

[45] *Pravda*, April 7, 1932. For the reaction of the Polish press see *Kurjer Warszawski*, April 7-8, 1932.

Count Szembek[46] during their personal meetings with the Rumanian officials proved of no avail.[47] While the Rumanian government assured Warsaw that it had no objections to the conclusion of a Polish-Soviet pact, it started at the same time a delaying action, asking the French to discourage Poland from any undue haste, and reportedly received assurances from Paris that the Poles would not sign any treaty without the consent of their allies.[48] A part of the French press also gave vent to its displeasure and bitterly accused the Polish leaders of having betrayed the interests of Western civilization.[49] All these efforts, including a desperate last-minute appeal of Rumanian envoy Cadere to Marshal Piłsudski, remained fruitless, and the Polish-Soviet pact was duly signed in Moscow on July 25, 1932, by Stanisław Patek for Poland and N. N. Krestinskii for the USSR.[50]

The two governments reaffirmed their wish to maintain the existing state of peace between their countries and stated that the Treaty of Riga constituted the basis of their reciprocal relations and undertakings.[51] They renounced war as an instrument of national policy in their mutual relations and promised to "refrain from taking any aggressive action against or invading the territory of the other party, either alone or in conjunction with other powers." In addition to this, each of the contracting parties bound itself to remain neutral if the other signatory became a victim of aggression, and gave a solemn pledge not to take part in any agreement directed against the other contrahent. A remarkable feature of the pact was the omission of any reference to arbitration procedure; future disputes were to be settled by conciliation, in accordance with a special convention which was to be signed separately at a

[46] Polish minister to Bucharest, 1927-32; since November, 1932, under secretary of state for foreign affairs and Beck's chief adviser.

[47] Laroche, p. 110, accuses Beck of "brutality" in dealing with the Rumanians, but the latter asserts that he never went beyond "expressing most friendly suggestions to the Rumanian government." See his *Przemówienia*, p. 61, and *Final Report*, p. 9.

[48] *The New York Times*, June 22, 1932.   [49] See Beck, *Final Report*, p. 19.

[50] Jaworznicki omits any mention of Krestinskii's name and asserts that the pact was signed for the Soviet Union "by Boris Stomoniakov, a member of the College of the People's Commissariat for Foreign Affairs." "Polsko-radziecki pakt," *Sprawy Międzynarodowe*, V, No. 5, 78. This singular error is apparently due to the fact that Krestinskii was executed in 1938, and Jaworznicki's study was published at the height of the Stalinist period.

[51] Excerpts from the text of the pact are quoted from League of Nations, *Treaty Series*, CXXXVI, 41-53.

later date.[52] The treaty was concluded for a period of three years, and an automatic renewal for another two years was provided for. Like all other nonaggression pacts signed by the Soviet Union at that time, it contained an "escape" clause, providing that, if one of the signatories committed an act of aggression against a third power, the other party had the right to denounce the treaty without a previous warning.

In spite of the fact that the signature of the pact received some faint praise from the Soviet press,[53] the inner circles in the Kremlin had probably serious doubts as to the real intentions of Poland, as was indicated by an outspoken article in a Comintern publication:

The obvious cooling off of France's friendship for the expensive ally and the increased strain visible in the relations between Poland and Germany are without doubt the reasons for the foreign political maneuver at present being carried out by the fascist dictatorship [in Poland]. Poland did not receive the promised . . . loan from France . . . and after the dissolution of Germany's Reichstag it was suddenly faced with the possibility of Hitler coming to power in Germany. In a great hurry and almost unexpectedly the pact of nonaggression with the Soviet Union was signed on the eve of the German Reichstag elections, although the necessary documents had lain in the safe of Poland's Foreign Ministry for six years. Is it possible that after having shown [himself] uncompromisingly hostile to the Soviet Union for years . . . Piłsudski has suddenly changed [his] opinion and now honestly desires to live in peace with the Soviet Union? Naturally, there can be no question of this sort. Poland's foreign political situation was difficult and complicated. In the general complex of imperialist contradictions and in view of the French attempts to come to an agreement with Germany, Poland was threatened with being pushed into an unfavorable position in the background. By signing the pact of nonaggression whilst at the same time leaving himself some loopholes (the questions of Rumania, of the ratification, etc.) Piłsudski aimed at exercising pressure on France and . . . strengthening

[52] As Zaleski declared in the Sejm on the eve of the initialing of the pact, Poland made known her preference for an arbitration convention, but since the Soviet government did not recognize arbitration, it was better "to conclude a conciliation pact than nothing." *Kurjer Warszawski*, Jan. 21, 1932. In Moscow's opinion, arbitration was not admissible in relations between the USSR and a capitalist state. See Beloff, I, 21.

[53] See the editorials in *Izvestiia* and *Pravda* on July 30, 1932.

his position towards Germany. His final aim is to restore and consolidate his old position in the general imperialist front against the Soviet Union. Thus it is clear that there has been no fundamental change in the foreign policy of fascist Poland. On the contrary, Poland's fascists are continuing their war preparation against the Soviet Union with all energy and they regard an attack on the Soviet Union as the only way out of the crisis.[54]

On the other hand, Polish official circles and the Polish press generally regarded the pact as a milestone on the way to a relaxation of tension throughout Europe.[55] Beck was later to describe it as a "sound form of agreement," which confirmed and consolidated the development of neighborly relations between Poland and Russia.[56] Privately, he went beyond these pleasant and somewhat trite generalities and confided to the British ambassador that he viewed the agreement with the Soviet Union as a "distinctly useful achievement," which came "at the right psychological moment to confirm and stabilize this state of things, which he hoped would endure for some time to come"; he realized, however, that the Russians would only adhere to the pact "so long as it suited them to do so."[57]

It may be taken for granted that Piłsudski and his associates were fully aware of the fact that the Soviet Union, by merely affixing its signature to an international document, did not give up its territorial and other ambitions with regard to Poland. They were not dazzled by the prospects of a rapprochement with Moscow and had no illusions as to the real significance of a pact which contained only very limited obligations and amounted to an "academic renunciation of war."[58] It was obvious that it would be risky to take it at its face value; it was by no means a true indi-

---

[54] I. Najda, "The External and Internal Difficulties of Fascist Poland," *International Press Correspondence*, XII (Aug. 25, 1932), 792. While Polish-Soviet negotiations were going on, Moscow intensified its charges that Poland was preparing a war against the USSR. See *Kommunisticheskii Internatsional*, XIII, No. 33/34 (Dec. 10, 1931), 3-9; *The Communist International* (English ed.), VIII, No. 21 (Dec. 15, 1931), 706-10. These accusations were repeated at intervals up to the conclusion of the Polish-Soviet nonaggression pact and have been revived by recent Soviet historiography. See *Istoriia Pol'shi*, III, 313-15.

[55] For a selection of the contemporary press comment see *Kurjer Warszawski*, July 26, 27, 28, and 30, 1932.

[56] Beck, *Przemówienia*, pp. 54-55; see also Harley, *The Authentic Biography of Colonel Beck*, p. 122.

[57] *DBFP*, 2d Series, VII, 284.   [58] Lukacs, p. 27.

cation of mutual feelings, but rather constituted a part of the "polite mummery of interwar Europe."[59] There is, however, no denying that it expressed a certain relation of forces and lost its importance only after that balance had been upset; it also lessened the danger of an immediate Polish-Soviet conflict and opened before the two nations the prospect of a precarious but nevertheless peaceful coexistence. It was in this spirit that it was welcomed by the Polish leaders; as the British Embassy in Warsaw reported on July 28, the Poles regarded the pact more "as a gesture of goodwill" than anything else; they did not "expect great things from it," but hoped that it might help to improve Poland's relations with her eastern neighbor.[60]

While some Polish circles expressed their disappointment over the fact that the treaty did not pay sufficient attention to the problems of subversion and the revolutionary propaganda "conducted on Polish territory by the agents of the Third International, so closely connected with the Soviet state apparatus,"[61] the most vocal opposition to the idea of a rapprochement with Russia came from the leaders of the Ukrainian minority in Poland. Some of them seemed to believe in the existence of a "secret agreement" between Moscow and Warsaw, directed against Ukrainian irredentism, and regarded the nonaggression pact as an attempt on the part of Poland and the Soviet Union to "petrify" the situation which came into being as a result of the Treaty of Riga.[62] The foreign press and public opinion abroad also showed an inclination to see in the pact some features which it did not possess, interpreting it as a new orientation of Polish foreign policy and crediting Piłsudski with appropriating the ideas of those opposition parties which had always preached the necessity of Polish-Russian friendship and regarded Germany as the hereditary enemy of their country.[63]

[59] Sharp, p. 146. As Beloff observes, the Poles retained their doubts as to the genuineness of the new orientation in Soviet foreign policy in spite of the fact that the USSR did not introduce, for the time being, the ticklish problem of the eastern marchlands (I, 143-44).

[60] *DBFP*, 2d Series, VII, 240.   [61] *Kurjer Warszawski*, July 27, 1932.

[62] See Poland, Sejm, *Sprawozdanie stenograficzne*, Okres III, Posiedzenie LXX [Stenographic Minutes, Third Convocation, Session LXX], p. 104; also *ibid.*, Posiedzenie LXXV, p. 34; LXXXV, p. 30; CIII, pp. 94-95; and Poland, Senat, *Sprawozdanie stenograficzne*, Okres III, Posiedzenie LIX, pp. 76-77.

[63] The National Democratic opposition had been arguing for years that Poland should base her relations with the USSR on a more reliable foundation than the

Surprisingly enough, the German press described the pact as a positive step and denied that it endangered the Rapallo policy in any way. A part of the neutral press asserted that the Poles decided to exchange nonaggression declarations with Russia in order to make a contribution to the cause of "moral disarmament" and to allay Moscow's fears that Poland might be used some day as a vanguard of a new intervention against the USSR.[64] The only discordant notes came from Bucharest and Paris. While some Rumanian newspapers denounced the pact as a breach of faith, in spite of an attempt by their own Foreign Ministry to clear the Poles from any charges of duplicity,[65] a part of the French press warned Poland to beware of dire consequences that might follow her "fateful" decision:

If Poland should attach any real value to the treaty concluded with Moscow, its existence would diminish rather than increase her security. . . . As regards doing business with the Russians, elementary prudence counsels not to believe a word of what they are saying. . . . Besides, when the Soviets are concerned, there can be not the slightest excuse for the conclusion of such agreements. It cannot but favor the activities of Bolshevism, which is working inside every country for a revolution and which is supporting in the diplomatic field all those who attempt to throw Europe into confusion.[66]

Fears that the pact might weaken Poland's ties with France and Rumania were intensified by Warsaw's apparent reluctance to take any steps that might jeopardize its rapprochement with the

---

Kellogg Pact. *Kurjer Warszawski,* Feb. 21, 1931. According to Stanisław Stroński, one of the party's chief spokesmen on foreign affairs, Soviet Russia was too much preoccupied with her internal problems to become a serious threat to Poland's independence. On the other hand, Germany's aggressiveness toward Poland could be regarded as a permanent feature of the European political situation. Hence, the Poles should concentrate their main effort on the defense of their western frontier and give up all adventurous schemes in the east which could only result in a German-Russian rapprochement at Poland's expense. See S. Stroński, "Niemcy-Rosja-Polska" [Germany-Russia-Poland], *ibid.,* Jan. 8, 1933.

[64] See the editorial "Il y a pacte et pacte" in *Journal de Genève,* July 29, 1932.

[65] *Kurjer Warszawski,* July 28, 1932. The text of the statement of the Rumanian government of July 25 is quoted in *Osteuropa,* VII (1931-32), 724-25; the declaration made in this connection by the Polish minister in Bucharest to the representatives of the Rumanian press can be found in *Kurjer Warszawski,* July 30, 1932.

[66] P. Bernus, "Les pactes avec les Soviets," *Journal des débats politiques et littéraires,* July 28, 1932; see also the editorial "La politique des pactes" in *Le Temps,* July 27, 1932.

USSR. Thus, for example, a memorandum was sent to the Vatican, urging the Holy See to discontinue the activities of the "Pro Russia" commission among Polish citizens, since its missionary work not only implied that Poland's eastern territories were actually a part of Russia but also could be regarded by the Kremlin as prelude for another intervention disguised as a religious crusade.[67] As a gesture of mutual good will, Warsaw and Moscow agreed to exchange political prisoners[68] and made arrangements for a visit to Poland by a Soviet trade delegation, but Polish public opinion seemed to be somewhat disturbed by a demonstration of Russia's naval might which occurred in October off Gdynia, just outside the limit of Polish territorial waters.[69]

Meanwhile, hopes for an early settlement of the remaining differences between Rumania and the USSR were dashed when Titulescu, then generally regarded as an inveterate enemy of the Soviet Union, resigned his post as minister to Great Britain and two weeks later took over the portfolio of foreign affairs in Maniu's cabinet. The meaning of this appointment was clearly understood in Moscow, and Litvinov warned in a special statement that the discussions with Rumania could not be changed into a "diplomatic play for unknown foreign aims."[70] The fruitless bargaining continued for another month, during which Titulescu displayed "inexplicable stubbornness" and "invented new arguments, every time more peculiar and every time less serious."[71] Finally, on November 23, Rumania announced that the negotiations with Russia had been broken off owing to the failure to reach a solution of the Bessarabian problem.[72] On the same day Litvinov and Patek signed in Moscow a conciliation convention for a peaceful settlement of any future disputes between Poland and the USSR. According to its provisions, a special mixed commission was to be set up to "clear up the questions at issue which have been submitted to it"; its recommendations were to be arrived at unanimously and then presented in a formal report to the two governments, which were free to accept or to reject them

[67] *Sprawy Narodowościowe,* VI (1932), 765-82.
[68] *Kurjer Warszawski,* Sept. 16 and 17, 1932.
[69] *Ibid.,* Nov. 2, 1932.   [70] *Izvestiia,* Oct. 16, 1932.
[71] Beck, *Final Report,* pp. 8-9; see also *DBFP,* 2d Series, VII, 284.
[72] *The New York Times,* Nov. 24, 1932.

within a period of three months. While the conciliation procedure was in progress, the contracting parties were to refrain from any steps that might hamper or obstruct the carrying out of the proposals made by the commission. The convention was to come into force at the same time as the nonaggression pact; it was to become an integral part of the pact and was to remain in force for the same period of time.[73]

While the provisions of the convention were being ironed out, an important change occurred in the Polish Foreign Office: on November 2, August Zaleski was replaced by Colonel Józef Beck, an able, sleek, and "rather Mephistophelean" figure,[74] who enjoyed the confidence of Marshal Piłsudski to a considerably greater degree than his independent and sophisticated predecessor. This event quite naturally gave rise to speculations that Zaleski's resignation was due to his opposition to the ratification of the Polish-Soviet nonaggression pact. The official Polish Telegraphic Agency was authorized to deny these rumors as completely unfounded, while Beck himself described the change as being of an entirely personal nature and stressed that the continuity of Polish foreign policy would be "absolutely maintained."[75] Nevertheless, the view that Piłsudski "threw over not only Rumania, but his own Foreign Minister . . . to secure Poland's eastern border" was held in some world capitals.[76] At the same time, one of the best-informed British publications credited Beck with the successful conclusion of the Polish-Soviet negotiations and pointed out that, while the policy of rapprochement with Russia had been initiated under Zaleski's auspices, it was Beck, the rising star of Polish diplomacy, who "had won over Marshal Piłsudski to this

[73] For the text of the convention see League of Nations, *Treaty Series*, CXXXVI, 55-71. A selection of press comments is given in *Kurjer Warszawski*, Nov. 25, 1932, and in *Osteuropa*, VIII (1932-33), 221.

[74] Roberts, "The Diplomacy of Colonel Beck," in Craig and Gilbert, eds., *The Diplomats*, p. 581.

[75] Beck, *Przemówienia*, p. 37.

[76] *The New York Times*, Dec. 11, 1932. Beck's appointment was greeted by the Polish press with caution, and most of the opposition newspapers were openly skeptical about his suitability. *Kurjer Warszawski*, Nov. 3, 1932. According to the Socialist *Robotnik*, the new minister's views on foreign policy were relatively unknown, but he was regarded by some circles as a sympathizer of fascist ideology. *Ibid.*, Nov. 4, 1932.

policy" and created, through his own efforts, a "decidedly better atmosphere" in Eastern Europe.[77]

The new Foreign Minister described the conciliation convention in his statement of November 26 as a "very real and very significant step" on the way to a further improvement and stabilization of relations between the two countries.[78] Both the nonaggression pact and the convention were ratified by President Mościcki on November 27, 1932, in accordance with Article XLIX of the Polish Constitution, which empowered the chief executive of the Republic to conclude treaties with foreign countries.[79] This method of ratification without recourse to the usual parliamentary procedure was used only to save time, since it was certain that an overwhelming majority would have supported both measures in the Sejm.[80] A simultaneous ratification took place in Moscow, followed by an exchange of the instruments of ratification in Warsaw on December 23, 1932. It was only now that the Soviet press gave its unreserved blessing to the pact, hailing it as a "victory for the cause of peace" and as Russia's "greatest diplomatic triumph"; it stressed, moreover, that the ratification was accomplished in spite of the efforts of foreign imperialists, who regarded small powers as mere pawns in their anti-Soviet schemes and hoped that Poland would become their mainstay in future intervention against the USSR.[81] The official organ of the Comintern also asserted that the treaties concluded by the Soviet Union with its neighbors and France[82] "testified to a tremendous change in the relationship of forces between the USSR and the capitalist world" and constituted an international recognition of this fact.[83]

---

[77] *The Economist* (London), Dec. 10, 1932, p. 1077.   [78] Beck, *Przemówienia*, p. 41.

[79] On January 18, 1933, the National Democratic group in the Sejm challenged the constitutionality of the procedure adopted by the government. See Poland, Sejm, *Sprawozdanie stenograficzne*, Okres III, Posiedzenie LXXV, pp. 23-32, and *Kurjer Warszawski*, Jan. 19, 1933.

[80] Some opposition newspapers maintained that the pact was not submitted to the Sejm in order to avoid a prolonged debate, dealing not so much with the treaty itself but rather with the personal changes in the Ministry of Foreign Affairs and with some other aspects of Polish foreign policy. See *Polonia* (Katowice) as quoted in *Kurjer Warszawski*, Dec. 2, 1932.

[81] *Izvestiia*, Nov. 28, 1932; see also *ibid.*, Nov. 30, 1932.

[82] France signed her nonaggression pact with the USSR on November 29, 1932.

[83] *Kommunisticheskii Internatsional*, XIV, No. 34 (Dec. 10, 1932), 3; *The Communist International* (English ed.), IX, No. 20 (Dec. 1, 1932), 701.

These developments raised expectations that political *détente* in Eastern Europe would result in a general improvement of economic conditions there.[84] It was hoped particularly that Poland's rapprochement with Moscow would have repercussions in the field of Polish-Soviet trade. Before 1914, industrial centers of the former Congress Kingdom depended to a large extent upon the Russian market. After the war, these commercial ties were severed and trade between Poland and her eastern neighbor declined to a mere trickle. The precarious state of the Polish economy induced the Warsaw government to make several attempts to persuade the Soviet Union to open its frontier for an exchange of goods, but Moscow's attitude was somewhat ambiguous. While the Kremlin was quite ready to admit that Russia "could provide a big market for a considerable part of Polish industry now idle" and that "certain industrial products . . . might be imported no less economically from Poland than from other countries,"[85] it also stressed that a trade agreement with Poland "could be of advantage only if it formed part of a general comprehensive agreement," which, in turn, would require "a decisive change in Poland's policy toward our Union."[86] Since the Poles felt that a propitious development of economic relations between the two countries should precede any political agreement, Poland's part in supplying the Soviet market remained limited to satisfying Russia's sporadic needs.[87] Under these circumstances, Warsaw could

[84] See Mr. Vereker's report to Sir J. Simon, *DBFP*, 2d Series, VII, 240.

[85] USSR, Tsentral'nyi Ispolnitel'nyi Komitet, *Sozyv III, Sessiia II, Stenograficheskii otchët*, pp. 1059-60; English translation in Degras, II, 111-12.

[86] USSR, Tsentral'nyi Ispolnitel'nyi Komitet, *Sozyv III, Sessiia II, Stenograficheskii otchët*, p. 1060; Degras, II, 112.

[87] *The Economist*, May 20, 1939, p. 432. The following table illustrates the fluctuations of Polish-Soviet trade (in millions of złotys):

Year	Imports from USSR	% of total	Exports to USSR	% of total
1928	39.1	1.2	38.6	1.5
1929	39.9	1.3	81.1	2.9
1930	45.8	2.0	129.0	5.3
1931	36.0	2.5	125.3	6.7
1932	19.3	2.2	29.1	2.7

See Poland, Główny Urząd Statystyczny, *Mały Rocznik Statystyczny, 1939* [Little Statistical Annual, 1939] (Warsaw, 1939), pp. 166-67; Mainz, pp. 158-61. It should be noted that, as a result of the First Five-Year Plan, Soviet imports of consumers'

only complain that Soviet foreign trade was but a tool in Moscow's hands, which was skillfully manipulated in accordance with the requirements of political expediency and with little respect for sound economic principles.[88]

The depression was one of the factors which prompted the Poles and most of the other western neighbors of the USSR to establish a political *modus vivendi* with Russia and thus open the door for an eventual development of commercial relations. Late in 1932 the prospects for an increase of Soviet purchases in Poland seemed so bright that the Polish government instructed its legation in Moscow to make exploratory steps toward the conclusion of a trade agreement.[89] It appeared, for a moment, that closer economic links between the two countries might help to bring about a thorough pacification of Polish-Soviet relations.[90]

---

goods from Poland were greatly reduced, with a corresponding rise in purchases of machinery. All Polish-Soviet commercial transactions took place under the sponsorship of the Sovpol'torg (Sowpoltorg), an international company, in which the Polish side was represented by a private association known as "Polros," and the Russian side by a Soviet government agency.

[88] See Zaleski, p. 156.

[89] *Osteuropa,* VII (1931-32), 724; *The New York Times,* Nov. 28, 1932.

[90] See Poland, Sejm, *Sprawozdanie stenograficzne,* Okres III, Posiedzenie LXXV, p. 34.

II. "Peaceful Coexistence": 1933-1934

During the first months following the ratification of the Polish-Soviet nonaggression pact, the steps taken by Warsaw and Moscow to improve relations remained guarded and somewhat hesitant. New Year's editorials in the Polish press which praised the treaty as a great diplomatic achievement also reflected an alarming increase of tension on Poland's western border.[1] German demands for equality of armaments were regarded in Warsaw as a prelude to an armed conflict over the Corridor, and the expected rise to power of the Nazis did nothing to dispel these apprehensions. Since Poland's alliances with France and Rumania were obviously inadequate to secure her against a simultaneous invasion in the west and in the east, the importance of the Polish-Soviet accord, which seemed to put an end to "the preceding period of blood and iron"[2] in the history of the two nations, could not be overestimated. During a lively debate in the Sejm in January, 1933, most of the deputies agreed that the pacification of Poland's eastern frontier was the best possible answer to Germany's aggressive intentions.[3]

Evidently, the time was now at hand for a thorough examination of the whole problem of Polish-Soviet relations in the light of the newly signed agreements. According to Beck, Poland's future policy toward her Russian neighbor was to be governed by the following three rules of conduct:

(1) to apply strictly the principles embodied in the nonaggres-

---

[1] *Gazeta Polska,* Jan. 1, 1933 (quoted in *Kurjer Warszawski,* Jan. 8, 1933).
[2] *Ibid.*
[3] See Poland, Sejm, *Sprawozdanie stenograficzne,* Okres III, Posiedzenie LXXV p. 34.

sion pact, while insisting on a complete reciprocity on Russia's part;

(2) to bring about a lasting improvement of the atmosphere of Polish-Soviet relations;

(3) to maintain wariness with regard to Moscow's political schemes, which could complicate Poland's relations with other countries without assuring her any real support by the USSR.[4]

The practical application of these rules was by no means easy. The extreme touchiness and suspiciousness of the Kremlin had to be taken into account, and each intended step had to be analyzed in the view of the possible reaction on the part of other neighbors of Poland and her western ally. Progress toward the goal of truly neighborly relations, which had to be slow and carefully planned by the two interested governments, was also encumbered by the fantastically exaggerated reports and erratic speculations of the world press.

In launching its drive for better relations with Russia, the Polish government considered it advantageous to manifest to the world that "something new had really happened," and that, in addition to solving various routine questions, the two countries were determined to cooperate "in all initiatives which aimed at showing the public at large that some of our former difficulties were fading away."[5] First signs of this hopeful development could be observed as early as the spring of 1933. In March, a Soviet art exhibition opened in Warsaw and was widely praised by the local critics as the most successful art event of the year.[6] About the middle of April, Bogusław Miedziński, editor-in-chief of *Gazeta Polska* and one of the most prominent figures among the "Colonels," left for Moscow, with Piłsudski's personal blessings, to conduct a series of informal talks with the Soviet leaders.[7] Al-

---

[4] Beck, *Final Report,* p. 33.   [5] *Ibid.,* p. 31.

[6] *Kurjer Warszawski,* March 5, 1933.

[7] In April, 1932, Miedziński and Ignacy Matuszewski (former finance minister) were instructed by Piłsudski to approach Vladimir Antonov-Ovseenko (then Soviet envoy in Warsaw) and convince him that Poland sincerely desired to establish loyal and neighborly relations with Russia. These informal discussions continued for several months but failed to bring any concrete results. It was only after the ratification of the Polish-Soviet nonaggression pact that Antonov-Ovseenko abandoned his suspicious attitude and helped to make arrangements for Miedziński's visit to Moscow. B. Miedziński, "Popioły są jeszcze gorące," *Wiadomości* (London), Oct. 26, 1952.

though the projected audience with Stalin did not materialize, Miedziński was treated in accordance with the best traditions of Russian hospitality. At the same time, a gala reception given by the Polish minister to Moscow, Łukasiewicz, was attended by the representatives of the Soviet government and the Red Army and several leading Russian writers and artists.[8] On May 1, Marshal Piłsudski granted a private audience to Antonov-Ovseenko, a favor which, as foreign correspondents were quick to point out, was reserved for a few diplomats on very important occasions, and the Soviet representative was said to have received assurances that the past was forgotten and that its consequences would not be allowed to poison Poland's future relations with Russia.[9] The beginning of May also marked the arrival in the Polish capital of a Russian trade mission, led by Deputy Commissar for Foreign Trade I. V. Boev.[10]

All these exchanges of visits and gestures of friendship were taking place against the background of increasingly troubled Polish-German relations, which even prompted some "private individuals" to aproach the Soviet minister to Warsaw in order to find out what attitude the USSR would take in the event of a war between Poland and Germany.[11] While the Nazi threat loomed over the western horizon, the conditions along the eastern frontier remained quiet, and it appeared that Moscow had no intention of reviving its old quarrels with Warsaw.[12] To be sure, Russia's desire for international cooperation was motivated by her fear of Japanese aggression rather than by the question of German rearmament and potential expansion,[13] but the weakening of the Rapallo connection prompted the Kremlin to intensify its efforts to establish a "community of interests" between the Soviet Union and

[8] *Kurjer Warszawski*, May 5, 1933.

[9] *Kurjer Warszawski*, May 2 and 5, 1933; see also Laeuen, *Polnisches Zwischenspiel*, p. 118. It is significant that Piłsudski granted a private audience to the Soviet envoy just on the eve of Wysocki's interview with Hitler (see below). It seems probable that the Marshal's friendly gesture toward Antonov-Ovseenko was calculated to impress Berlin rather than Moscow.

[10] See *Kurjer Warszawski*, May 1, 4, and 10, 1933; *Izvestiia*, May 8, 11, and 15, 1933.

[11] *DGFP*, Series C, I (Washington, 1957), 364. It should be noted, however, that the Hitler-Wysocki interview resulted in a certain relaxation of tension in German-Polish relations.

[12] *The New York Times*, May 7, 1933.

[13] *DBFP*, 2d Series, VII (London, 1958), 670; see also *DGFP*, Series C, II (Washington, 1959), 275.

the border states.[14] Poland, of course, occupied a prominent place in this campaign; she was, indeed, the chief beneficiary of the political situation which had been created by Germany's aggressive attitude.[15]

While Moscow was anxious to forge a bloc of friendly nations along its European boundaries, the Poles welcomed an opportunity of forming a "solid front of the western neighbors of Russia,"[16] though in a manner slightly different from that envisaged by Warsaw in the early 1920s. Thus the Polish delegation reacted favorably to a draft convention for the definition of aggression which was submitted by Litvinov to the general commission of the Disarmament Conference on February 6, 1933.[17] The Russian proposal was discussed in the subcommittee on security questions, and this body included most of Litvinov's ideas in its resolution on the definition of an aggressor, presented to the general commission on May 24, 1933.[18] The draft proved unacceptable to some of the delegations, but negotiations behind the scenes continued even after the adjournment of the Disarmament Conference on June 8. The Soviet proposal that the signatories of the Litvinov Protocol of 1929 should conclude a treaty based on the resolution of the subcommittee on security questions (the so-called Politis Report) was finally accepted by Afghanistan, Estonia, Latvia, Persia, Poland, Rumania, and Turkey, and the plenipotentiaries of these countries joined Russia in signing on July 3, 1933, the Convention for the Definition of Aggression.[19]

[14] See Litvinov's speech to the Central Executive Committee in USSR, Tsentral'nyi Ispolnitel'nyi Komitet, *Sozyv VI, Sessiia IV, Stenograficheskii otchët* (Moscow, 1934), Biulleten' No. 3, p. 12 (English translation in Degras, ed., III, 53).

[15] *DGFP*, Series C, I, 695.   [16] Beck, *Final Report*, p. 35.

[17] According to Litvinov, the Soviet delegation was interested primarily in the adoption of the second clause of its draft declaration which specified various political, strategic, and economic considerations that could not serve as justification for aggression. See League of Nations, *Records of the Conference for the Reduction and Limitation of Armaments*, Series B, Minutes of General Commission, II, 237-38. To H. L. Roberts, this indicated that the chief objective of the Soviet Union lay "in protecting its position as a revolutionary state in a presumably hostile world" rather than in establishing a criterion for aggression. See his "Maxim Litvinov" in Craig and Gilbert, eds., *The Diplomats*, pp. 351-52.

[18] "The Soviet Union and Non-Aggression," *Bulletin of International News*, X, No. 4 (Aug. 17, 1933), 97-107; see also Beloff, I, 51-53.

[19] On July 4, another convention was signed by the Soviet Union, Rumania, Turkey, Czechoslovakia, and Yugoslavia. Poland's refusal to join this agreement (probably caused by her reluctance to associate herself with Czechoslovakia) prompted the opposition press to some caustic comments. See *Kurjer Warszawski*, July 5, 1933.

The document stressed the adherence of the contracting parties to the Kellogg-Briand Pact and expressed their desire to consolidate the peaceful relations existing between them.[20] It defined as aggression various forms of direct and indirect attack, with or without a formal declaration of war, including the support of armed bands formed with the purpose of invading the territory of another state. The Convention represented an important development in the field of international law since it stated expressly that internal disorders, alleged defects in administration, and even the international conduct of a state could not be regarded as an excuse for aggression. It was, therefore, with some justification that Beck welcomed it in a press statement as a creative political act which embodied a "synthesis of individual efforts aimed at an effective organization of peaceful coexistence."[21] As far as Poland was concerned, the new accord was the logical sequence of a series of agreements concluded with the Soviet Union since 1929, and it was especially gratifying that it bore the signature of Rumania along with that of the USSR, thus placing Bucharest "once more on speaking terms" with Moscow. Now, as Beck confided to the British ambassador, the neighbors of Russia "would at least have some basis of security in their relations with that country"; heretofore they could not even count on the support of the League of Nations in case of a dispute with Moscow since the Soviet Union did not belong to that body.[22]

The favorable reception of the treaty in official quarters was echoed in sympathetic comments of the Polish and Soviet press.[23] Polish diplomacy, alarmed by the revisionist tendencies of the Four-Power Pact, could boast of having finally succeeded in its bid to restore the European balance of power which had been temporarily threatened by the "directorate" of Germany, Italy, France, and Great Britain.[24] Russia had an even more valid reason

[20] For the text of the Convention see League of Nations, *Treaty Series*, CXLVII, 67-77.

[21] Beck, *Przemówienia*, p. 71.   [22] *DBFP*, 2d Series, VII, 588.

[23] *Gazeta Polska* as quoted in *Kurjer Warszawski*, July 5, 1933; see also *Izvestiia*, July 5, and *Pravda*, July 6, 1933.

[24] The signature of the Convention was widely interpreted as "the Polish and Eastern European reply to the Four-Power Pact" (*The New York Times*, July 4, 1933); there were even some speculations that Poland, the Soviet Union, Rumania,

for rejoicing, now that her neighbors had shown in clear terms their unwillingness to participate in any anti-Soviet schemes.[25] The "great triumph" of the peaceful policy of the USSR, as it was hailed in *Pravda*,[26] also enabled the Kremlin to score a propaganda victory by posing as the unchallenged leader in the struggle for international security and gave it a chance to strengthen its shaky prestige in Asia.

The signature of the Convention created a propitious atmosphere for another series of Soviet visits to Poland. Russian diplomats and military leaders discontinued their long-established practice of avoiding Warsaw on their tours.[27] Soviet airmen and sailors were feted in Poland, and Polish fliers and seamen were treated with similar hospitality in Russia.[28] Polish scholars and artists were warmly received in the Soviet Union, and the Polish press and public reacted in a very friendly manner to the visits of the representatives of Russian science and art.[29] Indeed, it may be said that the relations between the two countries were never so satisfactory as in 1933 and early 1934, although even at that time some Polish circles warned against the growing intimacy of the friendly intercourse between the official representatives and private citizens

and Turkey were about to sign a security pact which would serve as the nucleus of a "new political system resulting from the necessity to oppose the Four-Power Pact" (*Kurjer Warszawski*, July 5, 1933). On the other hand, Beck claimed that there "had never been any idea of concluding a treaty of wider scope or anything of the nature of a reply to the Four-Power Pact." *DBFP*, 2d Series, VII, 588.

[26] It should be noted, however, that only one week after the signature of the Convention *Pravda* indicated Moscow's displeasure with the changing atmosphere of Polish-German relations by complaining that the anti-Soviet campaign incited by the Nazis was finding support among Poland's "ruling circles" (July 10, 1933). An article in the official organ of the Comintern charged at the same time that the "basic contradictions" between Poland and the USSR remained unchanged and that the "Sovietophile maneuvers" of the Polish government were designed to deceive public opinion. J. Bratkowski, "Pol'sko-germanskie protivorechiia i ugroza antisovetskoi interventsii" [Polish German Contradictions and the Threat of Anti-Soviet Intervention], *Kommunisticheskii Internatsional*, XV, No. 21 (July 20, 1933), 38.

[26] July 6, 1933.   [27] Beck, *Final Report*, p. 31.

[28] For detailed reports see *Kurjer Warszawski*, May 17-18, Sept. 12-13, and Nov. 7, 1933; July 20, 26, and 31, Aug. 2, and Sept. 4-8, 1934; *Izvestiia*, Sept. 14, 1933; July 24 and 27, Sept. 6 and 8, 1934; *Pravda*, May 17, July 19-20, and Nov. 10, 1933; July 24, 26, and 29-30, Sept. 5 and 8, 1934. See also Singer, p. 181.

[29] Further information about these cultural exchanges can be found in *Kurjer Warszawski* Aug. 22 and 26, and Nov. 13, 1933; *Izvestiia*, Nov. 11, 14, and 23, 1933; *Pravda*, Nov. 15, 1933.

of Poland and the USSR.[30] On the other hand, some Party publications in Russia continued to describe Poland as a "fortress of world imperialism in its struggle against the Soviet Union" and accused the Warsaw government of trying to reach a "compromise with Hitlerite Germany" at the expense of the USSR.[31]

One of the most prominent Soviet guests to visit Poland in the summer of 1933 was Karl Radek, leading editorial writer of *Izvestiia,* a native of Galicia and an expert on Polish affairs. The official purpose of his trip, which was regarded by some Polish newspapers as a "symbol" and a landmark of a new epoch in Poland's relations with Russia, was to repay Colonel Miedziński's visit to Moscow; it seems pretty certain, however, that he acted as Stalin's personal emissary.[32] During his talks with the Poles, he showed a great interest in the problem of Polish-German relations, and was especially anxious to ascertain whether Poland would be willing to join Hitler in an anti-Soviet expedition. Miedziński's assurances that the Poles would take up arms to defend their neutrality apparently made a deep impression upon Radek, the more so since they had been given to him in Piłsudski's name.[33] He had less success, however, with his proposal of a common Soviet-Polish "protection" of the Baltic states, which was unacceptable to the Poles not only because they were afraid of a possible violent reaction on the part of Germany but also on account of Warsaw's general policy not to share anything with Russia. Nevertheless, Radek's visit proved helpful in establishing

[30] Thus, for example, *Słowo* (Wilno) urged public opinion to beware of Communist propaganda spread from the Soviet Union under the cover of "correct neighborly relations" and pleaded with the Polish government to stop all visits and cultural exchanges which "overstepped the limits of prudent reserve" and might prove dangerous "to the future of the people and the state." Quoted from *Kurjer Warszawski,* Nov. 18, 1933.

[31] *Bil'shovyk Ukrainy,* VIII, No. 11 (Sept., 1933), 102-3.

[32] Beck, *Final Report,* p. 32; Miedziński, "Popioły są jeszcze gorące," *Wiadomości,* Oct. 26, 1952. See also Singer, p. 141.

[33] It would seem, however, that Radek's apprehensions were not entirely dispelled. Only a few months later, he expressed in a private conversation his fears that, in the event of a Russo-Japanese war, Germany would "pounce on Poland," and, having conquered the Poles, would "soothe" their national pride by offering them compensation for the Corridor in the Ukraine. Accordingly, the chief objective of Soviet policy was to prevent this "barter transaction" beween Germany and Poland. *DGFP,* Series C, II, 297.

new cultural and economic contacts between Poland and the USSR.[34]

The honeymoon of Polish-Russian friendship continued through the fall of 1933, and the spirit of amity was maintained by such thoughtful gestures as Poland's presentation to the Soviet government of Lenin's personal papers left behind after his stay at Poronin in 1914 and Stalin's gift to Piłsudski of a dossier of Tsarist police documents dealing with the Marshal's underground activities. A contribution to the development of a normal commercial intercourse between the two countries was made by the conclusion of a river-freight traffic treaty and a tariff agreement,[35] while the settlement of future frontier incidents was simplified by the mutual acceptance of a new international convention.[36] Finally, on September 15, the London Convention was ratified simultaneously in Moscow and Warsaw, and these diplomatic formalities were accompanied by an exchange of usual polite phrases and amicable statements.[37] The world press reacted to this show of neighborly good will with speculations that Polish-Russian friendship would find its consummation in the signature of a military pact; it was also rumored that Marshal Piłsudski would visit Moscow as an official guest of the Soviet government to take part in the celebrations marking the anniversary of the October Revolution.[38] Meanwhile Poland was trying once more to bring

[34] After his return to Russia, Radek discussed the problem of Polish-Soviet relations with a surprising amount of frankness in *Izvestiia* (Aug. 29, 1933), stressing that Soviet public opinion did not harbor any hostile intentions with regard to Poland's independence, although it would rather see the Poles living under a different social system. This expression of good will was accepted in Poland with "sincere satisfaction." See a statement of the telegraphic agency "Iskra" and excerpts from a *Gazeta Polska* editorial as quoted in *Osteuropa*, IX (1933-34), 30.

[35] The former accord, signed by Beck and Antonov-Ovseenko in Warsaw on June 19, 1933, was supplemented by the additional protocol of July 9, 1933. The first tariff agreement between Poland and the USSR, necessitated by the dissolution of the Sovpol'torg, took the form of an exchange of notes on September 18 and October 9, 1933; the second agreement was concluded on June 22, 1934. See Makowski, p. 192.

[36] This convention, replacing all previous agreements and protocols dealing with that subject, was signed on June 3, 1933.

[37] See *Kurjer Warszawski*, Sept. 16, 1933; *Pravda*, Sept. 18, 1933; *Osteuropa*, IX (1933-34), 79.

[38] *The New York Times*, Sept. 4, 1933. Early in September there appeared reports about a "secret Polish-Rumanian-Russian conference," allegedly taking place at Zaleszczyki (a summer resort on the Dniester), and the formation of a "Polish-

about a Russo-Rumanian rapprochement under Warsaw's sponsorship,[39] and it seemed that a stabilization of international relations between the Baltic and the Black Sea and between the Carpathians and the Ural Mountains was definitely in the making.[40]

In the fall of the same year an attempt was made to put an end to the Polish-Russian "entente" by means of an assassination. Ukrainian nationalist circles in Poland, who were responsible for this scheme, had been alarmed for some time by the ever closer ties linking Warsaw and Moscow.[41] The reports of a famine in the Ukraine, though officially denied by the Soviet government, prompted the leaders of the Organization of Ukrainian Nationalists (OUN) to resort to a violent action which, they hoped, would turn the attention of the world to the plight of their compatriots.[42] Mykola Lemyk, a freshman at the University of Lwów, was instructed to kill Soviet Vice-Consul Golub "to demonstrate the solidarity of all Ukrainians in their struggle against Moscow,"[43] but shot instead a secretary of the consulate.[44] The incident failed

Soviet anti-German front, with Rumania likely to join," was expected as a result of this meeting. *Ibid.*, Sept. 8, 1933.

[39] See *Kurjer Warszawski*, Oct. 11, 1933, and *Osteuropa*, IX (1933-34), 79. These efforts were intensified during Titulescu's visit to Warsaw in October, 1933, when the Poles succeeded in arranging two meetings between the Rumanian Foreign Minister and Antonov-Ovseenko.

[40] *Gazeta Polska* as quoted in *Osteuropa*, IX (1933-34), 79-80.

[41] According to *Gazeta Warszawska*, an improvement in Polish-Soviet relations was bound to strike at the very roots of the Ukrainian independence movement and to deprive it of its main political basis. Quoted from *Kurjer Warzawski*, July 27, 1933.

[42] Legal Ukrainian parties in Poland also engaged in a protest action and used the tribune of the Sejm to criticize the conditions in the Soviet Ukraine. See Poland, Sejm, *Sprawozdanie stenograficzne*, Okres III, Posiedzenie CIII, pp. 91-94, 123. On June 25, 1933, twenty-five Ukrainian organizations in Lwów formed a relief committee for the victims of the famine, which then appealed for help to the League of Nations. The Council of the League asked the International Committee of the Red Cross to organize a relief action, but all these efforts failed as a result of Moscow's refusal to accept any kind of aid. *Sprawy Narodowościowe*, VII (1933), 389-93, 545-46, 552-53; VIII (1934), 64-66; see also *Entsyklopediia Ukrainoznavstva* [Encyclopedia of the Ukraine], I, Part II (Munich, 1949), 562.

[43] Lemyk's statement to the police as quoted by Makar, "Stril v oboroni mil'ioniv," in *Al'manakh-Kalendar Homonu Ukrainy na 1956 rik*, p. 152.

[44] According to Makar this secretary, a certain Mailov, was "Stalin's special emissary," and his official functions served merely as a cover-up for his extensive activities as Soviet master spy (*ibid.*); however, another Ukrainian nationalist author describes Mailov as "an ordinary clerk of the Consulate." Z. Knysh, "Boiovi dii

to produce the results expected by the plotters: local authorities in Lwów sent their regrets to the Vice-Counsul, the Ministry for Foreign Affairs apologized to the Soviet legation, and although the Russians dispatched a stiffly worded note to Warsaw,[45] Beck and Antonov-Ovseenko agreed on October 25, only four days after the assassination, to regard the whole incident as closed. The Polish police proved efficient in rounding up some fifty suspects allegedly connected with the plot. Lemyk was duly sentenced to life imprisonment by an emergency court,[46] and the Polish press could state with a feeling of relief that the defendant had missed in his shot at Polish-Soviet friendship.[47] Litvinov, discussing the whole complex of Russia's relations with Poland in his speech before the Central Executive Committee of the USSR on December 29, 1933, reciprocated by completely ignoring the Mailov affair, and instead devoted a long passage of his address to the mutual "confidence" and understanding between Moscow and Warsaw:

We are particularly satisfied with the progress which we have observed in the attitude of Polish public opinion toward our Union—and this progress indicates that wide circles of Polish public opinion are also gradually coming to the conclusion we arrived at long ago, that between the Soviet Union and Poland the closest cooperation is both possible and necessary, and that there exist no objective reasons to hinder its development.[48]

Litvinov's views were warmly endorsed by a part of the Polish

---

OUN na ZUZ v pershomu desiatylitti ii isnuvannia" [Fighting Activities of the OUN in the Western Ukraine—The First Decade], in *Orhanizatsiia Ukrains'kykh Natsionalistiv, 1924-1954*, p. 98.

[45] For the text see *Izvestiia*, Oct. 24, 1933. The note alleged that a close connection existed between Mailov's assassination and the anti-Soviet campaign being conducted in some Polish provinces, and "especially in Lwów." See *Pravda*, Oct. 22-24, 1933. A resolution adopted by the Central Committee of the Communist Party of the Ukraine in November, 1933, singled out for personal vituperation a number of Ukrainian leaders in Poland, allegedly connected with "Polish fascist circles," and charged them with instigating anti-Soviet terroristic acts. *Pravda*, Nov. 27, 1933.

[46] For an account of Lemyk's trial see *Kurjer Warszawski*, Oct. 31, 1933; see also Poland, Sejm, *Sprawozdanie stenograficzne*, Okres III, Posiedzenie CIII, p. 94.

[47] *Kurjer Warszawski*, Oct. 26, 1933.

[48] USSR, Tsentral'nyi Ispolnitel'nyi Komitet, *Sozyv VI, Sessiia IV, Stenograficheskii otchët* (Moscow, 1934), Biulleten' No. 3, p. 12 (English translation quoted from *International Press Correspondence*, XIV [Jan. 5, 1934], 23).

press,[49] but it was becoming increasingly obvious that the Poles would not be satisfied with Platonic declarations of good will. *Kurjer Warszawski,* one of the most outspoken advocates of the idea of Polish-Soviet rapprochement, commented:

It would be desirable not to limit our mutual cooperation to insignificant tourist and intellectual interests which smack a little of sensationalism and which we regard in all frankness as the least valuable manifestation of the new situation. There are many unsolved questions between Russia and ourselves arising from the Treaty of Riga, there are unsettled financial accounts which should not be forgotten, there is, finally, a frontier which is dead from the economic point of view and which we would like to revive. Mr. Litvinov's declarations should produce an immediate effect upon all these problems. The settlement of these issues will fill the new situation with a real substance.[50]

Doubts as to the actual value of close contacts with the Soviet Union were being voiced with increasing frequency.[51] The view that a workable agreement with Germany and, possibly, France was preferable to an entente with Russia was expressed especially by those vociferous and influential groups who still subscribed to the belief that the destinies of the Polish nation lay in the vast areas of Eastern Europe.[52] In their opinion, Moscow was to be regarded not as a partner in the diplomatic game but as the center of a fanatic militant church, and the idea that the growing power of the Reich could be opposed by a Polish-Soviet league was a ridiculous absurdity.[53] Some of them believed that the question of nationalities was Russia's most explosive problem and was bound, in the long run, to bring about the dissolution of the Soviet empire

[49] *Gazeta Polska,* Jan. 6, 1934, as quoted in *Osteuropa,* IX (1933-34), 304.

[50] *Kurjer Warszawski,* Jan. 4, 1934.

[51] See *Le Monde Slave,* X, Part IV (Nov., 1933), 289.

[52] The ideas of Poland's eastward expansion were advocated by the so-called Wilno Circle, headed by Prince Eustachy Sapieha, one-time minister of foreign affairs, and Stanisław Mackiewicz, editor-in-chief of the daily *Słowo;* they were also supported by Jerzy Giedroyc, editor and publisher of the periodicals *Bunt Młodych* and *Polityka.* For a discussion of these ideological conceptions and of their implications in the field of Polish-Soviet relations see K. Symmons-Symonolewicz, "Polish Political Thought and the Problem of the Eastern Borderlands of Poland (1918-1939)," *The Polish Review,* IV, No. 1/2 (Winter-Spring, 1959), 65-81; see also W. Bączkowski, "Sprawa ukraińska" [The Ukrainian Problem], *Kultura,* 1952, No. 7/57–8/58, pp. 64-69.

[53] *Słowo* (Wilno), June 30, 1932, as quoted in *Bil'shovyk Ukrainy,* IX, No. 1 (Jan., 1934), 97.

and thus enable Poland to regain her leading role in that part of the continent.[54]

Official Polish circles openly disavowed the anti-Soviet aspects of this plan and dissociated themselves from its authors.[55] At the same time, however, Marshal Piłsudski had no intention of binding his country irrevocably to the Soviet Union,[56] and instead decided to assert Poland's independence of both Moscow and Berlin by maintaining a state of balance between the opposing influences of her two powerful neighbors. All plans for a "preventive" war against Germany seemed utterly unrealistic.[57] Thus, having regulated and pacified the relations with the USSR, the Marshal proceeded to make a determined effort to come to terms

[54] These circles established close ties with the so-called Promethean movement, an émigré organization which purported to represent the "oppressed peoples of the USSR" and which included among its members some former Russian citizens (mostly of Ukrainian and Georgian origin) serving as officers in the Polish Army. For details see *Osteuropa*, XIV (1938-39), 230-31, and Shandruk, p. 150. It was under the influence of this group that Włodzimierz Bączkowski, editor-in-chief of the periodicals *Biuletyn Polsko-Ukraiński*, *Myśl Polska*, and *Wschód-Orient*, developed the idea of "Polish Prometheanism," which he described as "an expression of Poland's *raison d'état*" and "a weapon of defense and of aggression" against Russian imperialism. *Wschód-Orient*, VII (1935-36), 12. Bączkowski had many sympathizers in the camp of Piłsudski's followers, especially among the Soviet and East European experts working in the Institute of Minority Affairs and the Eastern Institute in Warsaw and in the East European Research Institute in Wilno. Some of them actively cooperated with the Ukrainian Scientific Institute in Warsaw, an institution staffed with Ukrainian scholars, but founded (in 1930) and supported financially by the Polish government. The Polish "Prometheans" were frequently criticized by the National Democrats, who maintained that Poland, threatened by an implacable enemy in the west, "could not afford the luxury" of provoking Russia. R. Dmowski in *Przewrót* [The Upheaval] (Warsaw, 1934), p. 455.

[55] *Gazeta Polska*, Sept. 15, 1933, as quoted in *Kurjer Warszawski*, Sept. 18, 1933; see also *Izvestiia*, Sept. 16, 1933.

[56] In May, 1933, Piłsudski stated in a secret communication to Kemal Atatürk that "in spite of all appearances and of the settlement of Poland's eastern frontiers, he did not trust Soviet Russia and would always regard her as the most dangerous enemy"; he also tried unsuccessfully to sound the Turkish leader about the possibility of Polish-Turkish cooperation in dealing with the Russian problem. See W. Jędrzejewicz, "Piłsudski i Kemal" [Piłsudski and Kemal], *Wiadomości* (London), May 23, 1954, and M. Sokolnicki, "Polityka Piłsudskiego a Turcja" [The Policy of Piłsudski and Turkey], *Niepodległość*, VI (1958), 19-21.

[57] For a detailed discussion of the question of "preventive war" see B. Čelovsky, "Piłsudskis Präventivkrieg gegen das nationalsozialistische Deutschland," *Die Welt als Geschichte*, 1954, Heft 1, pp. 53-70; Z. J. Gąsiorowski, "Did Piłsudski Attempt to Initiate a Preventive War in 1933?" *Journal of Modern History*, XXVII (June, 1955), 135-51; Roberts, "The Diplomacy of Colonel Beck," in Craig and Gilbert, eds., *The Diplomats*, pp. 612-14; H. Roos, "Die 'Präventivkriegspläne' Piłsudskis von 1933," *Vierteljahrshefte für Zeitgeschichte*, III (Oct., 1955), 344-63.

with Hitler "as long as the Reich was still weak and ready to pay a good price."[58]

It was, incidentally, during these fateful months of decision and revaluation that the first speculation about the possibility of a Polish-German alliance directed against the Soviet Union began to appear in the world press. The Führer's sweeping "Eastern conception" and his determination to abandon the colonial and commercial policies of the past for the sake of the *Bodenpolitik* of the future[59] indicated that Poland had a key role in the realization of his plans, either as an associate sharing the spoils of victory or as an enemy who had to be put out of the way before the beginning of a military expedition against Russia. Rumors circulating in Europe during the summer and fall of 1933, especially after the presentation of the so-called Hugenberg memorandum to the World Economic Conference in London,[60] saw a possible solution of the Polish dilemma in an arrangement whereby Poland would cede the Corridor to Germany and receive as compensation a large part of the Soviet Ukraine in the direction of the Black Sea.[61] It was also suggested that the Russians knew all about this scheme and were irritated by the Polish "duplicity," in spite of the formal correctness of the relations between the two countries. These reports were usually denied almost as soon as they originated, but they seemed to make a lasting impression upon public opinion in the West, although few experts in Polish affairs were willing to believe that Poland would be prepared to surrender a vitally important part of her territory in exchange for vague promises and ambiguous pledges.[62]

The first references to the "Soviet danger" made by an official German spokesman to a representative of Poland were probably Hitler's statements during his conversations with Polish envoy

[58] Roos, *Polen und Europa*, p. 109.

[59] A. Hitler, *Mein Kampf* (New York, 1940), pp. 950-51.

[60] This memorandum dealt with the subject of Germany's need for territorial expansion. Text in *DGFP*, Series C, I, 562-67.

[61] According to Rudolf Nadolny, the German ambassador to Moscow, this "project" was supported especially by Alfred Rosenberg, the director of the Foreign Policy Office of the National Socialist Party (*ibid.*, II, 319); see also M. Sokolnicki, "Archiwum Ministra Szembeka" [The Archives of Minister Szembek], *Kultura*, No. 9/59 (Sept., 1952), p. 120.

[62] See *DGFP*, Series C, II, 326.

Wysocki on May 2 and July 13, 1933.[63] The Führer was even more outspoken in his prolonged interview with the new Polish minister, Józef Lipski, on November 15, 1933, during which he described Poland as an "outpost against Asia," whose destruction by the forces of Communism would bring "misfortune" to her neighbors.[64] According to some sources, Hitler was interested at that time in the creation of a buffer zone between Germany and Russia,[65] and wanted to secure Poland's cooperation for the realization of this scheme. Similar ideas were expressed by Goebbels during his meeting with Beck at Geneva in October, 1933, when he mentioned the possibility of a German-Polish alliance, "with the view of a common action in the east, and especially in the Ukraine." The Polish Foreign Minister took a skeptical attitude toward these projects; he was more concerned with the menace of German penetration in the direction of the Baltic states, and dismissed with a shrug "ces histoires d'Ukraine."[66]

These apprehensions were apparently shared by Moscow, and soon after the start of the Polish-German negotiations for a non-aggression declaration in November, 1933, the Kremlin made a renewed attempt to win Poland as a partner in "guaranteeing" the Baltic states; the obvious purpose of this offer was to stop the spread of Berlin's political influence along the shores of the Baltic by establishing a Polish-Soviet condominium over the area. While the Polish government was interested in the continued independence of its small neighbors, it did not wish to reject the Soviet proposal out of hand; it insisted, however, that the policy of "protecting someone against his will" could lead to dangerous consequences.[67] In Poland's opinion, the action proposed by the Russians could be taken only with the express agreement of the

[63] *Polish White Book*, pp. 12 and 16. During these conversations, Hitler seemed to be perturbed over the "astonishing fertility" of the Russian nation which "caused him to reflect seriously on the dangers to Europe and, therefore, to Poland" that might arise from this fact.
[64] *Ibid.*, p. 17.   [65] Laroche, p. 142.   [66] *Ibid.*, pp. 143-44.
[67] Beck, *Przemówienia*, p. 152. According to J. Łukasiewicz, then Polish minister to Moscow, the Soviet government insisted that the text of the joint declaration to be issued by the USSR and Poland be approved secretly by the two powers and only then communicated to the Baltic states. The Soviet draft was formulated in such ambiguous terms that any change in the internal life of one of the Baltic countries could serve as pretext for intervention. Umiastowski, p. 136.

countries concerned, and she hoped that their negative reaction would give her a chance to extricate herself from a difficult situation which could have easily compromised the chances for her *détente* with Germany.[68]

In December, Estonia, Finland, Latvia, and Lithuania were formally approached by Moscow and Warsaw and asked how they would regard a Polish-Soviet declaration to the effect that their "political and economic independence" was in the interest of Poland and the USSR, and that, should this independence be threatened, "those two governments would discuss possible action."[69] This joint *démarche* was viewed with some uneasiness not only by the countries concerned but also by the Western powers, and the British ambassador to Warsaw believed that the Poles, by associating themselves with Russia, "had fallen into a trap" laid for them by the Kremlin.[70] In order to clarify this misunderstanding, Beck deemed it necessary to give to the Western diplomats an authoritative explanation of his policy in the Baltic question.[71] Meanwhile the situation continued to develop according to Warsaw's expectations. Although Estonia, Latvia, and Lithuania adopted a favorable attitude toward the Soviet-Polish proposal, the Finnish cabinet decided to reject the whole scheme as "unnecessary." In view of the negative reply of one of the interested countries, the Polish government informed Moscow that further negotiations on the subject "had no longer any point."[72]

At the same time a more serious attempt to ascertain Poland's views with regard to the Soviet problem was made by Hermann Rauschning, the president of the Danzig Senate. During Rauschning's secret meeting with Piłsudski on December 11, 1933, the Marshal allegedly expressed his belief in the inevitability of a Russo-Polish and a Russo-German war, and showed interest in the

[68] As Beck confided to the German envoy, the Soviet proposal "amounted to the formation of a political bloc . . . which was all the less desirable to Poland as it might be pointed against Germany" (*DGFP*, Series C, II, 774-75; see also *ibid.*, pp. 879-80).

[69] *DBFP*, 2d Series, VII, 632.   [70] *Ibid.*   [71] *Ibid.*, p. 633.

[72] *Ibid.*, pp. 632 and 635; see also *DGFP*, Series C, II, 367-68. It should be noted that only a few months later, on March 28, 1934, Litvinov proposed to the German ambassador in Moscow the signature of a joint protocol guaranteeing the "independence" of the Baltic states. On April 15, Ambassador Nadolny informed the Narkomindel that this proposal was unacceptable to his government. See *DGFP*, Series C, II, 684-85, 731-34, 746-47, 763-64.

possibility of an alliance between Poland and the Reich, which would eventually create an entirely new basis for the settlement of the frontier dispute between the two nations. According to Rauschning, Piłsudski realized that neither the Poles nor their allies could stop the rearmament of Germany, and decided that the best way to promote Poland's interests lay in a close military cooperation with the Nazis. Unsupported by any other sources, however, this evidence can be easily refuted by the Marshal's studiously reserved attitude toward all more or less subtle offers of Polish-German entente which emanated from Hitler's entourage.[73] In any case, Rauschning's report on his talks with Piłsudski does not seem to have impressed the Führer, who responded by merely indicating his preference for "an eastern policy of agreement with Poland" and by stressing his willingness to "give the Poles a chance." At the same time he added that he had "little use" for Poland as a new great power on Germany's frontiers; what he was thinking of was "an eastern alliance between Poland, the Baltic states, Hungary, the Balkan states, the Ukraine, the Volga basin, Georgia. An alliance, but not of equal partners; it will be an alliance of vassal states, with no army, no separate policy, no separate economy."[74]

Meanwhile the negotiations conducted by Lipski with the Wilhelmstrasse continued to develop favorably, and a German-Polish declaration of nonaggression was duly signed in Berlin on January 26, 1934.[75] On that very day Stalin observed in his speech to the Seventeenth Congress of the CPSU that changes for the better had recently occurred in relations between Russia and Poland and that

[73] Rauschning's account of his conversation with Piłsudski is contained in an unsigned memorandum of January 14, 1934, in the files of the Auswärtiges Amt, No. 6601/E495072-77, and in a letter to Richard Breyer, dated October 1, 1951. Breyer, pp. 175-76.

[74] Rauschning, p. 128. In Rauschning's opinion, Poland and the Reich could have reached an understanding with regard to their common interests in Russia, but this was made difficult by Rosenberg's plans to organize a German dependency in the Ukraine.

[75] For a comprehensive discussion of this agreement and its background see Z. J. Gąsiorowski, "The German-Polish Nonaggression Pact of 1934," *Journal of Central European Affairs*, XV (April, 1955), 3-28, and B. Czarnecki, "Gdy Niemcy chciały z Polską pokoju," *Sprawy Międzynarodowe*, XI, No. 12 (Dec., 1958), 69-82. The advantages and disadvantages of the pact for both partners are summarized in K. Lapter's article "Polityka Józefa Becka," *Sprawy Międzynarodowe*, XI, No. 5 (May, 1958), 50-52.

the mutual distrust was beginning to disappear. His conclusions were, however, rather ambiguous:

Surprises and zig-zags in policy, for example, in Poland, where anti-Soviet sentiments are still strong, can by no means be regarded as precluded. But a change for the better in our relations, irrespective of its results in the future, is a fact worthy of being noted and singled out as a factor in the advancement of the cause of peace.[76]

Moscow's first reaction to the German-Polish pact was extremely cautious, although some undertones of uneasiness were discernible in the Soviet press, which suggested that the Poles must have promised Germany certain "compensations" in return for her renunciation of aggressive designs on Polish territory.[77] A *Pravda* editorial stated that Russia was always ready to welcome any agreement which reduced the danger of "war in general and war in Eastern Europe in particular," but it noted that the Polish-German declaration "raised a number of questions" and that neither the text nor the aims of the accord were quite clear.[78] Privately, some Soviet sources went much further and expressed fears that Poland might eventually "enter Germany's orbit and seek a new orientation in European affairs."[79] It was, as yet, "premature to speak about a bloc of Polish and German imperialism against the USSR as an accomplished fact"; the Kremlin felt, however, that "a serious step had been made in that direction" and that it might be followed by other steps.[80] The opposition parties in Poland also showed some signs of anxiety, and while a prominent Socialist leader described the Berlin declaration as a "turn-

---

[76] CPSU, *XVII S"ezd VKP(b), Stenograficheskii otchët*, p. 13; English translation quoted from Degras, pp. 69-70. It is of interest that a welcoming message from the Communist Party of Poland, which received "stormy applause" from the Congress, openly charged the Polish government with duplicity and with using "secret negotiations and pacts" in order to "reconcile imperialistic contradictions between Poland and Germany at the expense of the USSR." CPSU, *XVII S"ezd VKP(b)*, pp. 218-19.

[77] *Izvestiia*, Jan. 29, 1934. At the same time, the Soviet minister in Warsaw reportedly engaged in "nervous activities" and tried to obtain more information about the alleged agreement "whereby the joint Polish-German war of conquest against the Soviet Ukraine [was] supposed to be in preparation." *DGFP*, Series C, II, 459.

[78] *Pravda*, Jan. 29, 1934.   [79] *The New York Times*, Jan. 30, 1934.

[80] Communist International, *XIII plenum IKKI, Stenograficheskii otchët* (Moscow, 1934), p. 79; see also *KPP w obronie niepodległości Polski*, pp. 194-97.

ing point in Polish foreign policy" which could conceivably lead to dire consequences,[81] the chief spokesman of the National Democratic group in the Sejm warned the ruling circles to beware of any "ambiguity" in the conduct of Polish policy and to avoid any measures which might be misunderstood by the Soviet government.[82]

In order to prove that all these suspicions and apprehensions were unfounded, it was decided that Beck should go personally to Moscow to allay any Soviet fears of German-Polish collusion, and the time between the signature and the ratification of the Berlin declaration was chosen as most appropriate for this purpose. As the Polish Foreign Minister put it himself in his memoirs,

The simultaneous timing of these two events [the signature of the pact with Germany and the Moscow visit] was to stress our position in Eastern Europe more clearly. It was necessary to make it known that our direct contacts, negotiations, and agreements with each of our big neighbors were to clear the situation, aiming at positive results, i.e., the improvement of political relations in that European region, and that they were by no means diplomatic plots and could not be interpreted as a submission of Polish politics to influences coming either from Berlin or from Moscow. . . . I attached great importance to the necessity of stressing that there was no contradiction between the two pacts, as the improvement of our relations with Germany and Russia was limited by the impossibility of making our policy dependent on any of these dangerous partners.[83]

Beck's intention to visit the Soviet capital was disclosed for the first time in his address to the Foreign Affairs Committee of the Senate on February 5, 1934. The sensational news of the first official trip to the USSR by a Polish cabinet minister climaxed an optimistic account of the relations between Poland and Russia:

The lack of aggressive tendencies as between ourselves and the Soviet

[81] *Kurjer Warszawski*, Feb. 5, 1934.

[82] *Ibid.*, Feb. 7, 1934; Poland, Sejm, *Sprawozdanie stenograficzne*, Okres III, Posiedzenie CXI, pp. 58-59; see also Poland, Senat, *Sprawozdanie stenograficzne*, Okres III, Posiedzenie LIX, p. 88. During the debate the representatives of all major political parties emphasized the necessity of maintaining and consolidating Poland's good relations with Russia. Poland, Sejm, Posiedzenie CX, pp. 23, 36; Posiedzenie CXI, p. 61.

[83] Beck, *Final Report*, pp. 31, 51; see also his conversation with the German envoy as reported by the latter in *DGFP*, Series C, II, 458-59.

Union has produced an atmosphere in which the disappearance of opposed political trends made itself felt in a number of other fields. It was also possible to establish an identity of views in quite a number of matters. This, for instance, was revealed several times during the Disarmament Conference, and on the frontier itself a neighborly friendliness made itself felt, as was reflected in a number of technical matters. [Our] Government attaches great importance to that evolution of relations and to the contacts initiated with the Soviet government, which I hope shortly to be able to keep up personally.[84]

When Beck, accompanied by his wife, left Warsaw on the morning of February 12, it was emphasized that he was merely going to return the visit paid to the Polish capital by Chicherin in September, 1925, but it was obvious to everybody that the trip had been planned as a practical demonstration that Poland's rapprochement with Germany was no obstacle to the strengthening of Polish-Russian amity. The Warsaw press wished the Foreign Minister success in his difficult mission, and the newspaper comments ranged from a moderate editorial in *Gazeta Polska* to a frankly optimistic leading article in *Kurjer Warszawski*.[85] Perhaps the only discordant remark was made by German Minister von Moltke, who observed, with some cynicism, that "les amours de la Pologne ne durent pas longtemps."[86]

According to one of Beck's closest associates, the Polish guests initially encountered a cold reception in Moscow, but this uneasy atmosphere was entirely changed during the second and third days of the visit.[87] As soon as the ice was broken, the Russians showered Beck with innumerable tokens of attention and high esteem, and *Izvestiia* reminded its readers that he, as the closest adviser of Marshal Piłsudski, deserved full credit for the idea of Polish-Soviet rapprochement; it was also his special merit that

[84] Beck, *Przemówienia*, p. 98; English translation in Harley, *The Authentic Biography of Colonel Beck*, pp. 127-28. For more details on the background of the visit see *DGFP*, Series C, II, 525.

[85] *Kurjer Warszawski*, Feb. 11, 1934; for quotations from *Gazeta Polska* see *ibid.*, Feb. 13, 1934.

[86] Laroche, p. 152. The German envoy was annoyed by Beck's "evasiveness" in answering his questions about the purpose of the trip, notwithstanding the Foreign Minister's assurances that "nothing would be done that was contradictory to the German-Polish statement or that could otherwise injure German interests." *DGFP*, Series C, II, 458.

[87] Laroche, p. 152.

he was able to defend Poland's independent international role against the encroachments of imperialist powers.[88]

Beck's first official statement to a Tass representative on February 14 was rather reserved and did not go beyond stereotyped phrases about "friendly neighborly cooperation."[89] He had some difficulty, however, in trying to maintain this restrained attitude during the glittery reception given by Litvinov in honor of the visitors, when the Foreign Commissar enumerated all the signs of a "successful and varied development of relations between the USSR and Poland" and expressed his conviction that various international problems which demanded mutual clarification and agreement would be solved in such a way as considerably to weaken the forces disturbing peace and order among the nations.[90] This veiled allusion to the policies of Nazi Germany was not entirely to the liking of Beck, whose speech dealt only in very general terms with the stabilization of Polish-Soviet relations and laid special emphasis on the "formation of bonds of acquaintance and better understanding" between the two countries.[91] In this way, Beck was carrying out faithfully the instructions received from Marshal Piłsudski: he tried to "create the atmosphere of an important, free and even friendly manifestation," while "remaining at the same time cautious in avoiding any pushing of Poland into the slippery track of political collaboration with the Soviets."[92]

During his stay in Moscow, Beck had several conferences with Litvinov[93] and met many other prominent personalities of Russia with the notable exception of Stalin, who held at that time no official position in the Soviet government. Generally speaking, the concrete achievements of these informal conversations were quite impressive from the Polish point of view, though perhaps less

[88] *Izvestiia*, Feb. 12, 1934; see also *Pravda*, Feb. 13, 1934.
[89] Beck, *Przemówienia*, p. 103.
[90] Litvinov, *Vneshniaia politika SSSR*, pp. 360-62; English translation in Degras, III, 73-75.
[91] Beck, *Przemówienia*, pp. 101-2; *Polish White Book*, pp. 177-78. Similar sentiments were expressed in Beck's statement to the press on February 15, 1934. *Przemówienia*, p. 104.
[92] Beck, *Final Report*, p. 51; see also *DGFP*, Series C, II, 525.
[93] According to a Polish Communist historian, Beck "answered evasively" Litvinov's proposal to discuss a "common action" against "the danger of German aggression." B. Jaworznicki, "Pakt Wschodni," *Sprawy Międzynarodowe*, II, No. 3/4 (July-Dec., 1949), 94.

satisfactory to the Russian side. An official communiqué issued on February 15 stressed that any future understanding between Poland and the Soviet Union must be founded on the existing agreements.[94] Both governments pledged themselves to cooperate with each other in the spirit of these documents, with the purpose of preserving and reinforcing general peace; in order to take full advantage of the "increasing possibilities" of that cooperation, the Polish legation in Moscow and the Soviet diplomatic mission in Warsaw were elevated to the status of embassies. The "community of views in regard to many . . . problems" was also reflected in the decision to "synchronize" the Polish-Soviet and Polish-German nonaggression pacts. All these results enabled Beck to state on his return that the trip to Russia had justified his expectations and confirmed the "just principles" of Polish policy.[95]

Early in April Iakov Davtian, the Soviet minister to Greece, was appointed as the first ambassador of the USSR to Poland,[96] and Juliusz Łukasiewicz, since 1933 Polish envoy in Moscow, was promoted to the ambassadorial rank. Both diplomats took an active part in the continuation of the negotiations which had been initiated by Beck and which finally resulted in the signature of the Polish-Soviet Protocol of May 5, 1934.[97] The two governments noted in this document that the nonaggression pact had had a beneficial influence on their mutual relations; they had decided, therefore, that it was to remain in force until December 31, 1945, with an automatic prolongation for another two years if not denounced by either of the signatories.[98] The agreement was to be regarded as a "fresh proof of the unchangeable character and solidity of the

---

[94] For the text of the communiqué see *Pravda*, Feb. 16, 1934, and Degras, III, 75.

[95] *Kurjer Warszawski*, Feb. 17, 1934; *The New York Times*, Feb. 18, 1934. On the political significance of the visit see *DGFP*, Series C, II, 526.

[96] *Kurjer Warszawski*, April 5, 1934. For an account of Davtian's audience with President Mościcki see *ibid.*, April 14, 1934. The first reception given by the new Ambassador is described in *Pravda*, April 22, 1934.

[97] For the text of the Protocol see League of Nations, *Treaty Series*, CLVII, 431-39. A selection of press comments is given in *Izvestiia*, May 6, 1934; *Pravda*, May 7-8, 1934; and *Kurjer Warszawski*, May 7-8, 1934.

[98] According to Beck, the Poles were anxious to leave an interval of at least one year between the final terms of expiration of their treaties with Berlin and Moscow. If the two pacts remained valid for the same period of time (ten years), then Poland would have to renegotiate them at the same time with Germany and Russia. *Final Report*, p. 51. Besides, Warsaw had to consider the fact that the Baltic states also prolonged their pacts with the USSR until the end of 1945. See *DBFP*, 2d Series, VII, 675.

peaceful and friendly relations" between the two countries and as a contribution to the stability and peaceful development of the international situation in Eastern Europe. In an annex to the Protocol both sides stated expressly that they were under no obligation inconsistent with the provisions of the Riga Treaty, and this declaration was widely interpreted as a refutation of all rumors about a secret understanding between Germany and Poland, including promises of territorial gains for the latter in the Soviet Ukraine and Belorussia. In addition to this, Moscow solemnly denied any intention on its part to interfere in the settlement of territorial questions between Poland and Lithuania. This important victory of Polish diplomacy was won only after hard bargaining,[99] and it considerably enhanced the value of the Protocol to Poland by serving notice to Kaunas that it could no longer count on Russia's direct support in the Wilno dispute.[100] The favorable impression created by the signature of the agreement was strengthened by the publication of the final communiqué of the mixed commission which had been entrusted with the return of Polish cultural treasures from the Soviet Union and had now completed its task after more than twelve years of arduous work.[101]

At the time when the cycle of Poland's negotiations with Russia was approaching a successful conclusion and when normal diplomatic relations were about to be established between Warsaw's closest ally, Rumania, and the USSR,[102] Piłsudski told a secret meeting of Polish political and military leaders that the agreements signed with the Soviet Union and Germany "created for Poland an exceptionally favorable conjuncture unknown in history";[103] he warned them, however, that the friendly relations with Moscow and Berlin could not continue indefinitely since

[99] Litvinov himself admitted that the Polish government "used every endeavor" to persuade the Russians "to give way over the Vilna question." *DBFP*, 2d Series, VII, 687.

[100] *Ibid.*; see also *DGFP*, Series C, II, 220-21, 801-3. For Polish press comment see *Czas* (Kraków) as quoted in *Kurjer Warszawski*, May 9, 1934.

[101] *Kurjer Warszawski*, May 9, 1934.

[102] The decision to recognize the Soviet Union was taken by the governments of the Little Entente countries during their conference in Zagreb on January 22, 1934. The diplomatic relations between Rumania and Czechoslovakia on one side and the USSR on the other were formally established on June 9, 1934. For the reaction of the Polish press to this event see *Kurjer Warszawski*, June 10, 1934, and *Pravda*, June 11, 1934.

[103] Beck, *Final Report*, p. 57; see also Szembek, pp. 2-3.

the internal situation of both Russia and Germany was subject
to changes and unpredictable fluctuations. It was, therefore, vitally
important to answer the question as to which one of these two
neighbors was, or could become in the future, more dangerous to
Poland, and "from which side should [the Poles] first of all expect
a threat to come."[104] All persons attending the meeting were requested to study this problem in detail in order to determine
their personal solution of the dilemma, but the results of the inquiry were inconclusive: it appeared that neither the Reich nor
the Soviet Union was as yet powerful enough to vanquish the
Poles, although it was generally expected that the USSR would
be able to launch an attack against Poland much sooner than
Germany. In any case, it was obvious that the fundamental issues
of Polish foreign policy demanded a much more thorough approach, including a careful and exact analysis of the changing
international situation. These considerations prompted the Marshal to create in June, 1934, a secret bureau, headed by General
Kazimierz Fabrycy and devoted to a specialized study of Germany
and Russia.[105] The first report of this "special cell" indicated that
at least some Polish military experts regarded the growing strength
of the German Army as the paramount threat to Poland's security,
but a vast majority of army leaders, supported by Piłsudski and
Beck, disagreed with this appraisal of the situation.[106] It seems
that the old Marshal, preoccupied with the Russian danger
throughout his life, tended to overestimate Hitler's internal difficulties and was not fully aware of the scope of German rearmament efforts, although he was by no means inclined to ignore the
potential threat of the Third Reich. In his opinion, Russia's
standing army of some 1,300,000 men was much more impressive

[104] Beck, *Final Report*, p. 59; K. Fabrycy, "Komórka specjalna" [The Special Cell],
Niepodległość, V (1955), 217.
[105] For a detailed account see Fabrycy, *Niepodległość*, V, 217-20; K. Glabisz,
"Laboratorium" [The Laboratory], *Niepodległość*, VI (1958), 220-27; S. Pstrokoński,
"Interna" [Internal Research], *Wiadomości* (London), June 4, 1950; see also Beck,
Final Report, pp. 60-61, and Pobóg-Malinowski, II, Part I, 556-57. The members
of this "brain trust" included, besides General Fabrycy, several other high-ranking
officers of the General Staff, Beck, Szembek, and the Polish ambassadors to Moscow
and Berlin. The activities of the "special cell" were discontinued soon after
Piłsudski's death owing to the lack of interest shown for this project by Śmigły-
Rydz, the new inspector-general of the Polish Army.
[106] Glabisz, *Niepodległość*, VI, 224.

than the largely inexperienced troops grouped around the core of the Reichswehr; the Soviet leaders, inspired with a fanatic belief in the inevitability of world revolution, seemed also more likely to start an international adventure than the more "reasonable" Nazi rulers.[107]

There were, moreover, other reasons which made it advisable to concentrate Poland's defensive effort on her eastern frontier. In the event of a war with Germany, the Poles would be supported by their French allies, and other European powers could also be expected to spring into action to defend France's bastion on the Vistula; on the other hand, no effective help from the West could reach Poland in time to protect her from a Russian onslaught.[108] Thus, in shielding their borderlands against a Soviet attack, the Poles could count only upon themselves and, to a lesser extent, upon the questionable assistance of the Rumanian Army. All their military preparations had to be based on this simple premise, and all the resources of Polish diplomacy had to be mobilized in order to avert the possibility of Poland's international isolation in the event of a conflict with Russia. Some of the steps taken by Beck and his associates with this purpose in mind led necessarily to Berlin; though quite harmless in themselves, they provoked Moscow's anger and displeasure, and eventually put an end to the short-lived Polish-Soviet *détente*.[109]

Meanwhile the Nazi wooing of Poland continued with an increased fervor, although it is not entirely clear whether the initiative for this persistent solicitation came from Hitler himself or

[107] *Ibid.* In Polish military planning, the eastern front enjoyed a high priority up to 1938. Toward the end of 1935, the Polish General Staff began to prepare a detailed operational defensive plan, based on a thorough study of terrain and other preparatory work, which was to become effective in the event of a Soviet attack. In accordance with this outline, the Polish Army began in 1936 to fortify the strategic region of Polesie, but failed to secure in a comparable way the country's western frontier. See Poland, Polskie Siły Zbrojne, Komisja Historyczna, *Polskie Siły Zbrojne w drugiej wojnie światowej*, I, Part I, 109-11, 129, and Akademiia Nauk SSSR, Institut Slavianovedeniia, *Istoriia Pol'shi*, III, 452.

[108] See Fabrycy, *Niepodległość*, V, 219-20.

[109] According to Miedziński, an anti-Polish group of Soviet leaders, allegedly headed by Litvinov, gained at that time the upper hand in the councils of the Kremlin and tried to undermine the confidence between Poland and the Western powers by spreading rumors about Warsaw's secret contacts with the Nazis. This propaganda action was centered in the Soviet Embassy in Paris and had the support of a part of the French press. "Popioły są jeszcze gorące," *Wiadomości* (London), Nov. 9, 1952.

from his subordinates. Rosenberg took a lively interest in the Polish visit of Dr. Insabato, Mussolini's Ukrainian expert, and in his reports about Piłsudski's alleged intention of destroying the Soviet Union and of winning for Poland a corridor to the Black Sea.[110] While the Führer and the Duce met in Venice in the middle of June, 1934, Goebbels paid an official visit to Warsaw and made a strenuous effort to inject some cordiality into German-Polish relations. These attempts to prepare the ground for future close collaboration between the two countries were checked, however, by the bullets of a Ukrainian terrorist who on June 15 assassinated Bronisław Pieracki, Polish minister of the interior. This renewed Warsaw's suspicions that the Nazis were playing a double game, courting Poland and at the same time encouraging and subsidizing extremist groups among discontented national minorities. The conviction spread widely that the Germans shared the moral responsibility for the murder, in spite of the fact that the Nazis promptly extradited to the Polish authorities the underground leader who had planned the assassination. Under these circumstances, it was hardly possible to promote the idea of an alliance between Poland and Germany, the more so as the Ukrainian nationalists reportedly refused to follow Berlin's advice to give up their anti-Polish activities in favor of an intensified propaganda campaign in the Soviet Ukraine.[111]

[110] Roos, *Polen und Europa*, p. 150.   [111] *Ibid.*, p. 148.

III. Poland and the Eastern Locarno

One of the most perplexing problems facing Polish diplomacy between the wars was the issue of the so-called Eastern Pact of Mutual Guarantee, better known under the name Eastern Locarno.[1] The whole project developed from a Soviet proposal for a secret agreement with France, strictly bilateral in its original version, but much broader in its scope than the prewar accords between the Third Republic and the tsars.[2] The idea of this sweeping Franco-Russian alliance seems to have assumed a concrete form during Herriot's visit to Moscow in August, 1933.[3] While the Soviet Union went at first so far as to demand France's backing "not only in Europe but throughout the world,"[4] the French showed more restraint, being interested chiefly in strengthening their defensive system in Eastern and Central Europe by utilizing Russia as a counterpoise to Germany. The uneasiness called forth by Hitler's rise to power, as well as increasing doubts about Poland's willingness and ability to continue successfully to play her role as the chief ally and bulwark of France on Germany's eastern flank, prompted some French leaders to look for a more satisfactory solution. It was quite natural that they turned their attention to Soviet Russia, in spite of the misgivings expressed

[1] For a more detailed discussion of this subject see J. Jurkiewicz, "Polska wobec planów Paktu Wschodniego w latach 1934-1935," *Sprawy Międzynarodowe*, XII, No. 3 (March, 1959), 18-51, and B. Jaworznicki, "Pakt Wschodni," *ibid.*, II, No. 3/4 (July-Dec., 1949), 91-109.

[2] *DBFP*, 2d Series, VI (London, 1957), 804; see also *DGFP*, Series C, III (Washington, 1959), 19.

[3] *DBFP*, 2d Series, VI, 804. Herriot himself is rather vague about his talks with Litvinov; see his *Jadis*, II, 368.

[4] *DBFP*, 2d Series, VI, 804.

by those quarters which two years earlier had been so critical of the Polish-Soviet rapprochement. The overtures of the Quai d'Orsay found the Kremlin in an unusually responsive mood. Faced with the failure of the Rapallo policy and with the persistent threat of a military conflict in the Far East, the Russian rulers were inclined to regard all attempts at the revision of the Versailles system as a potential menace to the security of the USSR, and openly proclaimed their readiness to join the ranks of the defenders of the status quo in Europe.[5]

The unofficial talks between Paris and Moscow opened in October, 1933, under the personal sponsorship of French Foreign Minister Joseph Paul-Boncour;[6] they had to be interrupted, however, early in February, 1934, as a result of the fall of Daladier's cabinet. Louis Barthou, Paul-Boncour's successor, originally far from enthusiastic about the project, now made it his pet idea, but only after letting the Russians cool their heels for two months "to show them that he was not in a great hurry."[7] The original draft of the Franco-Soviet compact had to be brought in line with the new world order based on the Covenant of the League of Nations; the bilateral pact had to be transformed into a regional treaty, "a kind of eastern pendant to the main treaty of Locarno," but its scope was to remain limited to those states which were vitally interested in the security of Eastern Europe.[8]

The first round of the negotiations proceeded rather propitiously. In May, 1934, Litvinov arrived at Geneva to meet the French Foreign Minister, and it was during their talks that there developed the concept of a collective pact of mutual assistance which was to be guaranteed, "in some way," by France.[9] Barthou's proposal to restrict pact membership to the Soviet Union, Poland, Germany,[10] and Czechoslovakia was dropped in view of the Kremlin's insistence that the Baltic states be included as being particularly vulnerable to a German attack.[11] The treaty was to be based on a mutual pledge of nonaggression; it was also to provide for con-

---

[5] *DGFP*, Series C, III, 177-78; see also *ibid.*, pp. 150-51.
[6] See his *Entre deux guerres*, II, 345.　　[7] *DBFP*, 2d Series, VI, 803-5.
[8] See *DGFP*, Series C, III, 19.　　[9] *DBFP*, 2d Series, VI, 754.
[10] At first Moscow was unwilling to agree to Germany's participation and consented only when France insisted that this was an indispensable condition.
[11] *DBFP*, 2d Series, VI, 754.

sultation between the partners and for mutual assistance in case of an unprovoked aggression committed by one of the signatories against another.[12] An additional agreement between France and the Soviet Union was to assure the Russians of French help if the USSR became the victim of an unprovoked aggression by one of the signatories of the pact; on the other hand, Moscow was to pledge itself to aid the Third Republic if it should be subject to an attack as a result of a violation of the Locarno Treaties. Since Soviet Russia had hitherto remained outside the pale of "respectable" nations, it was considered essential that she should join the League of Nations as soon as possible, preferably before the signature of the treaty.

Now that the project of the pact seemed to be moving slowly toward its realization, it became obvious that the success or failure of the whole scheme would be determined by Warsaw's attitude, since Germany could hardly refuse to join if Poland decided to come in.[13] It was for this reason that the French were so eagerly "encouraging" the Poles to move even further in their rapprochement with the Soviet Union.[14] The first serious step in this direction was made by Barthou during his visit to the Polish capital in April, 1934, although no concrete proposals were submitted to Poland at that time. The French Foreign Minister, anxious to see "how Warsaw would accept the decision to ally itself with its bitterest enemy, Russia,"[15] showed interest in Piłsudski's views concerning the internal situation in the Soviet Union and the possibility of Moscow's entry into the League of Nations. The Marshal's answers were rather evasive; he stated that he had discontinued his old practice of making a special study of Russian affairs twice a year, but the anecdotes with which he entertained his French guest illustrated in an unmistakable way his deep-seated antipathy toward the Soviet system.[16] He believed that the USSR would stop short of joining the League; in his opinion, the

[12] For the proposed text of the treaty see *ibid.*, pp. 827-28.

[13] *Ibid.*, p. 769; see also Lipski's report of his conversation with Hitler and Neurath on August 27, 1934, as quoted by K. Lapter in "Polityka Józefa Becka," *Sprawy Międzynarodowe*, XI, No. 5 (May, 1958), 54.

[14] *DBFP*, 2d Series, VI, 262.

[15] Mme Tabouis as quoted in Potemkin, ed., III, 502.

[16] Szembek, pp. 4-7.

Kremlin had no stable policy, and it would be risky to rely too much upon its good will in preparing any new plans for Europe's salvation.[17]

Piłsudski's apprehensions failed to dampen Barthou's ardor; indeed, the statement made by the French Foreign Minister in the Chamber of Deputies on May 25 showed that he was as determined as ever to make his scheme work.[18] Although the Quai d'Orsay had no illusions as to Poland's reserved attitude and complained to the British Foreign Office about Warsaw's "narrow and self-seeking policy,"[19] it believed that it would be able eventually to overcome all possible objections. As Barthou saw it, the Poles would be in an awkward position if they refused to join their neighbors in a pact that was designed to improve the international situation.[20] Similar views were voiced by some leaders of the Polish opposition parties, who rejected a direct alliance between Poland and Russia but advocated the idea of a "political triangle" based on a close cooperation between Paris, Warsaw, and Moscow. In their opinion, the preservation of the European balance and the safeguarding of peace were "very difficult and immense tasks," which required collective action on the part of all interested powers. If the USSR was ready to join France, Poland, and the Little Entente in a formal understanding, this step would represent a strengthening of the forces of peace and ought to be welcomed by all well-meaning people in Europe.[21]

On June 4 the French Foreign Minister met Beck at Geneva and acquainted him with the projected "North-Eastern pact," which was later to be supplemented by the conclusion of a "Mediterranean treaty."[22] Beck, when asked whether he was prepared to give his approval in principle to this plan, answered that he did not intend to obstruct the action of the French government but had to make some reservations as far as Poland's attitude was concerned; moreover, he made no secret of his skepticism regard-

[17] Laroche, p. 159.

[18] See France, Journal officiel, *Débats parlementaires*, 1934, No. 43, p. 1258.

[19] *DBFP*, 2d Series, VI, 755.   [20] *Ibid.;* see also *DGFP*, Series C, III, 20.

[21] S. Stroński, "Francja-Polska-Rosja" [France-Poland-Russia], *Kurjer Warszawski*, May 18, 1934.

[22] The latter agreement was to include Italy, Yugoslavia, Greece, Turkey, Bulgaria, Rumania, and the Soviet Union.

ing the chances for success of the French scheme.[23] Beck's doubts were probably aggravated by his conversation with Litvinov on June 5, during which the Foreign Commissar declared bluntly that the only way to prevent war was to isolate Germany and Japan, and that this could be done through a series of treaties, including an Eastern Locarno, a Meditarranean pact, and an accord of the Pacific powers; at the same time, he rejected Titulescu's plan of a separate treaty of guarantees between Russia, Poland, and Rumania.[24]

During the summer the French intensified their pressure on Warsaw, and the Poles were told in plain terms that the Quai d'Orsay planned to sign a pact with the Russians even if Piłsudski and Beck declined to join it in that undertaking.[25] Several Francophile newspapers in Poland echoed these warnings and admonished the government to follow Barthou's lead since those who refused to "join hands loyally" with him would later "bitterly regret the lost opportunity."[26] On the other hand, the Polish leaders regarded the danger of isolation from their Western allies as rather remote and were reluctant to support a scheme that was opposed to the very principles upon which the old Marshal and his collaborators were trying to base their foreign policy. To them, the Eastern Pact limited Poland's individual initiative in international affairs, degraded her to the role of a tool of other countries, and deprived her of that increased influence which she was able to acquire thanks to her agreements with Germany and Russia; it also tended to "dilute" the Franco-Polish accord and to diminish Warsaw's prestige by making the Soviet Union the undisputed arbiter of Eastern and East Central Europe.[27] Further-

[23] See Beck, *Dernier rapport*, pp. 281-83. According to Beck, the projected pact "aimed at pushing Eastern Europe . . . into the arms of Russian policy, and at tying up all that company with French politics." See his *Final Report*, p. 68, and *DGFP*, Series C, III, 753.

[24] Beck, *Dernier rapport*, pp. 280-81.

[25] See Moltke's report on the visit of General Debeney (a former chief of the French General Staff) to Warsaw. *DGFP*, Series C, III, 154-55.

[26] *Kurjer Warszawski*, July 11, 1934; see also *ibid.*, June 23 and 30, and July 14, 1934. The National Democratic and Socialist circles were particularly vocal in deploring the fact that the position taken by Poland not only dissociated her from France but also automatically brought her closer to Germany and other revisionist powers. *Ibid.*, Aug. 15, 1934.

[27] *Polska Zbrojna*, July 23, 1934, as quoted in *International Press Correspondence*,

more, the usefulness of the proposed pact depended to a large extent on the sincerity and military prowess of Russia, and the Poles had considerable doubts as to the reliability and internal stability of their eastern neighbor; they were also anxious not to offend the Third Reich, and for this reason could not be persuaded to become a party to a multilateral treaty which Germany was unwilling to join.[28] Poland stood now between Berlin and Moscow, on good terms with both but dependent on neither; in this way, she was able to occupy an advantageous position, "holding balance between Germany and the Franco-Russian combination and being courted on both sides."[29]

Under these circumstances it was hardly surprising that Warsaw was determined not to allow either Russian or German troops to enter Polish territory[30] and showed a marked reluctance to assume any new obligations which would bind it to protect the disliked Czechoslovakia or the intransigent Lithuania without giving any tangible benefits to Poland. Since their arguments were not likely to find an appreciative audience in Paris, the Poles had to resort to delaying tactics and evasiveness, the two lethal diplomatic weapons, which Beck was able to wield with an almost unequaled mastery. His numerous and ingenious subterfuges and his unwillingness to accept the proposed pact even in principle aroused the suspicions of the British and irritated the French, who openly threatened Poland with the consequences of an alliance between the Third Republic and the Soviet Union. It was,

---

XIV, No. 45 (Aug. 24, 1934), 1169, and Mackiewicz, *Colonel Beck and His Policy*, p. 51; see also Flandin, p. 116, and Jaworznicki, "Pakt Wschodni," *Sprawy Międzynarodowe*, II, No. 3/4, 98-99. In Piłsudski's opinion, Russia's ascendancy in the Eastern Pact would have resulted in a "complete subordination" of Poland, the Baltic states, and the Danubian countries to Moscow's will. Komarnicki, *Piłsudski a polityka wielkich mocarstw zachodnich*, p. 79.

[28] *DBFP*, 2d Series, VII (London, 1958), 735; see also Beck's conversations with Moltke and Neurath as reported in *DGFP*, Series C, III, 277-79 and 385-86. Obviously, the Poles did not discount the possibility that an Eastern Locarno could prompt Hitler to return to the Rapallo connection. See Wheeler-Bennett, *Munich*, p. 285, and Mackiewicz, *Colonel Beck and His Policy*, p. 53.

[29] *DBFP*, 2d Series, VI, 784.

[30] This technical problem played a very important role in determining Poland's attitude toward the Eastern Locarno. According to the British military attaché in Warsaw, the very idea of having foreign troops on Polish soil was "repellent to every Pole," even if these armies entered Poland in order to assist her against enemy invasion. *Ibid.*, p. 860; see also *DGFP*, Series C, II (Washington, 1959), 845.

however, difficult to imagine anything more likely to inflame Piłsudski's anger than "putting a pistol to his head in this manner."[31] Some Western observers considered with alarm the possibility that this tactless challenge to Polish pride might result in throwing the Poles into Hitler's arms, especially since Beck reacted with studied indifference to France's warning that she was determined to sign the treaty with Russia regardless of Warsaw's attitude.[32]

Meanwhile Soviet diplomacy was busy spreading rumors about the existence of a "gentlemen's understanding" between Piłsudski and the Nazi leaders and accused the Marshal of cherishing a dream that a new Russo-Japanese war might provide Poland with "an historic opportunity to rush to the rescue of the victor."[33] Poland's attitude toward the Eastern Locarno was gradually becoming the chief worry of the Kremlin, where it was regarded as the "most delicate point" of the whole situation.[34] The Soviet press tried to convince Warsaw that an Eastern pact was, in fact, "the best guarantee that Poland could have," and expressed hopes that the critical state of international affairs, combined with Beck's common sense, would eventually make the Poles more inclined to listen to the entreaties of their allies.[35] Polish official circles contended, however, that the nonaggression pacts between the USSR and its neighbors, reaffirmed by the London Convention of 1933, made any new agreements superfluous. The German press, going even further, decried the "foolishness" of the idea of making Moscow a guarantor of the Locarno Treaties and warned that the right of passage of Soviet troops through Poland would impair rather than enhance the security of that country.[36] Indeed, the Russian problem appeared more complex than at any

---

[31] *DBFP*, 2d Series, VI, 783.   [32] *Ibid.*, p. 800; see also *DGFP*, Series C, III, 386.

[33] *USFR*, 1934, I (Washington, 1951), 497-98; see also *DGFP*, Series C, II, 233. The visit of Japanese prince Kaya to Berlin and Warsaw in the summer of 1934 gave rise to rumors that negotiations for a tripartite agreement between Germany, Poland, and Japan were going on and that a secret clause in the German-Polish nonaggression pact formally bound those two countries to undertake a joint action against Russia in the event of a Soviet-Japanese war. See L. K. Rosinger, "Germany's Far Eastern Policy under Hitler," *Pacific Affairs*, XI (Dec., 1938), 428, and Presseisen, pp. 63-64.

[34] *USFR*, 1934, I, 504.   [35] *Izvestiia*, July 16, 1934.

[36] See the article "Barthous Ernte" in the *Frankfurter Zeitung und Handelsblatt*, July 12, 1934, and the report "Polnische Vorbehalte gegen den französischen Sicherheitsblock," *ibid.*, July 11, 1934.

time during the past decade, and even some of the most outspoken friends of France advised Poland's allies to approach this issue with prudence and caution:

The present Soviet game is dictated by tactical considerations which can radically change with the passage of time, along with the position of the Moscow government. Under these circumstances Russia's withdrawal from the "syndicate" of revisionist powers can and should be regarded as an absolutely advantageous and positive fact. . . . Soviet offers should be treated loyally and taken into consideration in so far as they really serve the cause of general security. There is, however, an infinitely wide gap between this strictly realistic attitude and throwing oneself into the arms of the Bolsheviks. . . . Let us do everything in order to keep the Soviet guarantees offered to Europe within proper limits. Otherwise Bolshevik Russia will come to play the role of the proverbial Trojan horse in the system of European security.[37]

Beck's visit to Tallin and Riga undertaken toward the end of July was widely interpreted as a last-ditch attempt on Poland's part to prevent Estonia and Latvia from joining the Eastern Pact. After his return to Warsaw, the Polish Foreign Minister assured the Western diplomats that he had done nothing to disrupt their political plans in that part of Europe, but he warned them against assuming a condescending attitude toward the Baltic states, which were apprehensive of being used as pawns in the schemes of the great powers. In his opinion, they were especially afraid of putting themselves under Russia's "protection," the more so since they could not expect any effective assistance from France and had to be doubly suspicious of Soviet intentions because the project of an Eastern Locarno followed so closely Litvinov's attempts to make them the subject of a Russo-Polish or a Russo-German "guarantee."[38]

The solidarity between Poland on one side and Estonia and Latvia on the other proved short-lived. Although Beck had appar-

[37] W. Sikorski, "Sowieckie gwarancje bezpieczeństwa" [Soviet Security Guarantees], *Kurjer Warszawski*, July 29, 1934.

[38] *DBFP*, 2d Series, VI, 885-86; see also *DGFP*, Series C, III, 278. Some of the opposition parties in Poland (notably the National Democrats) dissociated themselves from the government's policy in the Baltic question and were prepared to enlist Russia's cooperation in this issue. *Kurjer Warszawski*, Aug. 4, 1934.

ently been successful in persuading the Estonians to follow Warsaw's lead in the negotiations concerning the Eastern Pact, Tallin
was forced to change its attitude under pressure from France,
Russia, and Great Britain.[39] The reversal of Estonia's position
culminated in Foreign Minister Seljamaa's hurried journey to
Moscow, where he and Latvian envoy Bilmanis signed a declaration
expressing the readiness of their governments to join the Eastern
Locarno on condition that Poland and Germany would also associate themselves with the proposed treaty.[40] Litvinov could now
relish his victory, and was reportedly "in a state of triumphant
delight at the defeat he had administered to Beck," while Polish
Ambassador Łukasiewicz was reduced to "a state of disordered
agitation" and complained to Radek that the Soviet Union had
now "disinterested itself entirely in the maintenance of friendly
relations with Poland."[41]

Moscow's elation was subdued to a certain extent by sober
afterthoughts and apprehensions that Poland's wounded pride
might intensify her "hysterical opposition" to the pact, but the
Kremlin apparently supported the Quai d'Orsay in its decision
to take immediate advantage of the setback suffered by Polish
diplomacy. At the begining of August, Ambassador Laroche received fresh instructions which included detailed answers to all
chief objections voiced in the past by Warsaw. According to this
memorandum, it was meaningless to fear that the Eastern Pact
would lead to an increase in Russia's might since the Soviet Union had already taken its proper seat among the great powers with
the partial help of the Polish government which, by signing the
treaty of nonaggression with the USSR, assisted in making it a full
member of the community of European nations; similarly, Po-

---

[39] *USFR*, 1934, I, 506.

[40] Estonia and Latvia reaffirmed this declaration during the conference of the
three Baltic states in Tallin in December, 1934. Lithuania, which previously had
expressed her willingness to join the Eastern Pact without any reservations, now
promised not to take any decisive steps in that direction without an understanding
with her two neighbors.

[41] *USFR*, 1934, I, 506. According to Seljamaa's own account of his conversation
with Litvinov, the Foreign Commissar "had not been much enamored of Estonia's
attitude of reserve." *DGFP*, Series C, III, 270; see also *ibid.*, pp. 279-80. Litvinov
himself later told the Lithuanian chargé d'affaires that he was "extremely satisfied" with the results of Seljamaa's visit. *Ibid.*, p. 271.

land's lack of confidence in Moscow's good faith was countered
with the observation that Russia, as a member of a collective system, could be more easily controlled by other powers and would
be less likely to pursue her own "sinister" schemes.[42] Having thus
presented their case, the French demanded an early reply, to be
delivered before the September meeting of the Assembly of the
League of Nations, and bluntly warned the Poles that their refusal to cooperate would endanger the future of the Franco-Polish
alliance. Beck tried again to play for time and raised the question
of Rumania's participation in the pact,[43] but the Soviet press saw
through his delaying maneuvers and admonished Warsaw not to
listen to the instructions of its Berlin "governess."[44] As Radek,
the Kremlin's top expert on Polish affairs put it, the friendship
between Russia and Poland was "incompatible" with any attempt
to oppose the "valid interests" of the USSR:

It is hardly necessary to prove that a policy which directs itself against
the valid interests of the Soviet Union is a hopeless one. The Soviet
Union and France will continue to take such measures as they think
necessary to consolidate peace. . . . If Polish foreign policy were
to adopt the ideas of those people who believe that any serious rapprochement between France and the Soviet Union must be opposed
by Poland, then Poland would inevitably be led into the camp of
German imperialism. . . . A failure to sign the pact would
strengthen the suspicions of important political circles in Europe that
Polish foreign policy is not directed towards maintaining peace, but
rather towards supporting those tendencies which are making for a
redivision of Europe.[45]

If Moscow's exhortations had any tangible effect upon Warsaw's
policy, it consisted only in making the Polish leaders more willing
to listen to Hitler's arguments that neither Poland nor Germany
had any reason to "provide rear cover for Russia in her dispute
in the Far East" or to serve as "shield" for the Soviet Union in its
coming conflict with Japan which, as the Führer purported to believe, would inevitably lead to the military and political collapse
of the USSR.[46]

[42] *DBFP*, 2d Series, VI, 894.   [43] *Ibid.*, p. 892.   [44] *Pravda*, Aug. 24, 1934.
[45] K. Radek, "The Arguments of the Polish Press against the Proposed Eastern
Pact," *International Press Correspondence*, XIV, No. 45 (Aug. 24, 1934), 1169-70;
see also *DGFP*, Series C, III, 312.
[46] Hitler's remarks during his conversation with Lipski on August 27, 1934, as

Meanwhile, the critical Assembly meeting approached in an atmosphere charged with tension and anxiety. Perhaps never before had Poland's attitude been so much in the limelight as during the dramatic negotiations that preceded Russia's entry into the League of Nations. The French delegation, acting as the sponsor of the Soviet Union, did its best to prepare a triumphal reception for Litvinov. Now that Moscow had condescended to join the organization it had been denouncing for years, it had to be accorded all the honors that Geneva could bestow, including a permanent seat on the Council of the League. While many European and Latin American countries expressed doubts as to the desirability of admitting the USSR to an international body whose lofty principles had been habitually disregarded by the Kremlin, only a few of them were prepared to embarrass and antagonize France by carrying this opposition into the open. There was, however, some speculation that Poland would try either to block Russia's admission or to conclude a bargain involving permanent seats on the Council for both Moscow and Warsaw.[47] As Beck himself was later to declare,

At a time when the entry of the Soviets into the League of Nations was the subject of discussions . . . a considerable section of European opinion expected us, and even tried to persuade us, to put forward some conditions or demands. Our government did not think it advisable to complicate such an important matter by seeking advantages for ourselves at Geneva, as this might have obscured the straight and clear line of our policy, which consistently aims at the stabilization of a normal and healthy atmosphere on our eastern frontier.[48]

---

reported in *DGFP*, Series C, III, 360-61. The Führer also tried to persuade the Polish Minister that the "regrettable and undeniable differences" between Poland and Germany were meaningless in the face of the Russian threat and that all the nations of Europe ought to unite "against the Asiatic colossus."

[47] See *DBFP*, 2d Series, VII, 714, 719, 729, 731-33; *DGFP*, Series C, II, 846. Poland was at that time a semipermanent member of the Council.

[48] Beck, *Przemówienia*, pp. 143-44 (English translation in Harley, *The Authentic Biography of Colonel Beck*, p. 134); see also Beck, *Final Report*, p. 65. Some opposition newspapers had been urging the Polish government since the spring of 1934 to use its influence at Geneva in order to facilitate the entry of the USSR into the League of Nations, "with the prerogatives enjoyed by the great powers." *Kurjer Warszawski*, May 7, 1934. This attitude was denounced by the Ukrainian parliamentary representation and by the Belorussian National Committee in Poland, which protested to the President of the General Assembly of the League against the admission of Soviet Russia. *Sprawy Narodowościowe*, VIII (1934), 593, 618.

This was, however, only part of the story. While the Polish Foreign Minister did not make any objections to the admission of the USSR to the League, he withheld his formal approval pending the settlement of "certain questions" between the two governments. Beck was ready to concede that Russia's membership in the League was likely to check her "aggressive intentions," but he was afraid that the Soviet Union, having joined a world-wide international organization, might tend to disregard such bilateral agreements as its nonaggression pact with Poland.[49] These rather far-fetched apprehensions prompted him to insist on a formal exchange of notes, reaffirming the validity of the existing accords between Warsaw and Moscow, as a preliminary condition of Polish support for Russia's entry into the League. The Kremlin proved quite willing to accept this demand, and the prearranged exchange of letters took place in Moscow on September 10, 1934.[50] The Polish chargé d'affaires proposed, in the name of his government, a "reciprocal recognition" of the fact that relations between the two countries would continue to be based on the existing agreements; in its reply, the Narkomindel solemnly reassured Warsaw that the USSR would honor all of its obligations with respect to Poland. With these formalities out of the way, Beck joined his colleagues at Geneva in addressing an invitation to the Soviet Union which asked for that country's "valuable cooperation" in the activities of the League.[51] In a special statement to the Political Committee of the Assembly, the Polish Foreign Minister welcomed Russia's decision to assume a proper share of the heavy responsibilities shouldered by other member states,[52] but privately he told Eden of his fears that Russia's arrival at Geneva would "open a chapter of difficulties for the League."[53]

As a result of diplomatic wrangling which preceded Litvinov's arrival in the Palais des Nations, that event, hailed by many contemporaries as one of the most significant triumphs of Soviet

[49] Beck, *Final Report*, p. 65.
[50] For the text of the letters see *Polish White Book*, pp. 180-81.
[51] *Documents on International Affairs*, 1934, p. 99.
[52] Beck, *Przemówienia*, p. 132; see also *Kurjer Warszawski*, Sept. 20, 1934.
[53] *DBFP*, 2d Series, VII, 735.

foreign policy, was somehow stripped of the atmosphere of solemn dignity that was supposed to surround it.[54] Moreover, it took place only a few days after another important development which produced a general sensation at Geneva and deprived Moscow of the opportunity of using the forum of the League to attack the treatment of the Ukrainians and Belorussians in Poland.[55] The Minorities Treaties, for more than fifteen years a thorn in Poland's side, were likely to become a dangerous weapon in the hands of the Kremlin and an excellent excuse for continuous interference in Polish internal affairs. Beck therefore proposed that the obligations contracted by Poland and other states under the Minorities Treaties should be extended to all members of the League. After this project had been indignantly rejected by the great powers, the Polish Foreign Minister informed the Assembly on September 13 that his government would decline in the future to cooperate with any international bodies "in the matter of the supervision of the application by Poland of the system of minority protection" until a uniform scheme for dealing with this question was adopted by all countries.[56]

While some foreign diplomats failed to realize the true significance of Beck's declaration and tended to regard it as a kind of revenge against the initiators of the Eastern Locarno and of the Disarmament Conference,[57] the reaction of Polish public opinion was spontaneous and unanimous as seldom before.[58] This emotional outburst of national pride temporarily strengthened Beck's position and enabled him to take a firm stand in his memorandum to the French government of September 27. In it he ignored such ticklish issues as the passage of Soviet troops through Polish ter-

[54] See Beck, *Final Report*, p. 66.
[55] *DGFP*, Series C, II, 846. In the past, the USSR had frequently charged Poland with the violation of Article VII of the Riga Treaty, which guaranteed the rights of the Ukrainian and Belorussian minorities in Poland and the rights of the Polish minority under Soviet rule.
[56] League of Nations, *Official Journal*, Special Supplement No. 125 (Geneva, 1934), p. 43.
[57] Laroche, p. 178.
[58] See *Kurjer Warszawski*, Sept. 15, 1934. At the same time the opposition press, while agreeing with the essence of Beck's statement, questioned his choice of methods, which "tended to undermine the whole system of Versailles." *Ibid.*, Sept. 14, 1934.

ritory but reaffirmed Poland's unwillingness to participate in any
collective system from which Germany was excluded and restated
Warsaw's reluctance to assume any obligations with regard to Lithuania and Czechoslovakia.[59] The increasingly uncompromising attitude of the Polish leaders had the effect of stirring up the ranks
of the opposition, whose spokesmen charged that the rigid policy
pursued by Beck had only succeeded in alienating Poland's friends
abroad and that, instead of eliminating Russia from European
politics, it actually helped her to secure a position of an almost unprecedented prestige and influence.[60]

Meanwhile the assassination of the king of Yugoslavia and the
French foreign minister at Marseilles contributed to a further
hardening of Warsaw's hostility toward the scheme "conceived
by Litvinov, elaborated by Beneš, and advocated by Barthou."[61]
Laval, who took over the reins of French foreign policy on
October 13, did not share his predecessor's ideas about the
future political alignment of Europe and "looked at the Eastern
Locarno from a somewhat different angle."[62] Since France's enthusiasm for the project showed some signs of slackening, in spite of
the agreement concluded between Litvinov and Laval at Geneva
on December 5, 1934,[63] it was now obviously Moscow's turn to
launch a new campaign in favor of the treaty, but this operation
was delayed by the Kremlin's preoccupation with Kirov's assassination.[64] The opening gun was fired on January 4, 1935, when
Litvinov made a lengthy statement to a delegation of visiting
journalists from Czechoslovakia, praising the proposed guarantee
pact as a "considerable factor for the insurance of peace not only
in Eastern Europe but in all Europe."[65] On January 6 an *Izvestiia*
editorial regretted Poland's failure either to accept the draft treaty

[59] For the text of the Polish note see Beck, *Dernier rapport,* pp. 335-38, and
DGFP, Series C, III, 446-49. The French reply to this memorandum (*ibid.,* pp. 715-
19) failed to remove Beck's doubts and apprehensions (*ibid.,* p. 752).
[60] *Kurjer Warszawski,* Nov. 2, 1934.   [61] *USFR,* 1934, I, 522.
[62] *Survey of International Affairs,* 1935, I, 72; see also *DGFP,* Series C, III, 807.
[63] For the text of the protocol signed by Laval and Litvinov see *British Blue
Book,* Cmd. 5143 of 1936, No. 4.
[64] During this time the Soviet press published scathing attacks on the Polish
critics of the ruthless measures taken to "avenge" Kirov's death. See *Pravda,* Dec.
7 and 10, 1934.
[65] *Izvestiia,* Jan. 5, 1935.

or to offer any agreeable suggestions; at the same time it implied that Warsaw was responsible for the fiasco of the Soviet guarantee proposal for the Baltic states. These complaints against Polish intransigence were coupled with a veiled but unmistakable warning: "To come together is a form of movement. . . . Polish diplomacy, while showing great activity in other aspects of its international relations, made no steps forward in the field of Polish-Soviet relations. Whoever does not go forward, moves backward."[66]

Moscow's increasing mistrust was made even more obvious by Molotov's cool references to Poland in his report to the Seventh Congress of the Soviets on January 28, 1935:

I shall not now stop to discuss the pretexts on which Germany and Poland have so far refused to sign [the Eastern] Pact. . . . In spite of the resistance and objections so far offered by the countries mentioned, the Soviet government regards its attitude toward this matter as unchangeable. . . . As regards Poland, we have manifested in an adequate and clear form our desire for the further development of Soviet-Polish relations. We cannot, however, say that we are satisfied with the results so far obtained. As regards ourselves, we can say quite definitely that we intend to continue our efforts to develop neighborly relations between the Soviet Union and Poland.[67]

Beck's reply to his Russian critics was given in his address to the Foreign Affairs Committee of the Sejm on February 1. This speech contained some polite remarks referring to the USSR and was rather extravagant in its praises of the nonaggression pact and the London Convention; the passages dealing with the Eastern Pact were, however, considerably less friendly, and the proposed treaty was ridiculed as being "neither 'Locarno' nor 'Eastern' ":

The essential part of the Locarno pacts consisted in the guarantee of a definite frontier by Great Britain and Italy. The pact proposed now does not possess this characteristic feature. Besides, its name certainly is not attractive to us. . . . Nor is it an eastern pact, for the problems of the east are treated there only partially and inadequately. . . . All aspects of the problem, even the most trifling, are of special concern to us, since they relate to the sphere of our immediate

[66] Ibid., Jan. 6, 1935.
[67] USSR, VII S"ezd Sovetov, Stenograficheskii otchët (Moscow, 1935), Biulleten' No. 1, pp. 14, 19; English translation in Degras, ed., III, 106, 111.

and most vital interests. That is why we must carefully study all the details, being especially anxious that the results that have been achieved by collaborating with our neighbors, with the object of a real stabilization of conditions in the eastern part of Europe, should come to no harm.[68]

Though Beck was prudent enough to make no binding declarations of policy, his statement was too outspoken to leave any doubts as to Poland's future course. Thus, while the French reproached the Polish Foreign Minister for his "unreasonable" attitude, the Soviet press denounced him openly for his attempt to evade all thorny questions of international diplomacy.[69] Beck's failure to develop any constructive program with respect to the problem of European security and his overbearing and arbitrary conduct of foreign affairs were also criticized by those Polish circles who declared themselves for a "clear, open, and intelligible policy," based on friendly coexistence with all Poland's neighbors and on the alliance with France.[70]

Warsaw's growing alienation from Paris intensified the suspicions, both in the Quai d'Orsay and in the Kremlin, that a new diplomatic revolution was under way, cutting across the postwar system of alliances and enlisting Polish help for a German-led military expedition against Russia.[71] In any case, early in 1935 the Germans renewed their feelers to Poland, probably encouraged by her resolute opposition to the Eastern Locarno. On January 22 Hitler had a talk with Lipski during a reception in the Reichskanzlei and once more "discussed at length the Russian

[68] Beck, *Przemówienia*, pp. 148-49; English translation in Harley, *The Authentic Biography of Colonel Beck*, pp. 137-38.

[69] *Izvestiia*, Feb. 4, 1935.

[70] See Poland, Senat, *Sprawozdanie stenograficzne*, Okres III, Posiedzenie LXXI, pp. 72, 102-3; LXXIII, pp. 56-62.

[71] The Soviet press not only stressed the close relationship between Poland and Germany but also charged that Japan was relying in her plans of aggression upon Warsaw's military support. See *Leningradskaia Pravda* as quoted in *Kurjer Warszawski*, Feb. 17, 1935, and Poland, Sejm, *Sprawozdanie stenograficzne*, Okres III, Posiedzenie CXXX, pp. 12-13. According to the official organ of the Comintern, Germany, Japan, and Poland were in complete agreement concerning a "joint aggressive policy . . . supported by close military and technical cooperation, transparently masked under the guise of so-called cultural ties." *Kommunisticheskii Internatsional*, XVII, No. 8 (March 10, 1935), 7; *The Communist International* (English ed.), XII, No. 7 (April 5, 1935), 286.

question and the danger threatening from the East."[72] He called
the Ambassador's attention to the fact that the Soviet Union had
scored substantial gains in its military preparations, and warned
him that the day might come when both Poland and Germany
would be forced to defend themselves against Russian aggression.

A few days after this conversation Göring made one of his
famous "hunting trips" to Poland. The purpose of this "private"
visit which led him to Białowieża and to Warsaw was to ascertain
the reaction of Polish official circles to the project of a "crusade"
against the Soviet Union; this was to be "not a delicate feeler or
sounding, but a clear and urgent invitation."[73] As the *Polish White
Book* shows, Göring was "very outspoken in his conversations"
and "outlined far-reaching plans, almost suggesting an anti-
Russian alliance and a joint attack on Russia."[74] He went so far
as to divide Soviet territory into spheres of influence and offered
the Ukraine to the Poles while reserving northwestern Russia for
Germany.[75] These tempting proposals were coupled with a veiled
warning that, in theory, "one could imagine a new partition of
Poland by means of a German-Russian collaboration," although
Göring hastened to add that actually this alternative was not

[72] *Polish White Book,* p. 24.

[73] Cardwell, p. 31. At the same time, the official organ of the Nazi Party published a series of articles which suggested that Poland should take advantage of
Russia's preoccupation with the events in the Far East and make a determined
effort to put an end to Moscow's supremacy in Eastern Europe. Since Poland's
economic and political potential was not strong enough to allow her to achieve
the status of a great power, it was essential for her to obtain the support of Germany, whose own interests in the East could be easily reconciled with those of
her Polish neighbor. "Die politischen Kräfte im Osten," *Völkischer Beobachter*
(Norddeutsche Ausgabe), Feb. 3/4, 13, and 15, 1935; for Polish reaction see Poland,
Sejm, *Sprawozdanie stenograficzne,* Okres III, Posiedzenie CXXXIX, p. 27. Almost
simultaneously (on February 5, 1935) Dr. Dmytro Levyts'kyi, the leader of the
UNDO group in the Sejm, urged the Polish government to take an active part in
the coming process of "political reorganization" in Eastern Europe and thus help
the Ukrainians to achieve independence from Soviet rule. Poland, Sejm, Posiedzenie
CXXVIII, p. 31; see also Makukh, pp. 449-51. Later, the supporters of the government and the members of the opposition parties joined forces in a sharp criticism
of Levyts'kyi's ill-timed speech. Poland, Sejm, Posiedzenie CXXXIII, p. 32.

[74] *Polish White Book,* p. 26. A good description of Göring's skill as a negotiator
is given in S. Reeburg, "The Antecedents of the Polish Defeat," *Journal of Central
European Affairs,* I (Jan., 1942), 376.

[75] See Strzetelski, *Where the Storm Broke,* p. 15. According to the same author,
Piłsudski was offered at that time joint command of German-Polish armies in the
event of war with Russia. *Ibid.;* Mackiewicz, *Colonel Beck and His Policy,* pp. 25-
26.

feasible since a common frontier between the Reich and the Soviet Union would be "highly dangerous" to Germany.[76] Göring's enthusiasm for "une marche en commun sur Moscou"[77] seems to have carried him away even during his meeting with Piłsudski, but the Marshal had no trouble in handling his unceremonious visitor who had apparently forgotten or disregarded Lipski's advice to "observe some reserve."[78] The embarrassing suggestion of a "joint Polish-German attack on Russia" and allusions to "the advantages to Poland in the Ukraine in such an event" were deftly countered with the irrefutable argument that the Poles could not support any political schemes which might lead to a revival of tension on their eastern border. It was impossible to "stand continually at the ready on such a long line as the Polish-Soviet frontier";[79] the only policy which Poland could pursue toward Russia was that of calmness and moderation, and the Marshal steadfastly refused to contemplate any other course of action.[80]

The Polish rejection of the German project was thus stated in a direct and definite manner; nevertheless, the ambiguous attitude of Polish diplomacy, obscured by some of Beck's enigmatic pronouncements, continued to arouse mistrust and suspicions, both at home and abroad, as to the real objectives of Poland's foreign policy.[81] Meanwhile the Polish leaders were disturbed by certain signs of "nervousness" in the Kremlin; the problem of Russian "expansion" in the direction of the Balkans was also causing some anxiety,[82] and the deadly disease sapping Marshal Piłsudski's strength threatened to paralyze for a time Warsaw's initiative in international affairs. Under these circumstances, Beck was deeply gratified when Anthony Eden, who visited the Polish capital at the beginning of April, assured him of his intention "not to carry

[76] Polish White Book, p. 25.   [77] Szembek, p. 34.
[78] In Göring's own words, Piłsudski "tat gestutzt," or "stiffened." Polish White Book, p. 26. According to L. B. Namier, the Polish account "erroneously puts 'tat' in place of 'hat' and translates these words as 'stiffened'; but 'hat gestutzt' means 'was puzzled.'" Diplomatic Prelude, p. 21. Professor A. Dallin has helped the author to solve these semantic difficulties by translating "tat gestutzt" as "pretended to be puzzled."
[79] Polish White Book, p. 26.   [80] Beck, Final Report, p. 30.
[81] See Poland, Sejm, Sprawozdanie stenograficzne, Okres III, Posiedzenie CXXXIX, p. 27.
[82] Szembek, p. 42.

out any pro-Soviet propaganda."[83] The British Minister knew
that he could expect no change in Poland's position as far as the
Eastern Pact was concerned, and he disarmed his Polish colleague
by declaring that his recent journey to Moscow had been dictated
by "tactical necessity." Beck, on his part, emphasized Poland's
desire to keep a neutral attitude toward both Germany and Russia
while refusing at the same time to join any multilateral agreements which would tend to jeopardize this position of neutrality.[84]

Eden's self-confessed ignorance of Russia set off a lengthy discourse on Soviet affairs during which the Poles described the
Kremlin's policy as "somewhat hysterical," less logical, and more
difficult to estimate than the policy of the Third Reich.[85] These
observations were coupled with the warning that the Foreign
Office was playing a risky game in attempting to start negotiations
with Moscow. Eden's view that it would take Soviet Russia at
least fifty years to master her internal difficulties and to become
a serious threat to other countries was hotly contested by his Polish
hosts, who also did their best to convince him that the tremendous
military power represented by the Red Army was bound to become
a very important factor in any future conflict. The inclination of
some British circles to treat the reports about Russia's growing
strength as "German bluff" was extremely disquieting to the
Poles.[86] It was hard to believe that Eden's naïve appraisal of the
situation in the USSR was merely a maneuver aimed at diverting
Poland's attention from her eastern frontier and at making her
more conscious of the German threat; in any case, it convinced
the Polish leaders that Warsaw and Berlin were the only capitals
of Europe fully aware of the Russian danger.

Piłsudski himself was also concerned with the effects of the

[83] Beck, *Final Report*, p. 85. The official telegraphic agency "Iskra" welcomed
Eden's arrival with a statement asserting that Poland's attitude toward the Eastern
Pact was "well known" and would remain unchanged. This declaration was sharply
criticized by the Soviet press, which charged that Poland was unwilling to check
any "aggressive tendencies" directed against the USSR and was, in fact, supporting
anti-Soviet schemes contrived by the enemies of peace. *Izvestiia*, April 1, 1935.

[84] *USFR*, 1935, I (Washington, 1953), 222.   [85] Szembek, p. 55.

[86] See Szembek's conversations with Laroche, Józef Potocki, Bastianini, and Bullitt.
Ibid., pp. 57-60.

rapprochement between the Western powers and Russia, and the trips of the British and French "pilgrims" to Moscow were his "last great political worry."[87] The Franco-Soviet treaty of mutual assistance was signed on May 2,[88] and the old Marshal, deeply troubled with this "substitute for the Franco-Polish alliance," predicted that Laval's journey would bring disastrous consequences for the Third Republic. "Why is that fool going to Moscow?" was the agonizing question put to the physicians and friends assembled round the dying man's bed, and Beck was called from a diplomatic reception to report whether "that blockhead Laval" was showing signs of a change of heart.[89]

Official Polish reaction to the pact was much more restrained, although the Poles realized that they were affected by the new development more than any other European nation. The pro-government press was anxious to stress that the treaty involved no direct or indirect obligations on the part of Poland and that, consequently, there would be no change in Polish-Soviet relations.[90] While Warsaw was demanding "positive assurances" from Paris that the new agreement would not jeopardize the Franco-Polish alliance, it viewed with some relief the disappearance of the danger of a German-Russian entente.[91] Some optimistic politicians regarded Poland as an insurmountable geographical barrier whose very existence defeated in advance any plans for ideological crusades plotted by Russia and Germany against each other; other, more realistic observers expected only dangerous complications from the fact that Poland separated France's new ally from her potential enemy. The London *Times* commented:

When France, under certain conditions, contracts to accept military assistance from Soviet Russia, Poland feels that her vital interests are involved, because it would not be feasible for Russia to render effective military support against Germany without violating Polish ter-

[87] Beck, *Final Report*, pp. 87-89.
[88] For details on the final phase of Franco-Soviet negotiations and on Poland's attitude in this matter see Herriot, pp. 521-46.
[89] Beck, *Final Report*, pp. 87-88.
[90] See *Gazeta Polska* as quoted in *Kurjer Warszawski*, May 6, 1935. The National Democratic opposition regretted that the treaty was signed without Poland's participation. *Kurjer Warszawski*, May 8, 1935.
[91] Szembek, p. 68.

ritory. It is felt, moreover, that Franco-Soviet collaboration can be inimical to Polish interests and to the healthy promotion of peace in the East of Europe.[92]

It was hardly to be expected that Laval's talks with the Polish statesmen, held under such inauspicious circumstances, would result in a better understanding than the inconclusive negotiations between Beck and the French Foreign Minister which had taken place at Geneva in the middle of January.[93] The first of the three meetings (May 10, 11, and 18) amounted actually to a post-mortem on the Eastern Locarno. Laval's pledges that he had no intention of conducting a pro-Soviet policy did not impress his Polish colleague, who also responded rather passively to the plan of a new multilateral pact, backed by France, Great Britain, and Italy, open to all interested countries, and aimed at the reintegration of Germany into the international system of security. The fact that this treaty would have rendered the Franco-Russian accord "entirely worthless" failed to make it attractive to Beck, who probably regarded it as a new and even more awkward version of Barthou's abortive project.[94]

In the course of these negotiations, which consisted chiefly in replaying old, wearisome tunes, Laval considered it his duty to warn the Poles that their policy was arousing suspicions in Moscow because of its alleged "subordination" to Germany.[95] The Soviet leaders, including Stalin himself, were quite outspoken in expressing their fears that Poland was "fostering aggressive intentions with regard to the Ukraine," and thought they were able to discern close links between the actions of Warsaw and Berlin. This state of affairs was, of course, embarrassing to the Quai d'Orsay, and it was to prove even more troublesome in the future; for, as Beck rightly observed, the essential element dividing Polish policy from that of France was not the German question but the manner in which the two allies viewed the Russian problem.[96]

The differences between Paris and Warsaw increased consider-

---

[92] *The Times* (London), May 11, 1935; see also speculations on this subject in *Polska Zbrojna* as quoted in *Kurjer Warszawski*, May 9, 1935.

[93] For an account of the Geneva negotiations see Beck, *Dernier rapport*, pp. 283-85.

[94] *Ibid.*, p. 288.   [95] Szembek, p. 85.   [96] Beck, *Final Report*, p. 177.

ably as a result of the conclusion of the Soviet-Czechoslovak treaty of May 16, which was interpreted by Beck as an "introduction of Muscovite pressure into the center of Europe."[97] This outward manifestation of friendship between Moscow and Prague occurred only four days after the death of Marshal Piłsudski, the alleged "archenemy" of Russia. While the Kremlin refrained from paying any tributes to the author of the "Miracle of the Vistula" and sent no official representative to the Marshal's funeral,[98] Karl Radek wrote a sympathetic article which was given wide publicity in the Soviet press. It expressed what seemed to be a sincere desire to bury the last vestige of difference between Moscow and Warsaw, and assured the Poles that no action on the part of the USSR endangered in the slightest the independence of their country. Since new storms were gathering over the world, Radek argued, the generation who took from the hands of the late leader the "scepter of authority" ought to realize that there could be no better guarantee of Poland's independence than friendship with the peoples of the Soviet Union. The new situation was, according to him, an opportunity for the Slavs of Eastern Europe to work jointly for the cause of international security. Cooperation between the Poles and the Russians might save the two nations from the approaching tempest and become the cornerstone of peace in Europe.[99]

This warm declaration of good will toward Poland was obviously dictated by Moscow's desire to influence the policy of Piłsudski's successors. It appeared that the men in the Kremlin had a good chance of attaining their ends. Now that the old Marshal lay buried in a vault of the Wawel Cathedral, no one in Poland was able to wield his power or to enjoy his prestige. There was, indeed, "no other such human rock to dominate and direct the Polish tide."[100]

[97] Laroche, p. 195. For the reaction of the Polish press see *Kurjer Warszawski,* May 18, 1935.

[98] Beck, *Final Report,* p. 90; see also *International Press Correspondence,* XV, No. 21 (May 18, 1935), 561.

[99] *Izvestiia,* May 14, 1935; see also M. M. Popov, "Pislia smerti Pilsuds'koho" [After Piłsudski's Death], *Bil'shovyk Ukrainy,* X, No. 4/5 (April-May, 1935), 9-20.

[100] *The New York Times,* May 13, 1935.

IV. The Policy of Balance: Theory and Practice

The year 1935 was an important landmark in Polish foreign policy. While the relations between Piłsudski and Beck had been very close and while the confidence that the former reposed in his protégé had enabled the young and ambitious colonel to act with some independence and self-assurance, the ultimate responsibility for the conduct of foreign affairs rested with the Marshal. After his death, Beck became not merely the chief executor but also the principal architect of the country's foreign policy. He alone could claim to have had the most intimate insight into the plans and ideas of the late dictator, whose imaginative vision and sagacity had contributed so much to Poland's resurrection; hence, he alone could be depended upon to interpret the Marshal's will and to adapt it to the changing conditions of international life.

The main responsibility which now rested on Beck's shoulders was to preserve the independence of Poland between Moscow and Berlin.[1] While this task could be easily defined in theory,[2] however, it could be carried out only against tremendous odds.[3] The idea behind this policy was to lessen the danger of Poland's becoming once more a German-Russian battlefield; at the same time, the Poles had to do everything possible to prevent their two formidable neighbors from uniting their forces against Poland and settling their differences at her expense. In short, they had to bear in mind that their country "would be seriously endangered

[1] See Beck, *Final Report*, p. 34.   [2] Beck, *Przemówienia*, p. 171.
[3] A German historian describes this policy as "tacking between the danger of being crushed and the existence of a satellite." Breyer, p. 191.

if German-Russian relations deteriorated too far, and even more seriously if they became too intimate."[4]

In Warsaw's opinion, the interests of Poland could not be furthered by joining the Russians in their attempt to form an iron ring around the Third Reich or by following in the wake of France's new policy toward the Soviet Union. For the time being, the Polish leaders were disturbed by rumors about an impending agreement between the USSR and Rumania and by the speculations about the possibility of a general security treaty between Russia and the Little Entente, although they hoped that Moscow's preoccupation with southeastern Europe might tend to alleviate its pressure in the Baltic area.[5] Their uneasiness was intensified when Beneš, following in the steps of his distinguished Western colleagues, visited the Soviet capital in June, 1935, the more so since Polish diplomats discovered in his public pronouncements what they considered to be overt "Panslavist tendencies" and "a desire to subordinate himself to Russia."[6] Significantly enough, this visit coincided with noisy celebrations honoring the fifteenth anniversary of the defeat of the Polish Army in the Ukraine and the liberation of Kiev by Red troops in 1920. Popular manifestations were held to demonstrate the "unswerving loyalty" of the population to the Soviet regime and to warn the "Polish landlords" that it would be "unhealthy" to incur the risk of a new adventure. Soviet newspapers devoted their front pages to this topic and expressed hopes that the events of the past would deter any potential aggressor from repeating Piłsudski's mistakes—for, if the ragged Red Army of 1920 could defeat the invaders with sabers and rifles, how much more terrible a blow could be struck by the modern Red Army, with its thousands of airplanes, tanks, and machine guns![7]

[4] H. P. S. Matthews, "Poland's Foreign Relations," *The Fortnightly*, CXLIV (Aug., 1938), 162.

[5] See Szembek, p. 96.

[6] *Ibid.*, pp. 92-93. Beneš himself stressed that his country's attitude toward the Soviet Union was "based on entirely realistic foundations" and had "nothing in common with Panslavism." *Kurjer Warszawski*, June 7, 1935. Polish opposition circles also maintained that "neither Mr. Beneš nor Mr. Stalin was motivated by Panslavist feelings." *Ibid.*, June 16, 1935.

[7] *Pravda* and *Izvestiia*, June 12, 1935; see also *Kommunisticheskii Internatsional*, XVII, No. 18 (June 20, 1935), 14-44, and *The Communist International* (English ed.), XII, No. 11 (June 5, 1935), 502-8. A month later similar celebrations were held in Soviet Belorussia. See *Pravda*, July 11, 1935, and *Kurjer Warszawski*, July 13, 1935.

These defiant statements indicated an unfavorable turn in Polish-Soviet relations, and Beck's visit to Berlin in July, 1935, scarcely contributed to the relaxation of tension building up between Warsaw and Moscow. Beck's trip provided the Nazi chiefs with an opportunity to find out whether the changes in the Polish leadership could be converted to Germany's advantage. Their expectations that Piłsudski's successors would be easily swayed by Hitler's alluring promises were sorely disappointed when Beck could not be persuaded to budge from the rigid attitude adopted by the late Marshal; indeed, the very arguments he used were those with which Piłsudski had checked Göring's impetuous advances. The Führer's suggestions that the existing relations between Poland and Germany should be "consolidated" and that any dangers emerging in the future should be resisted in a spirit of friendship between Berlin and Warsaw were also passed over in silence, although Beck gave Hitler his personal assurances that Poland would never become "a tool of Russian policy."[8] At the same time, however, the official communiqué on the talks stressed a "far-reaching agreement of views" concerning "matters of special interest to Poland and Germany,"[9] and Moscow was visibly concerned over this cryptic phraseology.[10] Hence, when the Polish Foreign Minister made a trip to Helsinki early in August, the Soviet press began to spread rumors that Finland was about to join the "Polish-German bloc" directed against Russia.[11]

Similar accusations against Poland were voiced during the Seventh Congress of the Comintern (July-August, 1935), and one of the principal speakers reiterated the old charges about Polish-German "collusion":

All that is known of the pact between Poland and Germany goes to show that it is an aggressive pact serving the preparations for war.

[8] Szembek, p. 106; see also the excerpts from the memorandum on Beck's conversation with Hitler quoted by J. Jurkiewicz in "Polska wobec planów Paktu Wschodniego w latach 1934-1935," *Sprawy Międzynarodowe*, XII, No. 3 (March, 1959), 48.

[9] *Polish White Book*, p. 30.

[10] See *Izvestiia*, July 3 and 5, 1935, and *Kurjer Warszawski*, July 7, 1935.

[11] See *Pravda*, July 26 and Aug. 14, 1935; *Izvestiia*, July 26, 1935; *International Press Correspondence*, XV, No. 39 (Aug. 24, 1935), 1002. According to Beck's own account, he and his Finnish colleague discussed "the interests we had in common with regard to Russia, as a permanent element of our direct relations." *Final Report*, p. 99.

. . . It endeavors to establish a certain co-ordination between Polish and German propaganda and between the actions of these two countries among the bands of the counter-revolutionary Ukrainian bourgeoisie. All this means that by the signature of this pact Polish fascism has joined the plan of Germany's territorial expansion towards the East, the criminal plan for the invasion and colonization of the Soviet Ukraine.[12]

Accordingly, the Congress stated in its resolutions that "the fascist states—Germany, Poland, Hungary, Italy" were "openly striving for a new repartition of the world and a change in the frontiers of Europe," and that German imperialism had found "an ally in Europe—fascist Poland, which is also striving to extend its territory at the expense of Czechoslovakia, the Baltic countries, and the Soviet Union."[13]

The Polish press answered these attacks by censuring the Soviet government for its attempts to shirk all responsibility for the activities of the international Communist movement. It was, indeed, hard to assume that "Stalin, as Soviet dictator, and as a member of the Comintern, could be two different individuals," and to believe in Litvinov's ability to "change his personality every time he doffs his Geneva top hat to don a Moscow cap."[14] Since the Comintern did not hesitate to exert revolutionary pressure on foreign governments in order to force them to conclude or ratify certain treaties with the Soviet Union, it was obviously necessary to ask the Kremlin a few pertinent questions:

Do Mr. Stalin and the Soviet government intend in future to act in accordance with the agreements signed in their name by Mr. Litvinov concerning noninterference in the affairs of other states, or must it be understood that the resolutions of the Comintern Congress cancel these agreements? Does Mr. Litvinov intend to operate in the customary diplomatic manner through the ambassadors and ministers of

[12] M. Ercoli [P. Togliatti], *The Fight against War and Fascism* (London, 1936), pp. 19-20 (also included in Communist International, 7th World Congress, Moscow, 1935, *Report*, with separate pagination).
[13] Ercoli, *Fight against War and Fascism*, p. 21. On the role played by the Polish Communists during the Congress and on the attempts by the CPP to create a united front in Poland see Dziewanowski, *The Communist Party of Poland*, pp. 140-46.
[14] *Gazeta Polska* as quoted in *Kurjer Warszawski*, Aug. 28, 1935.

the Soviet government, or through internal pressure brought to bear on other states through the medium of the Comintern?[15]

A further deterioration of Soviet-Polish relations was highlighted by the expulsion from Russia of Jan Otmar-Berson, the Moscow correspondent of *Gazeta Polska* and the Polish Telegraphic Agency, for his alleged spreading of "malicious and slanderous information about the USSR, bordering in its form and tone on political hooliganism."[16] The Polish authorities retaliated by withdrawing the visa of the Tass correspondent in Warsaw,[17] and the Russians critized this move as "petty revenge" and "naked repression."[18] At the same time unfriendly utterances of the Soviet press referring to the coming election in Poland[19] and to Polish affairs in general provoked a sharp reaction in Warsaw which was reflected in Colonel Miedziński's outspoken article in *Gazeta Polska*:

It is rather unfortunate that the Soviet press is regularly publishing attacks on Poland. There is no comprehensible reason for this anti-Polish campaign. . . . The tone of these attacks is very unusual among neighboring countries which are maintaining friendly diplomatic relations. There is a Polish-Soviet nonaggression pact in existence. It is quite true that this pact does not refer to any control of the press, but it is clear that the attacks in the Soviet press on Poland and Polish policy are absolutely contrary to the spirit of this pact. What can Poland do? In the circumstances—and should the press attacks continue in Soviet Russia—the Polish efforts for good cultural and neighborly relations can hardly be continued. The campaign against Poland has no justification and should cease.[20]

The rapid decline of what had been once described as Polish-

---

[15] *Ibid.*

[16] *Izvestiia*, Aug. 20, 1935. Some quarters in Poland and abroad expressed the opinion that Berson was expelled because of his revealing reports on the underground activities of the Comintern. *Polska Zbrojna* as quoted in *Osteuropa*, XI (1935-36), 42-43. According to the London *Times*, Aug. 21, 1935, the real reason for the drastic action taken by the Soviet government was probably an article accusing Moscow of fomenting disturbances in France; see also *Pravda*, Aug. 9, 1935.

[17] *Kurjer Warszawski*, Aug. 21, 1935.   [18] See *Pravda* and *Izvestiia*, Aug. 22, 1935.

[19] *Pravda*, Sept. 7, 10-11, and 13, 1935; *Izvestiia*, Sept. 10, 1935.

[20] Quoted from *News Digest*, I (1934-35), 790. On the attitude of the Soviet press toward Poland see Szembek, p. 20.

Russian friendship manifested itself in many different ways,[21] but
it was dramatically brought to the attention of the world as a result of a personal clash between Litvinov and Beck in Geneva.
In addressing a plenary meeting of the Assembly of the League of
Nations on September 14, 1935, the Soviet Foreign Commissar
criticized a new "political conception" directed against the idea
of collective security and supporting bilateral pacts "between
states arbitrarily chosen for this purpose."[22] The Poles felt that
Litvinov's unflattering remarks were addressed to Warsaw as well
as to Berlin, and were particularly offended by the charge that
some nations secured their rears or flanks by nonaggression pacts
only in order to "obtain the facility of attacking with impunity
third states." Since these unnamed countries were condemned
"before the whole world" as "probable disturbers of peace," Beck
thought it impossible to accept Litvinov's challenge in silence.
His statement to the Assembly on September 16 was obviously
intended to clear the air, although he did not discuss Polish-Soviet
relations as a whole and limited himself to delivering a sharp
personal rebuke, addressed directly to Litvinov. The Soviet Foreign Commissar was accused of having passed a "biased and completely arbitrary judgment" upon certain "diplomatic acts" concluded by Poland. In addition to making the "most express reservations" to Litvinov's speech, Beck defiantly stressed that his government remained completely indifferent to such opinions on its
policy.[23]

In reply to this emotional outburst, Litvinov delivered what
was generally considered a diplomatic chef-d'oeuvre:

I regret not to be able to concur with my Polish colleague in the
opinion that an open discussion here of the existing conceptions on
the system of international relations would do harm to international
collaboration. . . . International collaboration, in my opinion,
can only gain from such an open discussion. For my part, I would not
say that my government is indifferent as to what other countries,

[21] See *Kurjer Warszawski*, Sept. 18, 1935, on the conflict between the Polish PEN
Club and *Literaturnaia Gazeta*.
[22] League of Nations, *Official Journal*, Special Supplement No. 138 (Geneva, 1935),
p. 73.
[23] *Ibid.*, p. 84.

especially our neighbors, think of its foreign policy. It seems to me that we should be nearer to international collaboration and the idea underlying the League of Nations if we took special care to see that our foreign policy was properly understood and interpreted by other countries, especially our neighbors. I wish to assure the Polish delegation that if it had chosen to express its views to the Assembly on the policy of peace of my government, I would have made no objection, and its judgment would in no case have affected our attitude to Poland, friendly relations with which have never ceased to be one of the essential aims of that policy.[24]

The encounter between Beck and Litvinov was described by the London *Times* as a "verbal duel whose vehemence exceeded its importance."[25] The Soviet press, while refraining from stating directly that Beck acted as Hitler's dupe, published reports to that effect which appeared in French and British newspapers. The opposition circles in Poland were also highly critical of Beck's "unnecessary dispute" with Litvinov and deplored the fact that the Polish Foreign Minister had publicly associated himself with some political doctrines which hitherto had been advocated only by the Nazis.[26] On the other hand, Litvinov was widely praised for his coolness nad moderation; the conviction that the Soviet Union was "not seeking offense from Poland" and that it "wanted nothing more than to be friendly with Poland" was gaining ground in the West, and Beck and his associates fought in vain against this misconception, which seriously handicapped the efforts of Polish diplomacy to win more understanding and sympathy for its wary attitude toward Moscow.[27]

In the meantime, the Polish government was greatly disturbed by Soviet "intrigues" and "machinations" in Bucharest, Prague, and Kaunas, which led to a certain strain in the relations between Poland and Rumania and aggravated the old disagreements and suspicions in Warsaw's dealings with Czechoslovakia and Lithu-

[24] *Ibid.*, p. 87.
[25] *The Times* (London), Sept. 17, 1935.
[26] For the Soviet press comment see *Pravda*, Sept. 17, and *Izvestiia*, Sept. 17-18, 1935. The official Polish reaction was given in a commentary of the "Iskra" agency whose text can be found in *Le Monde Slave*, XII, Part IV (Dec., 1935), 416-17; for opposition criticism see the editorial "Jaka to dyplomacja?" [What Kind of Diplomacy Is This?] in *Kurjer Warszawski*, Sept. 23, 1935.
[27] See *The New York Times*, Sept. 22, 1935.

ania.[28] The Soviet press, too, began to voice its apprehensions that a Polish-German-Hungarian alliance was in the making and that this new alignment of powers in East Central Europe constituted a deadly danger to the Little Entente. Special attention was paid to the threat of a complete encirclement of Czechoslovakia, and Hungarian Premier Gömbös was represented as the chief architect of a new bloc, allegedly aimed at coordinating the policies of Berlin, Budapest, and Warsaw.[29] A mouthpiece of the Comintern charged:

The Polish government fascists await with the greatest impatience for Hitler to get a chance of occupying Austria and in this creating a firmer foundation in Central Europe for anti-Soviet aims. The next step would be the partition of Czechoslovakia between Germany, Poland, and Hungary: the elimination, that is, of the last difficulties in Central Europe in the way of an anti-Soviet adventure.[30]

While the opposition parties in Poland were more moderate in their criticism, they also warned Beck against "tipping the balance in the western direction" and openly questioned his ability to maneuver adroitly in the difficult international situation.[31] At the same time disturbing signs of a progressive alienation in Polish-Soviet relations continued to multiply. On December 18 *Pravda* published excerpts from a speech by P. P. Postyshev, the first secretary of the Central Committee of the Communist Party of the Ukraine, which contained some provocative references to Poland.[32] Molotov, addressing the Central Executive Committee of

[28] Szembek, p. 119; see also *The Times* (London), Sept. 18, 1935.

[29] *Pravda*, Sept. 30 and Oct. 3, 1935.

[30] *International Press Correspondence*, XV, No. 43 (Sept. 7, 1935), 1113. The Soviet-inspired press spread at that time rumors about a conference which allegedly took place at Rominten in East Prussia with the purpose of coordinating the political and military planning of Germany, Poland, Hungary, and Finland. See *ibid.*, No. 50 (Oct. 5, 1935), pp. 1254-55.

[31] See the Socialist *Robotnik* and the National Democratic *Warszawski Dziennik Narodowy* as quoted in *Kurjer Warszawski*, Oct. 11 and 29, 1935. The Executive Committee of the Peasant Party also adopted at that time a resolution on foreign policy which opposed the attempts to "tie Poland to Germany" and to "loosen" friendly relations with France, the Little Entente, the Soviet Union, and the Baltic states. *Kurjer Warszawski*, Oct. 12, 1935.

[32] Postyshev urged "the workers and peasants of the Western Ukraine and Poland" to "overthrow the police regime of fascist Poland, liquidate Little Poland, and found in its place a free Western Ukraine, liberated from colonial oppression." His bitter personal attacks on the leaders of Ukrainian political parties in Poland

the USSR on January 10, 1936, hinted strongly at the existence of a secret understanding between Warsaw and Berlin, obviously directed against Moscow:

Reports recently appeared of the conclusion of a military agreement between Japan and Germany, and of Poland's complicity in this matter. There is nothing unexpected in this for us. . . . The fascist rulers of Germany sometimes endeavor to divert the attention of simple people from their plans of conquest with regard to the Soviet Union by referring to the absence of common frontiers between Germany and the USSR. But we know, on the other hand, that Germany, encouraged by certain foreign powers, is feverishly preparing to occupy a dominant position in the Baltic and has established special relations with Poland, which has fairly extensive common frontiers with the Soviet Union.[33]

In addition to these serious charges, the head of the Soviet government attacked by name various groups and individuals in Poland who were lending their support to the aggressive plans of the Nazis:

This criminal propaganda for the seizure of foreign territory has now found new followers outside Germany. All sorts of echoes of the German capital are to be heard in neighboring Poland, for example, from Mr. Studnicki[34] and the other harebrained gentry on the Kraków

---

indicated the annoyance of the Soviet government with the attempts of Premier Kościałkowski and the UNDO group to "normalize" Polish-Ukrainian relations. For a detailed but somewhat biased account of the policy of "normalization" see Makukh, pp. 425-27, 448-56.

[33] USSR, Tsentral'nyi Ispolnitel'nyi Komitet, *Sozyv VII, Sessiia II, Stenograficheskii otchët* (Moscow, 1936), Biulleten' No. 1, pp. 32-33; English translation in Degras, ed., III, 156. Similar accusations were made by P. P. Liubchenko, chairman of the Council of the People's Commissars of the Ukrainian SSR. See USSR, Tsentral'nyi Ispolnitel'nyi Komitet, Biulleten' No. 3, pp. 24-27.

[34] A reference to Władysław Studnicki, the leading ideologist of Polish-German cooperation and the author of the controversial book *System polityczny Europy a Polska*. According to Studnicki, Europe's security required a further "amputation" of Russia in the west, the south, and the east. He suggested a "rectification" of the Polish-Soviet frontier, proposing that the new boundary should run along the Berezina and reach the mouth of the Pripet; other territorial changes he envisaged included the separation from Russia of the Ukraine (where the Ukrainians from Poland would be resettled), the Crimea, the Caucasus, Turkestan, and eastern Siberia as far as Lake Baikal. In order to accomplish these objectives, Poland was to ally herself with Germany and attack Russia in the event of a Soviet-Japanese conflict. In addition to his militant anti-Russian program, Studnicki advocated the *Anschluss* of Austria and the dismemberment of Czechoslovakia, with the resulting common Polish-Hungarian-German frontier as the first step toward the creation

newspaper *Czas*[35] who go so far as to battle openly in the press for the seizure of certain territories belonging to the USSR.[36]

When Beck made his annual report to the Foreign Affairs Committee of the Sejm on January 15, 1936, the usual friendly references to Russia were conspicuously absent from his speech. He failed, however, to answer Molotov's accusations, and thus laid himself open to renewed criticism of the opposition press:

Did not some passages in Premier Molotov's last speech call for an official denial from the Polish side? Can we remain indifferent to the fact that at least a part of public opinion abroad . . . is convinced that there exists some "German-Polish revisionism" . . . that Poland has already dissociated herself from the nations which desire to preserve the postwar status quo at any price?[37]

Tension between Warsaw and Moscow was intensified also as a result of an acrimonious press dispute concerning Russia's unfulfilled obligation under the Riga Treaty to pay Poland the sum of 30,000,000 gold rubles.[38] At the same time the approaching ratification of the Franco-Soviet pact of 1935 called forth a new flood of rumors about a five-power accord, allegedly to be concluded by Germany, Poland, Italy, Austria, and Hungary in order to counterbalance the treaties of mutual assistance binding the Kremlin to Paris and Prague.[39] Berlin and Warsaw were reported to be working on "secret deals," and the chancelleries of Europe occupied themselves with conjectures concerning Poland's future attitude:

The role of Poland is of primary importance. It is giving the deepest concern not only to the French but to the British and the Little Entente. It is an enigma which is the more puzzling because of the

---

of a "Central European bloc." While his book caused some sensation abroad, it remained relatively unnoticed in Poland, where it sold only a thousand copies. See *Wiadomości* (London), Dec. 11, 1949.

[35] The Conservative *Czas* supported the policy of Polish-German rapprochement and was markedly cool, though not openly hostile, toward the Soviet Union. It reflected the views of Prince Janusz Radziwiłł, chairman of the Foreign Affairs Committee of the Sejm and one of Beck's closest associates.

[36] USSR, Tsentral'nyi Ispolnitel'nyi Komitet, *Sozyv VII, Sessiia II, Stenograficheskii otchët,* Biulleten' No. 1, p. 30; English translation in Degras, III, 154.

[37] *Kurjer Warszawski,* Jan. 16, 1936; see also *ibid.,* Jan. 17, 1936.

[38] See *Gazeta Polska,* Feb. 20, 1936, as quoted in *Kurjer Warszawski,* Feb. 21, 1936; *Izvestiia,* Feb. 28, 1936.

[39] *The New York Times,* Feb. 25, 1936.

baffling personality of Beck. . . . Speculations as to Poland's position are many and varied. There are those who believe that it may definitely throw in its lot with Germany in an attempt to seize the Ukraine and permit Germany to dominate Central Europe.[40]

The Soviet leaders appeared to share these apprehensions, and their fears were obviously aggravated by their awareness of the advantages which Poland's geographical position would offer to an aggressor. As Litvinov revealed to Bullitt, the Russians realized that Germany could not invade the Soviet Union "except by way of Poland" and believed that the Poles might cooperate with Hitler in an attack on the USSR.[41]

While Moscow viewed its western neighbor with distrust and foreboding, suspecting anti-Soviet motivation even in Beck's harmless trip to Belgium,[42] Warsaw also found ample reason for misgivings with regard to the diplomatic and military maneuvers of the Kremlin. Contrary to the expectations of the Quai d'Orsay, Beck made no dramatic moves to indicate his displeasure with the ratification of the Franco-Soviet treaty; he and his associates showed definite anxiety, however, over other developments which might prove dangerous to Poland's security and lessen her weight in international affairs. Toward the end of February, Ambassador Łukasiewicz arrived in the Polish capital to report on the situation in Russia, and the confidential information which he had been able to collect did not augur well for the future of Polish-Soviet relations. While his talks with the Russian rulers did not reveal any radical change in their attitude toward Poland, he was concerned over a large-scale concentration of Soviet troops along the Polish border and over the tendency of the Kremlin to shift its main attention from the Far East to the western frontiers of the USSR.[43] It was especially the numerical and technical superiority of the Red Army that presented the Poles with some perplexing and frustrating problems.[44]

[40] *USFR*, 1936, I (Washington, 1953), 186-87.

[41] *Ibid.*, p. 201.

[42] According to the Soviet press, the visit of the Polish Foreign Minister was inspired by his plans to establish contact with "reactionary Belgian groups" opposed to the Franco-Soviet treaty of mutual assistance. *Pravda*, March 7, 1936.

[43] Szembek, p. 164.

[44] In 1934 the Soviet Union increased the peacetime strength of its standing army

Under these circumstances it appeared advisable for Poland to continue her policy of rapprochement with the Third Reich; in fact, Łukasiewicz was prepared to go even further and to support Germany's southeastward expansion.[45] The allusions to the necessity of a common stand against the Soviet danger had by now become the standard feature of almost every German-Polish conversation on the governmental level.[46] In the opinion of the Nazi chiefs, European solidarity "ended at the Polish-Soviet frontier," and it was the duty of all "civilized nations" to put an end to "Bolshevik savagery"; as Reichsminister Hans Frank expressed it during his visit to Warsaw in February, 1936:

Polish-French-German collaboration was the only way to an effective struggle against the barbarism which would come from the East. The Russian nation had to be pitied for being lost in the confusion of Bolshevism, but against it "we must defend ourselves with all our strength, since it aimed at destroying everything which had been most sacred to us for a thousand years."[47]

These sentiments were undoubtedly shared by some responsible Polish politicians, though they were understandably reluctant to regard Nazi Germany as the champion of Western civilization and had no intention of embroiling their country in "religious wars" between the representatives of opposing ideologies.[48] At the same time, however, they realized that standing "à l'écart des grands

---

to 940,000, and in 1935, to 1,300,000 men. After 1935 the Russians accelerated the motorization of the Red Army and intensified the build-up of their armor, air force, and artillery. See White, p. 358, and Liddell Hart, ed., p. 61. At the same time, the numerical strength of the Polish Army remained stationary at about 280,000 men. The level of motorization and mechanization was extremely low; there were only a few armored units, composed mostly of reconnaissance vehicles, and practically no antiaircraft or antitank weapons. The number of combat airplanes was very limited, although the country was relatively advanced in aircraft construction. Kirchmayer, p. 23; Norwid-Neugebauer, pp. 15-19; Poland, Polskie Siły Zbrojne, Komisja Historyczna, *Polskie Siły Zbrojne w drugiej wojnie światowej*, I, Part I, 110, 146-47; see also "Materiały do zagadnienia przemysłu wojennego w Polsce w latach 1919-1939" [Materials Concerning the Question of War Industry in Poland, 1919-1939], *Niepodległość*, VI (1958), 148-87, and Akademiia Nauk SSSR, Institut Slavianovedeniia, *Istoriia Pol'shi*, III, 451.

[45] Szembek, p. 164. According to W. Zbyszewski, Łukasiewicz hated both the Soviet Union and France and regarded Russia as Poland's "mortal and eternal enemy"; his appointment as his country's ambassador to Moscow was, therefore, a "tragic blunder." "Józef Lipski," *Kultura*, No. 12/134 (Dec., 1958), p. 64.

[46] See Breyer, p. 187.   [47] *Polish White Book*, p. 31.   [48] Szembek, pp. 181-82.

enjeux européens" was not necessarily the best solution of Poland's troubles.[49]

While Piłsudski's heirs were thus engaged in a reappraisal of their policy toward Russia, Moscow continued to accuse Warsaw of attempting to intimidate the USSR, and Stalin himself made an obvious reference to Poland in his interview with Roy Howard on March 1, 1936. When asked how Germany could attack Russia without having a common frontier with her, the Soviet dictator replied he did not know what "specific frontiers" the Nazis were planning to use for this purpose, but he thought that those willing to "lend" them a frontier could be found.[50] Molotov showed a more conciliatory attitude toward the Poles in an interview granted to Jacques Chastenet, editor-in-chief of *Le Temps,* on March 19, but he also gave them to understand that they could count on no consideration if they refused to follow the policies advocated and supported by the USSR. He stated that an improvement in Polish-Soviet relations was both "desirable and possible," and that one way to bring it about would have been Poland's participation in the Eastern Pact; this opportunity was not yet irretrievably lost, however, and new chances to improve the situation could be found if the Polish government really desired "to strengthen peace in Europe."[51] When Chastenet wanted to know whether putting an end to Communist propaganda in Poland could not be regarded as one way of improving Polish-Soviet relations, the Soviet Premier parried this query with the remark that he had "no information" about such propaganda and that this was an "artificial question," evidently "dragged in" by his visitor's Polish informants.

In spite of its uneasiness over the true intentions of the Kremlin, Warsaw preferred to ignore Moscow's thinly veiled allusions and unacceptable suggestions; it did, however, reaffirm its determination to maintain correct relations with the USSR, the more so since the remilitarization of the Rhineland cast an ominous

[49] *Ibid.,* p. 208.
[50] *Pravda,* March 5, 1936; Degras, III, 164. According to *International Press Correspondence,* it was "perfectly obvious" that Stalin referred to "the Sanacja fascists in Poland" (XVI, No. 16 [March 28, 1936], 422).
[51] Molotov, pp. 230-31; English translation in Degras, III, 183-84.

shadow over Europe and markedly increased the possibility of an eventual armed conflict between Germany and the Western powers. Beck, in his statement to the Council of the League of Nations on March 18, 1936, made an attempt to define his government's views concerning current international problems and to clarify its attitude toward Russia:

The entry of German military effectives into the demilitarized zone is a fact which nobody disputes and which the Council must place on record. It rests, I think, with the signatories of the Rhineland Pact to judge of the circumstances in which that event has taken place. . . . Recent events have given rise to lively discussions on the subject of the Franco-Soviet Pact. I wish to say that that Pact, concluded between France and the Soviet Union, to which, as to the Rhineland Pact, Poland is not a party, could not in any way modify the obligations and rights which Poland derives from her previous engagements. As regards the Soviet Union, Poland's engagements have been formulated during the last few years in the Pact of Nonaggression and in the London Protocol on the Definition of Aggression. Those two agreements, which were signed by my country in order to consolidate the security of Eastern Europe, still represent the expression of our resolve to maintain lasting relations of friendship with our eastern neighbor.[52]

However, while Beck was still interested in maintaining "une certaine détente" with the USSR,[53] he also displayed an increasing concern over the policy of the Quai d'Orsay, with its allegedly pro-Soviet tendencies, and attributed some moves of French diplomacy to the crafty intrigues of the Kremlin.[54] Wishing to avoid or minimize any risks in Poland's contacts with Russia, he adopted a passive attitude toward Moscow and waited for the Soviet Union to make new overtures, but the expected gestures

[52] League of Nations, *Official Journal*, XVII, No. 4, Part I (April, 1936), 328-29. The Comintern sources answered Beck's statement with insinuations that the Polish government was "fairly well informed" about Germany's plans and that during the fortnight preceding the German march into the Rhineland "there was much coming and going between the Wilhelmstrasse and the Polish Ministry for Foreign Affairs." *International Press Correspondence*, XVI, 422.

[53] Szembek, p. 180. This was shown, for example, by the signature of a commercial agreement with the Soviet Union on March 5 and of an understanding defining the legal status of the Soviet trade mission in Poland on June 14. See *Kurjer Warszawski*, March 5 and June 15, 1936.

[54] Szembek, p. 180.

of friendship from that direction failed to materialize. Instead, the Kremlin turned its attention to Poland's Baltic neighbors and invited the chiefs of the General Staffs of Estonia, Latvia, and Lithuania to a series of talks which took place in the Soviet capital toward the end of April. The three military leaders met with a cordial reception, and this conspicuous show of Russo-Baltic friendship was widely regarded as a serious blow to Polish diplomacy.[55] As General Sikorski commented in *Kurjer Warszawski:*

A rapprochement between the Baltic bloc and the Soviets would radically change our military situation in the east. Poland's frontiers with Russia as fixed by the Riga Treaty guaranteed to us a continuous front stretching from the Baltic to the Black Sea, provided that we maintained an understanding with Latvia and Estonia and an alliance with Rumania. Today the northern sector of that front is breaking down and falling to pieces, shifting . . . the starting point of a possible Russian invasion far westward, to the gates of Suwałki and Grodno.[56]

Beck's feverish search for new friends and his visit to Yugoslavia in May,[57] which followed closely Premier Kościałkowski's trip to Budapest, indicated a desire on Warsaw's part to counterbalance this setback. In spite of their persistent efforts, however, the Polish leaders were unable to change the fact that the Soviet Union was now playing an increasingly active role in world affairs, where its proper weight was unduly enlarged through the influence of international Communism. Moscow was widely credited with the victories of the Popular Front in the Spanish and French elections (February and May, 1936), and during the dramatic summer of that year emerged as the foremost power throwing its unqualified support behind the Spanish Loyalists.

[55] See *Le Monde Slave,* XIII, Part III (Aug., 1936), 227, and *Osteuropa,* XI (1935-36), 609.

[56] *Kurjer Warszawski,* May 24, 1936.

[57] Moscow reacted to this trip by charging that Beck was trying to split the Little Entente by breaking Yugoslavia away from it. See *Kommunisticheskii Internatsional,* XVIII, No. 14 (Aug., 1936), 39; *The Communist International* (New York ed.), XIII, No. 10 (Oct., 1936), 1286. According to *International Press Correspondence,* the Polish Foreign Minister went to Belgrade "as an envoy of Hitler" in order to form "a bloc opposed to the bloc of the powers desirous of organizing collective security" (XVI, No. 27 [June 6, 1936], 708).

This increase in Russia's might and prestige was viewed with apprehension by the Polish government and the conservative circles, but it prompted the Socialists to intensify their demands that Poland should join the "antifascist block extending from Madrid to Moscow."[58] In Poland itself, the growing activity of the Communists was demonstrated by numerous riots which took place in several Polish cities.[59] The May Day celebrations in the capital assumed a menacing character and served as an indication of a dangerous state of mind prevailing among the workers, who, in the words of Beck, seemed to be "much more revolutionary and bellicose" than in the past.[60]

Soon after his return from Belgrade, Beck decided to make two important changes in Polish diplomatic service abroad. Ambassador Łukasiewicz, who had spent three years in Russia, was to take charge of the embassy in Paris, and the vacant post in the Soviet capital was to be occupied by Wacław Grzybowski, formerly Poland's representative in Czechoslovakia. The latter appointment was regarded as especially significant since the new ambassador to Moscow combined a high degree of practical skill with a thorough understanding of the Soviet system and the Russian mentality.[61] His first experiences in the USSR were, however, hardly encouraging, and Krestinskii, who received him in Litvinov's absence soon after his arrival,[62] told him "in plain terms" that his mission was beginning "at a most unfortunate time":

The political relations between us could not be worse. We are working . . . to increase the prestige of the League of Nations, and

---

[58] *Kurjer Warszawski,* June 15, 1936.

[59] A bloody clash between the police and striking workers occurred in Kraków on March 23; similar incidents took place in Częstochowa and Chrzanów. The CPP also claimed credit for the disorders and street fighting in Lwów on April 14 and 16.

[60] Szembek, p. 175; see also F. Sławoj-Składkowski, "Opowieści administracyjne czyli pamiętnik niebohaterski" [Administrative Tales; or, Non-heroic Memoirs], *Kultura,* No. 9/47 (Sept., 1951), pp. 114-15.

[61] See the tribute paid to him by Ambassador Noël in the introduction to Szembek's diary. Szembek, p. ix.

[62] Grzybowski himself states in his final report that this interview took place on July 1 (*Polish White Book,* p. 194), but according to the press reports the Ambassador left Warsaw on July 1 and arrived in Moscow on July 2. See *Kurjer Warszawski,* July 3, 1936.

for collective security; we are combating all forms of aggression and all forms of fascism. At the present time we are pursuing an anti-German, anti-Italian, and anti-Japanese policy. Poland is pursuing a diametrically contrary policy, tending to weaken the League of Nations, combating attempts to realize collective security, supporting Italy and sympathizing with Japan. Poland is within the orbit of German policy.[63]

Grzybowski's assurances that such suspicions were unfounded and that Poland's main objective was to achieve "correct and good relations" with her neighbors remained ineffective; he was more successful, however, in his conversation with Kalinin, to whom he presented his credentials on July 4.[64] Both sides seemed to agree that the development of closer economic ties between Poland and Russia might lead to an improvement of political relations, but no concrete proposals were advanced at this stage. This rather friendly encounter ended on a somewhat sour note as a result of Kalinin's complaints that the Poles were isolating themselves from cultural contacts with the USSR and that the achievements of Soviet art and literature were not made accessible to the Polish people.[65]

In Grzybowski's opinion, the ideas expounded by the Soviet leaders expressed Moscow's tendency toward expansion and indicated that Poland was to be treated as a mere object of that expansion.[66] His subsequent impressions were even more pessimistic; after only a few months in the Soviet Union he was able to observe there "signs of a growing dynamism," and he expected that Russia's "doctrinal imperialism" would eventually assume the form not only of expansion but also of aggression. It was only a matter of time as to when the Kremlin would launch an attack against Europe—and at a moment of its own choosing, for the Soviet rulers were the "masters of the situation."[67] Expansion was the sole reason and justification for the existence of the Soviet regime and, in spite of all vague promises and paper declarations of friendship, Moscow's basic hatred and hostility toward Poland remained unchanged: "By its very nature Soviet

---

[63] Polish White Book, p. 195.   [64] Kurjer Warszawski, July 5, 1936.
[65] Polish White Book, pp. 195-96.   [66] Ibid., p. 196.   [67] Szembek, p. 215.

expansion is directed against us, for we constitute a natural barrier to the realization of their designs."[68]

The gloomy reports from Russia served only to strengthen Warsaw's anti-Soviet sentiments, and some Polish diplomats were rather impressed by Ribbentrop's and Göring's assertions that "Poland was menaced by the danger of Bolshevism equally with Germany," that this threat could be forestalled only "by crushing at their roots even the smallest signs of Communism,"[69] and that both countries might be eventually forced to "march together" against the Soviet Union.[70] Count Szembek, who had always harbored some illusions about the real nature of the Nazi regime, came now to the conclusion that the policy of equilibrium between the Third Reich and the USSR should be given up and that an attempt should be made to harmonize the views of Warsaw and Berlin with regard to the Soviet problem.[71] His memorandum prepared in support of this conception was, however, disregarded by Beck, and General Śmigły-Rydz also refused to abandon his skeptical attitude toward Germany, although he was ready to admit that the Poles could never declare themselves "pour le parti bolcheviste."[72]

At the same time the hopes that Poland and Russia could be brought together as friends of France proved impracticable, as was shown by the cool reaction of Śmigły-Rydz to the proposals of Polish-Soviet cooperation advanced during General Gamelin's visit to Warsaw in August, 1936.[73] When the French Chief of Staff mentioned informally the possibility that Poland might accept some military assistance from the USSR, his hosts categorically refused to discuss the subject.[74] They also objected to

[68] *Polish White Book*, p. 197; Szembek, p. 215.
[69] *Polish White Book*, p. 34.   [70] Szembek, p. 199.
[71] See W. A. Zbyszewski, "Fragmenty pamiętnikow min. Szembeka" [Excerpts from Minister Szembek's Memoirs], *Kultura*, No. 6/56 (June, 1952), p. 50. The corresponding passage of Szembek's diary is not included in the French translation of his *Journal*.
[72] Szembek, p. 208.
[73] For Polish press comments on this visit see *Kurjer Warszawski*, Aug. 13-17, 1936.
[74] Germany, Auswärtiges Amt, *Documents and Materials Relating to the Eve of the Second World War*, I, 117. According to some reports, Gamelin was also made to feel that the close relations between the Red Army and the Czechoslovak armed forces "definitely embittered Polish feelings." *Neue Zürcher Zeitung*, Aug. 17, 1936.

the plans of a Russian action against East Prussia through Lithuanian territory in the event of a Franco-German war and expressed their fears that the entry of Soviet troops into any country was likely to lead to its permanent occupation by the Red Army.[75] The attempts of the Quai d'Orsay to make a French loan to Poland dependent on Warsaw's concessions in favor of the Soviet Union and Czechoslovakia were likewise firmly opposed by Śmigły-Rydz, who was eventually able to secure substantial credits from France without accepting any humiliating conditions.[76]

The Poles were also able to score an important diplomatic victory in Bucharest. On August 30 Titulescu was removed from his post as Rumania's Foreign Minister, and his dismissal was accompanied by unusual tributes and expressions of regret in the Soviet press.[77] The man who had brought about the collapse of the Russo-Rumanian talks in 1932 was now emulating Beneš in his attempts to harmonize the policies of the Little Entente with those of the USSR, and his pro-Soviet orientation left no doubt in Warsaw that "du point de vue polonais, la nécessité d'abattre Titulesco s'imposerait."[78] Accordingly, Polish influence in Bucharest was used to undermine Titulescu's position and to achieve a closer cooperation between Poland and her Rumanian ally.[79]

While combating Soviet diplomatic moves in Paris and Bucharest, Warsaw continued to assure Moscow of its determination to keep aloof from any aggressive plans directed against Russia, and the Polish press condemned almost unanimously a series of anti-Soviet speeches delivered by the Nazi leaders during the

[75] Gamelin, II, 230. The only form of cooperation with the Red Army which Śmigły-Rydz was willing to accept was in the field of aviation. While refusing to offer the Russians any permanent bases, he was prepared to consider the possibility of granting them temporary landing rights on Polish territory. *Ibid.*

[76] Among other things, the French wanted to obtain the dismissal of Beck, but withdrew this demand at the last moment. See Noël, p. 145; Beck, *Final Report*, p. 122. The loan granted to Poland was to enable her to finance the mechanization of the army and the development of war industry.

[77] See *Izvestiia*, Sept. 1, 1936. For the reaction of the Polish press see *Kurjer Warszawski*, Sept. 7 and 10, 1936.

[78] Szembek, pp. 95-96.

[79] For details see S. Mikulicz, "Wpływ dyplomacji sanacyjnej na obalenie Titulescu" [The Influence of the Sanacja Diplomacy on Titulescu's Overthrow], *Sprawy Międzynarodowe*, XII, No. 7/8 (July-Aug., 1959), 104-23; see also *DGFP*, Series C, III (Washington, 1959), 621, 1012, and Szembek, pp. 203-4.

Party Congress at Nuremberg in September, 1936.[80] There was no doubt, however, that the position of Poland as a barrier between Germany and Russia was becoming increasingly precarious as the military power of her two dangerous neighbors continued to grow at an alarming rate and her own limited economic strength rendered her unable to keep abreast of the tremendous strides made by Berlin and Moscow in the field of rearmament.[81] This became especially obvious when the saber-rattling performance of Hitler and his associates was followed by an impressive display of the armed might of the Soviet Union during the fall maneuvers of 1936. The Red Army demonstrated its preparedness in a series of exercises that took place over a vast territory from the Baltic to the Black Sea and from the Leningrad area to the Far East,[82] but the greatest assemblage of elite troops, supported by strong armored and mechanized units, took place along the Polish frontier, in the Belorussian Military District. The maneuvers around Minsk were attended by four marshals of the USSR and by delegations from Czechoslovakia, France, and Great Britain, their progress received extensive coverage in the Soviet press,[83] and foreign observers were inclined to interpret them as a distinct warning to Poland not to get involved in any aggressive combinations directed against the Russians or their Czech allies.[84]

This fairly transparent device to exert pressure on Warsaw was accompanied by some moderately worded though not exactly

---

[80] *Kurjer Warszawski,* Sept. 16 and 25, 1936.

[81] While Soviet expenditures for defense increased from 5 billion rubles in 1934 to 8.2 billion in 1935, 14.8 billion in 1936, 17.5 billion in 1937, and 27 billion in 1938 (see USSR, Verkhovnyi Sovet, *Second Session, Verbatim Report,* p. 532), the Polish military budget was kept for four successive years (1934-35–1937-38) at 768,000,000 złotys, and even then was raised to only 800,000,000 złotys, or about $151,000,000. See Poland, Sejm, *Sprawozdanie stenograficzne,* Kadencja IV, Posiedzenie XIII, p. 3, and Poland, Senat, Komisja Budżetowa, *Sprawozdanie o preliminarzu budżetowym na okres od 1 kwietnia 1938 do 31 marca 1939* [Report on Budget Estimates for the Period from April 1, 1938, to March 31, 1939], VI (Warsaw, 1938), 1. In 1932-39, between 36 and 37 percent of the Polish budget was earmarked for defense expenditures ("Materiały do zagadnienia przemysłu wojennego w Polsce w latach 1919-1939," *Niepodległość,* VI, 163); the corresponding figures for the Soviet Union were 18.6 percent in 1937 and 23.5 percent in 1938 (USSR, Verkhovnyi Sovet, p. 532).

[82] *Osteuropa,* XII (1936-37), 54.

[83] See *Pravda,* Sept. 9-11, and *Izvestiia,* Sept. 9-12 and 14, 1936.

[84] *Osteuropa,* XII, 54; see also *ibid.,* pp. 114-15.

conciliatory statements to the effect that the halfhearted attempts of Polish leaders to emancipate themselves from Hitler's tutelage were as yet unsatisfactory, but that a reversal of Beck's policy would surely bring about an improvement of Poland's relations with Moscow and Prague and thus make a "definite contribution to the struggle for the preservation of peace in Europe."[85] The developments of the next few months were to prove to the Kremlin, however, that its scheme to intimidate the Poles and its rather dubious offers of friendship were equally ineffective. Poland's reluctance to give up her role as an independent factor in the European balance of power and her determination to preserve her freedom of action prompted Beck to pay a visit to London, where he reportedly tried to persuade the British that Warsaw rather than Moscow must be reckoned with in any attempt to safeguard peace in Eastern Europe, that his country was pursuing quite sincerely a policy of "positive" and "conditional" neutrality, and that it ought to be supported in this endeavor.[86] As *The Manchester Guardian* subsequently observed,

Poland entirely shares the British instinct against any kind of participation in the so-called ideological or holy wars. She has no intention whatever of incurring the enmity of Russia—or, for that matter, of Germany. . . . She has chosen the best course between an absolute neutrality and membership of an anti-German coalition. . . . The conditional neutrality of Poland keeps Russia and Germany apart (both as foes and as allies) and so averts the main cause of war in Eastern Europe.[87]

According to *Pravda,* on the other hand, the Anglo-Polish negotiations merely showed that Poland was "by no means willing to relinquish her role as wirepuller of German aggression," since they aimed at isolating the Soviet Union and at delivering up Czechoslovakia and other countries of Central and Southeastern Europe to the tender mercies of the Nazis.[88] These accusations were coupled with charges that the cultural agreement negotiated

---

[85] *Pravda,* Sept. 25, 1936.
[86] *The New York Times,* Nov. 8, 1936. According to the Polish press, Beck's visit was directed primarily against the revival of the idea of the Four-Power Pact. *Kurjer Warszawski,* Oct. 23, 1936.
[87] *The Manchester Guardian,* Dec. 31, 1936.
[88] *Pravda,* Nov. 21, 1936.

by Poland and Japan[89] constituted but "a new link in the bloc of alliances forged by the warmongers" and that it "threw new light on the objectives pursued by Poland in her talks with Rumania."[90]

While Moscow's allegations lacked any factual basis, Polish official circles felt that, in view of the conclusion of the anti-Comintern treaty by Germany and Japan on November 25, 1936, Poland's attitude toward this new "ideological alliance" should be stated with clarity and precision for the benefit of all interested parties. As an editorial in *Gazeta Polska* affirmed, the agreement between Berlin and Tokyo was "of no mean significance" to Warsaw:

Poland constitutes a buffer state between the Soviets and Germany, and nothing but the utmost caution can ensure peace and neutrality for her citizens. There are many theories about the real nature of this agreement. Whatever the case may be, Poland cannot participate. If it is a plain alliance, it would be against the very fundamentals on which our foreign policy rests. If it is not an alliance but a kind of an anti-Red International launching a crusade against the Comintern, it would not be less foolish to join. We wish to abstain from any move which may hurt the feelings of our eastern neighbor. This, of course, does not mean that German fears on account of Bolshevist activities are entirely unfounded. We are fully aware of the existence of Soviet propaganda abroad in spite of the most solemn promises on the part of Moscow, but there is sufficient power in the government's hands to deal with it. We do not believe that one International could be successfully suppressed by another International.[91]

At the very time this conciliatory statement was published in Warsaw, the Kremlin was intensifying its pressure on the Baltic

[89] Documents relating to this agreement are listed in C. H. Uyehara, comp., *Checklist of Archives in the Japanese Ministry of Foreign Affairs, Tokyo, Japan, 1868-1945* (Washington, 1954), p. 54.

[90] *Pravda*, Dec. 17, 1936. The latter remark refers to the visits paid to Poland by Rumanian Foreign Minister Antonescu and Chief of Staff Samsonovici in November and December, 1936, which were intended to review and revivify the alliance between Warsaw and Bucharest. See *Kurjer Warszawski*, Nov. 24, 1936; *Osteuropa*, XII, 238.

[91] *Gazeta Polska*, Nov. 28, 1936, as quoted in *Czas*, Nov. 29, 1936, and in *News Digest*, III (1936-37), 234; see also *Czas*, Nov. 20, 1936. The opposition press in Poland took an even more outspoken stand against the pact. See *Kurjer Warszawski*, Nov. 26, 1936.

states, and A. A. Zhdanov, one of the most prominent leaders of the CPSU, in his strongly worded speech to the Eighth Congress of the Soviets, issued a warning to the small countries "not to get entangled in big adventures" and not to allow the "fascists" to use their territories for aggressive purposes.[92] While Beck preferred to ignore several direct anti-Polish attacks made by the representatives of the Ukrainian and Belorussian Soviet Republics,[93] he made a reference to Zhdanov's address in his report to the Foreign Affairs Committee of the Senate on December 18, 1936:

Public opinion has recently been rather shocked by the utterances of one of the speakers during the Eighth Congress of the Soviets, whose words appeared to contain threats to the western neighbors of the Union. Though these utterances did not concern Poland but rather our Baltic friends, I could understand the stir caused in public opinion. . . . It gives me great satisfaction to confirm that the explanation received does not give ground for any concern[94] . . . [and] that the Soviet government, just like ourselves, continues to attach equal importance to good and normal relations with all the states situated on its western borders.[95]

In spite of the tension created by the Zhdanov incident, Beck thought it possible to assure the Senate that the work done by Poland in cooperation with the USSR continued to "yield useful results" and that Warsaw and Moscow were settling their neighborly affairs "in a normal way, giving no cause for shocks or serious misunderstandings."[96] This attempt to minimize or ignore the differences between Poland and Russia met with a sharp rebuff in the Soviet press, which ridiculed Beck's statement and

[92] *Pravda*, Dec. 1, 1936; Degras, III, 226. The unofficial text of the speech circulated in the West was much sharper than the official version and contained threats of direct military action against the Baltic states. *Kurjer Warszawski*, Dec. 3, 1936, and Beloff, II, 78.

[93] See *Izvestiia*, Nov. 27 and Dec. 1, 1936.

[94] Here Beck probably refers to the explanations given by the Soviet envoy in Riga to Latvian Foreign Minister Munters. See *Kurjer Warszawski*, Dec. 3, 1936. According to *Pravda*, Dec. 21, 1936, Poland received no explanations from the Soviet government.

[95] Beck, *Przemówienia*, p. 264; English translation in Harley, *The Authentic Biography of Colonel Beck*, p. 154.

[96] Beck, *Przemówienia*, p. 264; Harley, *The Authentic Biography of Colonel Beck*, p. 154.

treated the whole passage of his speech referring to Polish-Soviet relations as a masterpiece of deception:

What Mr. Beck said and what he neglected to say bear witness equally to the fact that his policy has remained unchanged and that he invariably continues to follow the trail of German fascism. Mr. Beck is free to assume mysterious airs and to put on a Sphinx-like mask. The riddle of that Sphinx has been solved long ago.[97]

From now on Soviet propaganda exerted much energy to discredit Beck's reputation by labeling him a "German agent" and "Hitler's traveling salesman";[98] it also denounced Poland's interest in the fate of the Baltic states as inconsistent with her alleged desire to preserve neighborly relations with Moscow and to maintain a neutral position between Germany and Russia.[99] Thus, as the crucial year 1936 drew to a close, it was becoming increasingly obvious that the Kremlin's attitude of sullen suspiciousness toward Warsaw was being replaced by one of open and implacable enmity.

[97] *Izvestiia,* Dec. 21, 1936; see also *Pravda,* Dec. 21, 1936.
[98] As Noël observes, p. 169, Beck had by now become "la bête noire de Moscou."
[99] *Pravda,* Dec. 21, 1936.

V. The Cold War

The beginning of 1937 seemed to be particularly inauspicious in the field of Polish-Russian relations. Early in January the Soviet press responded with a torrent of abuse to the charges of inhuman treatment of the Polish population in the USSR voiced in the Sejm by a prominent member of the government bloc,[1] but its most violent outburst of indignation was reserved for the Polish newspapers for their refusal to accept uncritically the accusations against Piatakov, Radek, and other defendants in the trial of the so-called Anti-Soviet Trotskyite Center.[2] It was alleged that the Warsaw press was closely connected with the German Ministry of Propaganda and that it gave wide publicity to "all anti-Soviet monstrosities prepared in Goebbels' department"; this was, however, hardly surprising since Poland had no legal independent press, and the fascist newspapers did everything in their power to cover the Moscow trial with a "curtain of lies."[3]

Amidst this uproar, during the first half of February, Göring went again to Poland and had a long conversation with Śmigły-Rydz who had recently received a marshal's baton and was gradually assuming dictatorial airs. This time the German visitor tried to convince his hosts that the danger to Poland and the rest of Europe existed "not only in the form of a Bolshevik and communized Russia, but of Russia generally, in any form, be it

---

[1] Poland, Sejm, *Sprawozdanie stenograficzne,* Kadencja IV, Posiedzenie XXXVIII, p. 41; *Pravda,* Jan. 15 and 19, 1937. According to the census of 1926, the number of Poles in the USSR was 782,338, but by 1939 it decreased to 626,905.

[2] Similar charges had been made by the Soviet press in the summer of 1936 in connection with the trial of Zinov'ev and Kamenev. See *Pravda,* Aug. 31, 1936.

[3] *Ibid.,* Feb. 9, 1937. For editorial comment of the Polish press see *Kurjer Warszawski,* Feb. 4, 1937.

Monarchist or Liberal"; he also stressed Berlin's dependence on Warsaw and voiced his apprehension that an isolated Poland could be easily subdued by Soviet troops, and then "the whole Russian avalanche would strike directly against the German frontier."[4] Göring's thesis that the interests of Poland and Germany were "entirely one" in opposing Russia was, however, not acceptable to Piłsudski's heirs, who saw no urgent necessity of aligning their policy with that of the Third Reich.[5]

Meanwhile Soviet diplomacy continued its attempts to undermine Poland's influence in the Baltic states by sending Marshal Egorov on a good-will tour to Kaunas, Riga, and Tallin.[6] At the same time no opportunity was missed to blame Warsaw for the deterioration of Polish-Russian relations, and a relatively harmless incident in Gdynia, during which a Soviet sailor was allegedly beaten up by the Polish police, was inflated to the dimensions of an international crisis.[7] The Kremlin was also irritated by Beck's visit to Bucharest in April, 1937, especially since the Polish press began to speak openly of the dangers threatening Rumania from the side of the Soviet Union and advised her to rely on Poland for protection and support.[8] Moscow's own interpretation of the objectives pursued by Beck and of the general line of Polish foreign policy was presented in *Pravda:*

Everywhere Mr. Beck is carrying out the same task: he is preparing the ground for the subversive work of fascist warmongers. . . . At one time, people used to say that Beck was sitting on two stools. . . . Now even the French newspapers, known for their benevolent attitude toward Poland, admit with bitterness that Beck has firmly settled down at Hitler's feet and is openly demonstrating his devotion to his German master. . . . Thus, gradually, Beck has turned into an acrobat balancing himself on the Berlin-Rome axis. . . . Mr. Beck is now operating under the fashionable slogan of creating "neutral blocs." The question concerns the so-called neutral bloc consisting of Poland, Rumania, and some Baltic states, a bloc which, according to the intention of its initiators, should "separate" the USSR

[4] *Polish White Book,* p. 37.   [5] *Ibid.,* p. 38.

[6] See the editorial "Misja Marszałka Jegorowa" [Marshal Egorov's Mission] in *Kurjer Warszawski,* March 8, 1937.

[7] See *Izvestiia* and *Pravda,* Feb. 20, 1937.

[8] *Gazeta Polska* as quoted in *International Press Correspondence,* XVII, No. 19 (May 1, 1937), 447; see also *Izvestiia,* April 24, 1937, and *Pravda,* April 25, 1937.

from Germany throughout the distance from the Baltic to the Black
Sea.[9] In fact, this amounts to the establishment of joint-stock company Hitler & Co., with the purpose of "lending" frontiers to the
German aggressor, or, to put it more exactly, for providing him with
a jumping-off place for an attack against the USSR. Beck is playing
the role of the chief broker in that deal.[10]

This appraisal of Polish policy showed that Warsaw's refusal
to be drawn into any anti-German combination was misconstrued
in Moscow as a token of Nazi-Polish collusion against the Soviet
Union, and it was apparent that nothing short of a complete
reversal of this attitude would appease the Kremlin's apprehensions. An exchange of visits by President Mościcki and King
Carol in June, 1937, brought a new series of complaints about
Polish-German "intrigues" in the Balkans, allegedly aimed at
destroying the system of collective security in Southeastern Europe
and at disrupting the "policy of peace" pursued by the Soviet
government.[11] On the other hand, the Polish press welcomed the
Rumanian monarch with editorials stressing that both countries
were in the unfortunate position of being immediate neighbors
of Russia; as long as the USSR refused to give up its schemes of
ideological and military conquest of the rest of the continent,
Poland and Rumania would continue to act as guardians of
civilization and as an unassailable barrier against the onslaught
of Communism.[12]

[9] For a detailed treatment of this subject see Roos, *Polen und Europa*, pp. 260-
73. The concept of a "Third Europe" (sometimes referred to as the "Helsinki-
Bucharest axis") did not originate with Beck; see H. Batowski, "Rumuńska podróż
Becka w październiku 1938 roku," *Kwartalnik Historyczny*, LXV (1958), No. 2, 435.
It was frequently discussed both in the Polish press (see General Sikorski's article
"O polską tezę bezpieczeństwa" [For a Polish Thesis of Security] in *Kurjer Warszawski*, Feb. 2, 1936, and *Czas*, July 13, 1938) and from the rostrum of the Sejm
(Poland, Sejm, *Sprawozdanie stenograficzne*, Kadencja V, Posiedzenie III, p. 7). The
notion of a "bloc of antibloc states" was developed into a coherent system by
Wojciech Wasiutyński in his book *Między III Rzeszą i III Rusią*. Beck's own interpretation of this idea is given in his *Final Report*, p. 118.
[10] *Pravda*, April 27, 1937; see also *Izvestiia*, April 24, 1937; Potemkin, ed., III, 603;
and Akademiia Nauk SSSR, Institut Slavianovedeniia, *Istoriia Pol'shi*, III, 424-25.
[11] *Pravda*, June 9 and 30, and July 19, 1937; *International Press Correspondence*,
XVII, No. 28 (July 3, 1937), 624. Litvinov also stated in a private conversation
with Ambassador Davies that King Carol's Polish visit was "distinctly anti-Soviet,"
but described it at the same time as "not of serious consequence." USFR, *The
Soviet Union, 1933-1939* (Washington, 1952), p. 387.
[12] *Goniec Warszawski*, June 27, 1937, as quoted in *News Digest*, III (1936-37),
976; see also *Czas*, June 21, 1937, and *Kurjer Warszawski*, June 26, 1937.

While Soviet diplomacy counteracted all Polish attempts to establish a closer cooperation between Warsaw and Paris,[13] the Poles tried to frustrate the Kremlin's designs by arguing with their friends in the West that they would be well advised to revise their attitude toward Russia and to reconsider her value as an ally.[14] They were helped in this undertaking by the wave of shock which spread throughout the world as a result of the execution of Marshal Tukhachevskii and his associates. Seldom before had the Polish press been so unanimous in expressing its horror at what was happening in the Soviet Union; at the same time it argued, however, that the developments across the border were not without certain advantages to Poland:

The events in Russia are bound to have strong repercussions in the field of international relations. Some circles in Western Europe used to regard Russia as a strong military and economic power. . . . Recent events will undoubtedly cool the enthusiasm of Soviet friends in the West. For Poland, the developments in the Soviet Union are of special interest. . . . The exposure of the weakness of the Soviets is particularly advantageous to us, not because we are taking pleasure in somebody's misfortune, but because these facts demonstrate clearly who is the stronghold of order and power in the east of Europe.[15]

During the summer of 1937 Soviet diplomacy concentrated its efforts in the Far East, trying to stall the Japanese invasion of China by concluding, on August 21, a nonaggression treaty with the Nanking government.[16] The possibility of an armed clash between the USSR and Japan loomed larger than ever, and Poland made no effort to conceal the fact that, in the event of a Russo-Japanese conflict, her sympathies would lie on Tokyo's side.[17]

---

[13] See *Osteuropa*, XII (1936-37), 584-85.

[14] In this connection see Beck's conversation with Churchill at Cannes, during which the Polish Foreign Minister tried to persuade the British statesman that "Europe could have no confidence in Soviet Russia" and that the Poles "had more data than anyone else to judge this phenomenon [the Soviet regime] with skepticism." *Final Report*, p. 174.

[15] *Czas*, June 14, 1937; see also *ibid.*, June 15-16 and 21, 1937, and *Kurjer Warszawski*, June 15, 27, and 29, 1937.

[16] The repercussions of these developments in Europe, including a Japanese attempt to enlist Germany's help in forcing Poland to cooperate with the Anti-Comintern Pact, are discussed in *DGFP*, Series D, I (Washington, 1949), 750-52.

[17] Polish-Japanese relations had developed very favorably since the early 1930s and many gestures of friendship were exchanged by the two countries in the field

On October 1 Poland and Japan raised their missions in Tokyo and Warsaw to the status of embassies,[18] and the ceremonies honoring this event were marked by a pronounced cordiality.[19] Poland's support for Japan in the League of Nations signified Beck's determination to check the Kremlin's active policy in Europe by forcing it to devote all its attention to the problems of Asia.[20] Warsaw declined, however, "in a determined and consistent manner," several Japanese offers to make its association with Tokyo even more intimate by giving it the form of an anti-Soviet alliance; moreover, Count Tadeusz Romer, Polish ambassador in Japan, received from Beck categorical instructions to maintain friendly relations with that country but to avoid getting involved in any agreements, even of the most general nature, which would tend to restrict in any way Poland's freedom of action.[21]

Although Beck stopped short of committing himself to an openly anti-Soviet course of action, his policy of flirting and collaborating with the adversaries of the USSR was bound to irritate and exasperate Moscow and to prompt it to assume an increasingly defiant and uncompromising attitude toward Poland. In the summer of 1937 the Soviet government informed Warsaw in a curt note that all Polish citizens in the Caucasus and in the Ukraine beyond the Dnieper had made use of their right of option, and that the process of their repatriation had been completed; consequently, there was no longer need for any Polish

---

of cultural cooperation, especially after the founding of the Association of Poland's Friends in Tokyo in 1934. In addition to this, Warsaw was occasionally visited by Japanese military missions, and informal consultations concerning current international problems were held at irregular intervals by Polish and Japanese diplomats. Since 1936, however, this relationship tended to become complicated by Japan's participation in the Anti-Comintern Pact and her involvement in China, as well as by Poland's difficulties in maintaining the balance between Germany and the USSR.

[18] *Kurjer Warszawski*, Sept. 28, 1937.

[19] See *ibid.*, Nov. 11, 15, and 30, and Dec. 20, 1937; *Osteuropa*, XIII (1937-38), 122.

[20] Roos, *Polen und Europa*, p. 286.

[21] Quoted from Count Romer's letter to the author dated Aug. 31, 1958. It would seem that the reports about the existence of an "informal understanding" between Tokyo and Warsaw (J. C. Grew, *Ten Years in Japan* [New York, 1944], p. 155) had no factual basis; as E. L. Presseisen observes, "It cannot be too strongly emphasized that till this day no real evidence has come to light to substantiate these rumors" (p. 64).

diplomatic posts in those areas.[22] Late in August the Polish government gave in to the insistent demands of the Kremlin and agreed to close, as of December 1, its consulates in Tiflis (Tbilisi) and Kharkov.[23] Soon it became apparent that the process of alienation and progressive severing of all "superfluous" links between Poland and Russia was approaching its climax. At the beginning of October, Ambassador Davtian together with his press attaché and some minor officials of the Soviet Embassy were recalled from Warsaw and soon afterwards became victims of the Great Purge.[24] Frontier incidents began to multiply,[25] and the tension prevailing along the border increased after two unsuccessful attempts to set on fire the Soviet train running between the Polish station Zdołbunów and Shepetovka in the USSR.[26] The Soviet chargé d'affaires in Warsaw protested against these "provocations," demanded a severe punishment of the guilty, and reserved the right to claim damages from the Polish government, but there were certain indications that the incidents were staged by the Russians in order to provide them with an excuse for stopping traffic on the only railroad line connecting Poland with the Soviet Ukraine.[27] This was not an isolated occurrence but a part of an extensive and deliberately planned action aimed at insulating the Soviet citizen from all external influences by blocking most of the remaining ways of communication between the USSR and the neighboring countries.[28] Moscow's foreign policy, too, was undergoing a reappraisal. Litvinov's policy of collective security was losing its essential meaning, and the return of the Soviet Union to neutrality and isolation was foreshadowed not only by official declarations and warnings but also by some subtle manipulations in the background.

[22] Polish Research Center, *Poland and the USSR, 1921-1941*, p. 111.

[23] See the official communiqué in *Kurjer Warszawski*, Aug. 18, 1937. Poland's diplomatic posts in the Soviet Union were now limited to the embassy in Moscow, the consulates-general in Kiev and Minsk, and the consulate in Leningrad, while the USSR maintained an embassy in Warsaw and a consulate in Lwów. Odrowąż-Wysocki, pp. 840, 850.

[24] *Kurjer Warszawski*, Oct. 7, 1937, and *The Times* (London), Nov. 13, 1937; see also Szembek, p. 281, and *Osteuropa*, XIII (1937-38), 198-99.

[25] An increase in border clashes had been registered already during the summer of 1937. See *Pravda*, July 26, 1937.

[26] For details see *Czas*, Dec. 19, 1937; *Kurjer Warszawski*, Dec. 19, 1937; *Pravda*, Dec. 3, 5, 18, and 21, 1937; Jan. 4, 1938. See also *Vneshniaia politika SSSR*, IV, 323-25.

[27] Szembek, p. 264.   [28] *Polish White Book*, p. 199.

The stepping up of the "cold war" against Poland gave rise to rumors that the Kremlin was about to create a zone of devastation along Russia's European frontiers;[29] it also aggravated the fears about the personal safety of Polish diplomats in Moscow.[30] At the same time, the Russians intensified their propaganda campaign against Warsaw and increased the schedule of radio programs in Ukrainian and Belorussian and of other anti-Polish broadcasts beamed at Poland from Kiev, Minsk, and several other stations close to the western border of the Soviet Union.[31] In spite of these efforts, however, the last months of 1937 marked a definite decline of Communist strength inside Poland. The Great Purge involved most of the prominent Polish Communists living in the USSR; others were recalled to Russia from abroad only to be summarily executed or to disappear behind prison bars.[32] The Communist Party of Poland, deprived of its best brains and most enthusiastic organizers, was rapidly disintegrating and losing even that rather limited measure of popularity which it had been able to win during the two decades of its existence. Many of its underground propaganda centers had been liquidated as a result of concerted police action; Socialist and Populist groups and organizations were making a determined effort to purge themselves of Communist influences, and most of the former fellow-travelers, deeply embarrassed and disturbed by the ruthless extermination of the leadership of the CPP and by the wave of unprecedented terror sweeping the Soviet Union, were severing their connections with the Party and leaving it to its own fate.[33] The national minorities were also showing an increasing resistance

<hr/>

[29] *USFR*, 1937, I (Washington, 1954), 164.   [30] Szembek, pp. 264-65.
[31] Poland, Sejm, *Sprawozdanie stenograficzne*, Kadencja IV, Posiedzenie LXVII, pp. 100-1, 104.
[32] For details see A. Burmeister, "Tragedia polskich komunistów" [Tragedy of Polish Communists], *Kultura*, 1952, No. 1/51, pp. 101-9; Dziewanowski, *The Communist Party of Poland*, p. 149; and Pobóg-Malinowski, II, Part I, 644. Ironically, only the Party chiefs serving prison terms in Poland succeeded in escaping Stalin's vengeance.
[33] The Communist Party of Poland was officially dissolved by the Executive Committee of the Comintern during the early summer of 1938. *Istoriia Pol'shi*, III, 434. For the reasons behind the dissolution and the mysterious circumstances surrounding it see L. Honigwill, "Dlaczego Stalin rozwiązał K.P.P." [Why Stalin Dissolved the CPP], *Wiadomości* (London), May 20, 1956; M. K. Dziewanowski, "Rozwiązanie i rehabilitacja Komunistycznej Partii Polski" [The Dissolution and Rehabilitation of the Communist Party of Poland], *ibid.*, Aug. 5, 1956, and the same author's account in *The Communist Party of Poland*, pp. 149-52.

to the blandishments of Soviet agents and Communist agitators.[34]

Meanwhile, in spite of the Kremlin's cavalier attitude toward the usages of international life,[35] Poland tried to maintain at least some outward appearances of correct relations with Russia. After the German-Japanese anti-Comintern agreement had been expanded by Italy's accession on November 6, 1937, the Polish leaders expected that they would be invited to join this tripartite declaration. In order to quash any rumors that the Poles would associate themselves with an anti-Soviet coalition, Beck on November 9 advised all Polish diplomatic missions abroad that no proposal to join the pact had been received by Warsaw and that "in any case, Poland could not be a party to that protocol in view of her special position as neighbor of the USSR, as well as her objection in principle to the formation of any bloc."[36] Moreover, at this time the Poles believed themselves to have no reason to worry about any direct threat of Russian invasion; as Marshal Śmigły-Rydz confided to Ambassador Bullitt,

He was convinced from his military intelligence reports that the Red Army along the European frontier was totally incapable . . . of taking the offensive; the staffs of the armies on the Polish and Rumanian frontiers of the Soviet Union had been so destroyed by the recent executions and so shaken in self-confidence that any offensive operations were out of the question. He felt, therefore, that the position of Poland vis-à-vis the Soviet Union was today much safer than it had ever been.[37]

[34] On the progressive increase of anti-Soviet sentiments among the Belorussian minority in Poland see *Sprawy Narodowościowe*, VII (1933), 559-60, 692-93; VIII (1934), 263, 618; IX (1935), 463-64; XI (1937), 652; Poland, Sejm, *Sprawozdanie stenograficzne*, Okres III, Posiedzenie CXXIX, p. 52; Vakar, pp. 135, 146. The attitude of the Ukrainian minority toward the USSR is discussed in *Sprawy Narodowościowe*, VII, 389-93, 545-46, 552-53; VIII, 64-66,593-94; X (1936), 64, 66, 256-57, 492, 609-10, 619-20; XII (1938), 101-2; Poland, Sejm, Okres III, Posiedzenie CXXVIII, p. 31; Kadencja IV, Posiedzenie XXX, p. 48; XLI, p. 25.

[35] Szembek, p. 264.

[36] *Polish White Book*, p. 181. At the same time the Polish government officially denied rumors about a Soviet *démarche* concerning Warsaw's possible participation in the Anti-Comintern Pact. *Kurjer Warszawski*, Nov. 10, 1937. Nevertheless, the pro-Russian press continued to allege that Beck had given "definite assurances" to a Japanese emissary that Poland would join the tripartite agreement "at the suitable moment." *International Press Correspondence*, XVII, No. 52 (Dec. 4, 1937), 1277. Diplomatic circles in Berlin also believed that the Poles would eventually be "compelled" to join the Anti-Comintern Pact. Dodd, p. 432.

[37] *USFR*, 1937, I, 164; see also Szembek, p. 268. Göring made similar remarks

Under these circumstances, Poland was not unduly troubled by the Kremlin's hostile reaction to the visit of French Foreign Minister Yvon Delbos to Warsaw in December, 1937. The Soviet press, obviously offended by the fact that Moscow was left out of Delbos's itinerary,[38] criticized him for his "indulgent" attitude toward Beck and tried to convince the Quai d'Orsay that the ties connecting Poland and Germany were much stronger than the bonds of affection uniting the Poles to France, in spite of Warsaw's eagerness in "swallowing up" French loans.[39] Beck himself presented to Delbos a rather optimistic picture of Polish-Russian relations which, in his words, were developing "in a normal way," but Soviet Chargé d'Affaires Vinogradov was quick to point out that the Kremlin had an entirely different opinion on that subject and viewed with concern the "progress of fascism" in Poland's domestic life.[40] Similar accusations were repeated by Moscow when the majority of the Polish newspapers threw their enthusiastic support behind Goga's short-lived government in Rumania and praised him as a "faithful and fervent friend."[41]

Beck's annual report to the Foreign Affairs Committee of the Sejm on January 10, 1938, was again answered with a barrage of hostile criticism from the USSR, although he studiously refrained from making any direct or indirect attacks against Russia and devoted only a brief passage of his speech to the problem of Polish-Soviet relations:

As regards our neighbor in the east, the Soviet Union, the past year has brought no essential changes. Our attitude and our policy con-

---

about the fighting qualities of the Red Army during his meeting with Śmigły-Rydz and Szembek on February 23, 1938, but his observation that it "would not be difficult to inflict a military defeat on the Soviets" met with a cool reception on the part of his Polish hosts. *Polish White Book,* pp. 44-45.

[38] For the reasons behind this decision see *Kurjer Warszawski,* Dec. 2 and 11, 1937.

[39] *Pravda,* Dec. 17, 1937; see also O. Dluski, "Delbos' Impending Visit to Warsaw," *International Press Correspondence,* XVII, No. 52 (Dec. 4, 1937), 1276-77, and G. Peri, "The Unpleasant Journey of M. Delbos," *ibid.,* No. 53 (Dec. 11, 1937), 1283-84. According to the German Embassy in Moscow, the Kremlin was irritated by Delbos's attempts to improve Franco-Polish relations because of Russia's own failure to achieve closer cooperation with the Western powers. *DGFP,* Series D, I, 122-23.

[40] Szembek, p. 260.

[41] *Kurjer Warszawski,* Jan. 5, 1938. For the Soviet reaction see *Izvestiia,* Jan. 5, 1938, and *Pravda,* Jan. 9, 1938.

tinue to be based on the nonaggression pact of 1932, with all its supplements, and the current problems have therefore been settled in an atmosphere of realistic negotiations.[42]

Referring to the treaties signed by Poland with Russia and Germany, Beck stressed that they were based on "well-considered reasons and political interests" and that their value remained unimpaired; he also restated his government's reluctance to join any doctrinal blocs or to follow blindly a policy whose objectives and means had been defined by other powers without Poland's participation.[43] Nevertheless the speech was described in the Soviet press as a rebuttal of Beck's own thesis about the independence of Warsaw's foreign policy and as a further proof that the Polish Foreign Minister was acting as an "obedient clerk" of his German and Italian masters.[44]

Meanwhile an approaching crisis in Polish-Soviet relations was indicated by Molotov's address to the Supreme Soviet on January 19, 1938,[45] in which he fully endorsed Zhdanov's earlier complaints that some foreign states, whose attitude toward the Soviet Union "could not possibly be regarded as friendly," maintained an excessive number of consulates in the USSR, although they in no way merited any special status or preferential treatment.[46] This statement, made only a few months after the preliminary agreement between Poland and the Soviet Union to close two Polish consulates in Russia, unnecessarily exacerbated and publicized the differences between Moscow and Warsaw. On the other hand, Molotov's charges that some foreign consuls in the USSR engaged in "illegitimate, unfriendly, anti-Soviet activities," including espionage and organization of acts of sabotage, seemed

[42] Beck, *Przemówienia*, p. 335; English translation in Harley, *The Authentic Biography of Colonel Beck*, p. 175. While Beck was reluctant to discuss Poland's complaints against Russia in order not to provoke any unnecessary disputes with Moscow, a moderate but frank appraisal of Polish-Soviet relations was given by Count Artur Tarnowski, one of the most influential Conservative leaders in the Sejm. *Czas*, Jan. 13, 1938.

[43] Beck, *Przemówienia*, p. 332; Harley, *The Authentic Biography of Colonel Beck*, p. 174.

[44] *Pravda*, Jan. 12, 1938. For Polish editorial opinion see *Kurjer Warszawski*, Jan. 11, 1938.

[45] USSR, Verkhovnyi Sovet, *Sozyv I, Sessiia I, Stenograficheskii otchët* (Moscow, 1938), p. 151; English translation in Degras, ed., III, 271.

[46] USSR, Verkhovnyi Sovet, *Sozyv I, Sessiia I, Stenograficheskii otchët*, p. 136.

to indicate that a concrete, well-documented indictment would be presented in the near future to prove the truth of the extravagant accusations which impugned the integrity of the whole diplomatic corps accredited to the Kremlin.

The evidence produced during the public trial of the so-called Bloc of Rights and Trotskyites[47] was hardly convincing, although all defendants were specifically charged with "espionage on behalf of foreign states."[48] According to A. I. Rykov, one of the alleged leaders of the "Bloc," some members of that organization had established as early as 1930-31 "connections with fascist Poland, and with the Polish intelligence service in particular."[49] The accused V. F. Sharangovich, former secretary of the Central Committee of the Belorussian Communist Party, was charged with having been an agent of Polish intelligence service since 1921; he was also denounced as one of the leaders of the "anti-Soviet organization of Belorussian National-Fascists," who allegedly planned to detach Belorussia from the Soviet Union and place it under the influence of Poland and Germany.[50] Another of the defendants, H. F. Hryn'ko (Grin'ko), former people's commissar of finance of the USSR, was described as a spy of the German and Polish intelligence services and a leader of the Ukrainian "National-Fascist organization."[51] According to the indictment, Hryn'ko and his associates

discussed the necessity of coming to an agreement with Poland about obtaining military assistance for an insurrection in the Ukraine against the Soviet government. As a result of these negotiations with Poland an agreement was reached and the Polish General Staff increased the quantity of arms and the number of diversionists and Petliura emissaries sent to the Ukraine.[52]

The purpose of the unusual attention paid to Sharangovich and Hryn'ko was obviously to discredit, in the persons of the two defendants, the Belorussian and Ukrainian nationalist movements

[47] This trial, conducted by the Military Collegium of the Supreme Court of the USSR, took place in Moscow on March 2-13, 1938.

[48] USSR, Narodnyi Komissariat Iustitsii, *Report of Court Proceedings in the Case of the Anti-Soviet "Bloc of Rights and Trotskyites,"* p. 5.

[49] *Ibid.,* p. 13. Rykov claimed that this group, acting under his personal instructions, was ready to make far-reaching territorial concessions to Poland.

[50] *Ibid.,* p. 12. [51] *Ibid.,* pp. 7, 11. [52] *Ibid.,* p. 11.

as the tools and agencies of Polish and German imperialists;[53] at the same time, the evidence submitted to the court was intended to "unmask" Poland and other foreign powers as the real patrons and protectors of the subversive organizations in the Soviet Union.[54] It was a consul of "one of the foreign states bordering on Belorussia" who allegedly directed Sharangovich to transmit information required by the Polish intelligence service and to establish "close connections" with the Polish General Staff;[55] the accused and their organizations were to provide the Poles, in case of need, with a "small but dangerous fifth column," and their work was allegedly carried on under the immediate direction of their superiors in Warsaw.[56] As Vyshinskii put it in his final address to the court, the Polish intelligence service was "the real and true master of the fate of the 'Bloc of Rights and Trotskyites.' "[57]

The trial, which resulted in the mandatory death sentence for most of the defendants, demonstrated in a dramatic way the lamentable state of Polish-Soviet relations. The court proceedings were publicized in the Soviet press, and the citizens of Russia were made to believe that Poland had now definitely joined the ranks of the "aggressor states," intent on attacking the USSR at the first opportunity.[58] This impression was considerably strengthened as a result of a dangerous flare-up on the Polish-Lithuanian border which seemed to pose a serious threat to the shaky structure of peace in Eastern and East Central Europe.

[53] According to Hryn'ko, the "Ukrainian National Fascist organization" headed by him "was, by resorting to bogus slogans of national 'independence,' leading the Ukrainian people to the yoke of German fascists and Polish gentry." *Ibid.*, pp. 719-20. Sharangovich made a similar "confession," claiming that the people of Belorussia, once they had been severed from the Soviet Union, would have to "languish under the yoke of the Polish landlords and capitalists." *Ibid.*, p. 743.

[54] Similar charges had been made by the Soviet press and the leaders of the CPSU and the CPP on several occasions. See Communist International, Executive Committee, *XI plenum IKKI, Stenograficheskii otchët* (Moscow, 1932), II, 48; *XIII plenum IKKI, Stenograficheskii otchët* (Moscow, 1934), p. 113. A Comintern publication claimed that the Second Division of the Polish General Staff had been implicated in all major trials against "saboteurs" and counterrevolutionary organizations in the Soviet Union. *International Press Correspondence*, X, No. 58 (Dec. 18, 1930), 1209.

[55] USSR, Narodnyi Komissariat Iustitsii, *Report of Court Proceedings*, pp. 201, 658.

[56] *Ibid.*, pp. 657-58.   [57] *Ibid.*, p. 662.

[58] For the reaction of the Polish press to these charges see *Czas*, March 8 and 10, 1938.

In the past the delicate relations between Warsaw and Kaunas had often provided the Kremlin with an opportunity to intensify tension between Poland and Lithuania and thus prevent the Poles from consolidating their influence in the Baltic countries.[59] The abnormal conditions existing along the Polish-Lithuanian frontier due to the Wilno dispute constituted a latent source of trouble and tended to create a situation in which even a relatively unimportant incident could explode into a major crisis. The refusal of the Lithuanian authorities to establish diplomatic relations with Warsaw and to open the frontier for trade and normal international intercourse became even more irritating to Poland when the project to hold unofficial talks in Danzig between the representatives of the two countries in February, 1938, came to nothing because of the pressure of some extremist groups on the Kaunas government.[60] Thus the killing of a Polish soldier by Lithuanian border guards on March 11, 1938, gave Poland a chance to exert pressure on her small neighbor and to "normalize" the situation in a way which would deprive Moscow of the possibility of making Lithuania a permanent playground for its anti-Polish intrigues. There were, moreover, other motives which prompted the Poles to take recourse to the methods of totalitarian diplomacy. The Lithuanian incident happened almost simultaneously with Hitler's occupation of Austria; for the first time since World War I the independence of a whole European country had been violated with impunity, and Beck apparently came to the conclusion that a passive attitude in the face of German expansion would have been inadvisable and even dangerous.[61]

The terms of the Polish ultimatum to be presented to Lithuania were ironed out during a dramatic night conference at the royal

[59] The Lithuanian problem and its effect on Poland's relations with the USSR and Germany are discussed in *DGFP*, Series C, II (Washington, 1959), 216-17. The Soviet government was generally believed to have prevented Polish-Lithuanian reconciliation on several occasions by promising Kaunas its support against Warsaw and by spreading rumors about Poland's alleged plan to partition Lithuania between herself and Germany. See *Survey of International Affairs*, 1938, III, 345-46; *International Press Correspondence*, XV, No. 47 (Sept. 21, 1935), 1193.

[60] For a detailed account see T. Katelbach, "Co poprzedziło polskie ultimatum do Litwy" [What Preceded the Polish Ultimatum to Lithuania], *Kultura*, No. 4/102 (April, 1956), pp. 111-18.

[61] See Beck, *Final Report*, p. 145, and Pobóg-Malinowski, p. 653. The possibility that Poland might occupy Kaunas in the event of a crisis developing in Central Europe had been mentioned by Beck as early as December, 1936. Szembek, p. 220.

castle in Warsaw on March 16. While the world press reported that the note demanded the abrogation of an article in the Lithuanian constitution referring to Wilno as the capital of Lithuania and the conclusion of a special convention guaranteeing the rights of the Polish minority in Lithuania,[62] the actual text of the ultimatum required only the establishment of "normal and direct" diplomatic relations between the two countries, to take place by the end of the month.[63] Before the Polish demands were made public, however, a wild flurry of speculation swept through the capitals of Europe. The diplomatic corps in Moscow was "excited" over the situation, and Lithuanian Min-

[62] *The New York Times,* March 18, 1938.

[63] See *Documents on International Affairs,* 1938, I, 302-3. Available documentary evidence fails to substantiate the official account of Soviet historiography about "two versions" of the Polish ultimatum and about a "revision" of its original text under Moscow's pressure. The origin of this fictitious story can be traced back to an article by André Leroux, a French foreign policy analyst, published in *La Populaire* on March 23, 1938, according to which the Kremlin informed the Polish ambassador in Moscow that the Soviet Union advised Warsaw against using force in the conflict with Kaunas and reserved its freedom of action in the event of an armed aggression against Lithuania; this, as the French newspaper claimed, contributed to the relatively moderate tone of the Polish note. On March 26, this news item was reprinted in *Pravda,* thus receiving Moscow's implicit approval; a few weeks later, it was quoted again in an article by a noted Soviet commentator, who also asserted that Russia's "cooperation" in the settlement of the dispute prompted the Polish government to change its ultimatum and to extend its original time limit. L. Ivanov, "Pol'sko-litovskii konflikt" [The Polish-Lithuanian Conflict], *Mirovoe khoziaistvo i mirovaia politika* (May, 1938), p. 119. According to other Soviet sources (all of them published after World War II), Moscow threatened the Polish ambassador that it would "denounce without notice" the nonaggression pact of 1932; as a result of this intervention, the Poles "limited their demands to Lithuania to one point—the establishment of diplomatic relations—and gave up their plans of armed invasion." Potemkin, III, 625; the same story appears in *Bol'shaia Sovetskaia Entsiklopediia* [The Great Soviet Encyclopedia] (2d ed.), XXV (Moscow, 1954), 259, and XXXIV (Moscow, 1955), 47, and in *Istoriia Pol'shi,* III, 427-28.

These claims have no factual foundation. Neither Beck nor Szembek make any direct or indirect mention of Moscow's "warning" to Poland; in fact, a Communist historian accuses the late Foreign Minister of having neglected to mention in his memoirs an "essential fact," namely the "energetic intervention" of the Soviet government, which allegedly forced Warsaw to "restrain its aggressive tendencies." G. Jaszuński in Beck, *Pamiętniki,* p. 115. The Soviet press remained silent about the whole incident until the story received some publicity abroad, and even then gave it a cursory treatment; a contemporary Comintern publication, while referring to "some feeble representations" over the Lithuanian crisis made to Warsaw by London and Paris, does not mention any Soviet action in this matter. *International Press Correspondence,* XVIII, No. 16 (March 26, 1938), 358-59. Ambassador Grzybowski, the alleged recipient of Litvinov's *note verbale,* in his letter to the author dated March 18, 1959, categorically denies the truth of the entire story.

ister Baltrušaitis admitted that "confidence in the Soviet government's protection was his only hope."[64] The main source of this
general anxiety was the fear

that Poland had some secret agreement with Germany whereunder
Germany would support a Polish purpose to absorb Lithuania and
find an outlet to the sea, in consideration for which Poland would
relinquish the Polish corridor to Germany. . . . If such were the
actual facts of the situation, there was a general conviction [in Moscow]
that the Soviet Union would be compelled to come to the aid of
Lithuania and that war would result.[65]

Wherever these rumors might have originated, their relationship to reality was rather remote, since Hitler himself was prepared to occupy Memel and a certain portion of Lithuania
proper if the Poles decided to march on Kaunas.[66] Moreover,
while a "special relationship" existed between the USSR and
Lithuania,[67] and while Baltrušaitis reportedly enjoyed the privi-
lege of being the only member of the diplomatic corps to have
direct contacts with the Kremlin,[68] the Soviet leaders were obviously reluctant to get involved too deeply in a controversy which
could have widespread international repercussions.

On the eve of the dispatch of the Polish ultimatum, Grzybowski approached the Narkomindel with the request to arrange a
meeting between Litvinov and himself during which both parties
could discuss various aspects of the Lithuanian problem; since
the Foreign Commissar was spending the day in the country, the
Ambassador went to see him in his *dacha* near the capital. In
the course of the conversation, Litvinov inquired whether Poland
intended to use force against Lithuania, to which Grzybowski
replied that he was unable to give a definite answer to that question; he could state categorically, however, and with the assumption of full responsibility for his words, that the Polish government had no intention of annexing Lithuanian territory. Litvinov
seemed to be satisfied with the formula used by the Ambassador
and repeated the phrase "so there is going to be no annexation";

[64] Davies, p. 289.   [65] *Ibid.*, pp. 293-94.
[66] See Roos, *Polen und Europa*, pp. 313-14.
[67] *DGFP*, Series D, II (Washington, 1949), 180.   [68] Coulondre, p. 158.

Grzybowski himself was pleasantly surprised by the conciliatory attitude displayed by the Foreign Commissar and emphasized this fact in his report to Warsaw.[69]

In a press statement issued after his return to Moscow on March 17, Litvinov made a passing reference to the "alarming situation" on the Polish-Lithuanian border; he also told the reporters that his government had informed the Poles, "in a friendly way," of its anxiety over the situation which was "dangerous for the peace of all Eastern Europe."[70] While the Foreign Commissar expressed his hope that a peaceful solution of the existing differences would be found, he did not indicate what action, if any, the Kremlin intended to take if Poland resorted to radical measures. After all, Russia had no mutual assistance pact with Lithuania, and the lack of a common frontier prevented her from giving that country any help short of direct military action. The Poles were, of course, aware of this state of affairs, and during the deliberations of the Polish leaders Beck stated flatly that, in his opinion, there was no danger of Soviet armed intervention.[71] The indignation felt in Moscow could be expressed only through a few sharply worded editorials in the Soviet press, describing the Polish ultimatum as "inspired by fascist powers" and aimed at creating an "atmosphere of conflict" in Eastern Europe:

Beck's methods in foreign policy have for a long time been a slavish imitation of the piratic ways of the big predators from the camp of the aggressors. But if up to now Beck's maneuvers had been patterned mostly after the German model, this time, in the case of Lithuania, Poland chose as her model the crude tricks of Japanese militarists. The Polish side staged an incident on the Polish-Lithuanian frontier which was immediately used by Poland as an excuse for an openly provocative pressure on Lithuania. . . . The conjectures that the Polish provocation with regard to Lithuania is a part of a single

[69] The account of this conversation is based on the information supplied by Ambassador Grzybowski in his letter to the author (see above).

[70] *Pravda*, March 18, 1938; Degras, III, 277; *The New York Times*, March 18, 1938. Litvinov was also reported to have made the following remark to a Polish correspondent: "Your government says it did not address an ultimatum to Lithuania, but it smells like one to me. If you say the situation is not serious I hope you are right; but it looks serious to me." *Bulletin of International News*, XV, No. 7 (April 7, 1938), 320.

[71] Szembek, p. 311.

plan contrived by the aggressors are completely justified. . . . To Poland has been assigned the task to start war in Eastern Europe by provoking a Polish-Lithuanian conflict. It is difficult to determine at this moment whether Poland is to receive territorial compensation for her services to the aggressors, or whether . . . Poland has been entrusted with instigating a conflict whose consequences the aggressors themselves have not yet foreseen.[72]

In order to avoid further complications in the crisis at an inopportune moment, the Soviet government exerted strong pressure on Lithuania and informed Kaunas that it would put its friends "into an impossible situation" if war should result from its refusal to establish diplomatic relations with Poland;[73] any further exacerbation of the conflict was fraught with dangerous consequences and had to be prevented at any price.[74] Throughout the critical period Litvinov remained in constant touch with Baltrušaitis and followed all new developments with a pronounced interest, but this was about as far as the Kremlin was prepared to go. "As to the attitude of the Soviet government," German Chargé d'Affaires von Tippelskirch commented, "it seems to consist in not committing itself and retaining its freedom of action."[75] Moscow was obviously unwilling to back its Platonic expressions of sympathy with any concrete deeds, and the Lithuanian military attaché could only regret that his country had not accepted in the past "the repeated offers of the Soviet Union to cooperate in foreign policy and military matters."[76] Now it was too late, and world opinion was prone to accept the view that the Polish-Lithuanian incident "tested Russia's willingness to back her supposed friends and found it wanting."[77]

While diplomatic circles in Western Europe expressed their relief at the acceptance of the Polish ultimatum by Kaunas, the Kremlin voiced its apprehensions lest Beck's swift and complete triumph over Lithuania tempt and embolden him to continue to employ "the most primitive, malicious, Hitlerite methods" in the

[72] *Pravda,* March 17, 1938; see also *International Press Correspondence,* XVIII, No. 14 (March 19, 1938), 324. Similar charges were made by the Central Committee of the CPP. *KPP w obronie niepodległości Polski,* p. 419.

[73] Coulondre, p. 139.   [74] *DGFP,* Series D, V (Washington, 1953), 442.

[75] *Ibid.,* p. 443; see also Roos, pp. 315-16.   [76] *DGFP,* Series D, V, 444.

[77] *The New York Times,* March 20, 1938.

conduct of Polish foreign policy.[78] The Soviet press devoted much attention to the theory that Warsaw's recent action represented only a step toward the transformation of Europe according to a scheme elaborated by Hitler and supported by Mussolini.[79] Since it was obvious that Czechoslovakia would be the next victim of aggression, Litvinov let it be known that, in the event of a German attack on that country, the treaty of mutual assistance between Moscow and Prague would oblige the Soviet Union to intervene, and that "means would be found" to help the Czechs in spite of the fact that they had no common frontier with Russia.[80] It was generally felt in Moscow that the USSR was, in this cryptic way, warning Poland and Rumania that, if necessary, the Red Army would not hesitate to violate their territory to reach Czechoslovakia.[81] Thus the problem of passage of Soviet troops through Poland, which was to trouble European diplomacy for many months to come, again made its appearance on the international stage.

British observers agreed that the only way in which the Russians could advance in full strength to the aid of Czechoslovakia would be through Polish territory, since neither Rumania nor the Baltic countries could provide the Red Army with sufficient space to utilize its numerical and mechanical superiority;[82] at the same time, however, it was generally realized that the Poles would not even consider allowing Soviet troops to operate through their country.[83] The advice of some hotheads in the French diplomatic service to "speak very strongly" to Warsaw, to bring about Beck's retirement, and to force Poland to yield found little support in either Paris or London, since most European capitals remained decidedly skeptical about the possibility of Russian intervention.[84]

[78] *Izvestiia,* March 20, 1938.

[79] See *International Press Correspondence,* XVIII, No. 16 (March 26, 1938), 369.

[80] *DBFP,* 3d Series, I (London, 1949), 65. According to some reports, Litvinov agreed that Russia's intervention in the defense of Czechoslovakia would involve the creation of a "corridor." *Ibid.*

[81] *USFR,* 1938, I (Washington, 1955), 465.   [82] *DBFP,* 3d Series, I, 173.

[83] *Ibid.* Colonel Firebrace, British military attaché in Moscow, asserted that, in the event of a Russian action through Polish territory, Poland "must be reckoned with as an enemy."

[84] *Ibid.* In April, the British Embassy in Moscow reported that Soviet troops were unable to carry the war into the enemy's territory and that any involvement of the USSR in war merely to fulfill the terms of the mutual assistance treaties appeared to be "contrary to reason." *Ibid.,* p. 161; see also *USFR,* 1938, I, 58.

Some Polish diplomats also shared the opinion that, in the event of an armed conflict, Russia "would not move a man" out of fear that a general mobilization might prove fatal to the Soviet system.[85]

While the Polish government had certain doubts as to whether Moscow would be willing or able to come to Czechoslovakia's assistance, it refused to participate even in a purely theoretical discussion of any scheme involving the passage of foreign troops through Poland.[86] If the Kremlin had any illusions on this point, they were dispelled by Warsaw's unequivocal and categorical statement to the French government that, if the Red Army should attempt to cross Polish territory in order to attack Germany or to aid Czechoslovakia, "Poland would at once declare war on the Soviet Union."[87] The Nazi leaders relied, in planning their bloodless conquests, on the information that it was "an intolerable thought for Polish policy, as well as for Polish public opinion, that Soviet troops should set foot on Polish soil."[88] The Czechs themselves were also fully aware of Warsaw's attitude but they apparently hoped that the Russians would use force in order to compel Poland to yield to their demands.[89]

Having made his position clear, Beck proceeded to eliminate another, indirect threat to Poland's security that could result from the passage of the Red Army through allied Rumania.[90] The very fact of the existence of a military convention between Warsaw and Bucharest strengthened Poland's hand in any conflict with Russia: it facilitated the cooperation of the Polish and Ru-

[85] *DGFP*, Series D, II, 203. General Stachiewicz, the chief of the Polish General Staff, also thought that, with the exception of a limited action by Soviet air force, the USSR "could be discounted as a factor beyond [its] own boundaries for some years to come." *DBFP*, 3d Series, I, 483-84.

[86] *USFR*, 1938, I, 4.

[87] *Ibid.*, p. 502. Ambassador Łukasiewicz, when told by the French foreign minister that Russia had asked for the right of passage through Poland, replied: "We will resist this by force, and this will mean war between Russia and ourselves." Bonnet, *Défense de la paix*, I, 134. The French Embassy in Warsaw sent a similar warning to Paris. Noël, p. 197.

[88] *DGFP*, Series D, II, 452.   [89] *USFR*, 1938, I, 523; *DBFP*, 3d Series, I, 172.

[90] It appears that the possibility of the passage of Soviet troops through Rumania to the aid of Czechoslovakia had been discussed by Prague and Bucharest as early as 1936. See Coulondre, p. 136; Čelovsky, p. 204. The Czechs had agreed at that time to help the Rumanians financially in repairing the railroad network in Bessarabia, Bukovina, and Transylvania, but the results of this arrangement turned out to be disappointing. Bonnet, *Défense de la paix*, p. 202; *DGFP*, Series D, II, 701, 847-48.

manian armed forces in spite of the lack of a joint command, placed any Soviet troops that might penetrate into Eastern Galicia under the threat of encirclement, and increased the chances of a successful counterattack.[91] The presence of the Rumanian Army checked in advance any overbold moves of enemy forces in the direction of the Carpatho-Ukraine or Slovakia, and also neutralized the threat of the "Czechoslovak wedge" in the rear of Polish troops.[92] These were the reasons why the Polish General Staff and the Warsaw government used all means at their disposal to prevent the southeastern approaches to their country from falling, even temporarily, under the control of the Russians. However, though Bucharest was understandably reluctant to allow the Red Army to enter Rumania and showed particular anxiety over the future of Bessarabia, its policy toward France was much less independent than that of Poland, and strong pressure exercised by Paris could be expected to weaken its resistance.

While the Quai d'Orsay tried to persuade the Poles and the Rumanians to open their frontiers to Russian troops, Moscow made its first contribution to the cause of collective security by sending a number of bombers to Czechoslovakia over Rumanian territory.[93] The prospect of the Red Army moving through Rumania and Czechoslovakia and blocking all routes connecting Poland with the Danubian region and the Balkans, though still rather remote, was disquieting enough to prompt Beck to energetic action, and the Polish ambassador to Bucharest was instructed to demand an explanation from the Rumanian authori-

[91] This convention, originally concluded on March 3, 1921 (League of Nations, *Treaty Series*, VII, 77-83) and renewed on March 26, 1926 (*ibid.*, LX, 161-67) and January 15, 1931 (*ibid.*, CXV, 171-76) in the form of a treaty of mutual guarantee within the framework of the Covenant of the League of Nations, was to retain its validity until March, 1941. According to its provisions, Poland and Rumania were to give each other assistance against all "external aggressive attempts endangering their integrity or political independence." The agreement was accompanied by a secret military convention which specified what precautionary measures were to be taken if Soviet military build-up indicated an imminent outbreak of war. If one of the allies was attacked by Russia, his partner was obliged immediately to move his armed forces against the invader. See Poland, Polskie Siły Zbrojne, Komisja Historyczna, *Polskie Siły Zbrojne w drugiej wojnie światowej*, I, Part I, 106-7, and *DGFP*, Series C, III (Washington, 1959), 621.

[92] *Polskie Siły Zbrojne*, p. 107.

[93] Coulondre, p. 136. At the beginning of June, Polish air space was also violated by Soviet planes on their way to Czechoslovakia. *DBFP*, 3d Series, I, 482.

ties, who seemed to show no undue alarm over the infringement of their country's sovereign rights. Foreign Minister Comnen answered this *démarche* with assurances about Rumania's determination to prevent the Russians from crossing her territory, but persistent rumors about a continued concentration of Soviet airplanes in Czechoslovakia did little to appease Warsaw's apprehensions.[94]

The impassioned pleas of the Poles encouraged King Carol to take a more resolute stand and to oppose France's attempts to break down his resistance with promises of territorial guarantees.[95] General Ionescu, the chief of the Rumanian General Staff, was dispatched to Warsaw toward the end of May, only a few days after the visit of Premier Cristea, and his discussions with Polish military and political leaders resulted in an agreement on joint measures designed to meet the possibility of a Soviet attack.[96] Having thus secured their southeastern flank, the Poles proceeded to strengthen their position in the Baltic region. Early in June, General Stachiewicz made a trip to Latvia, Estonia, and Finland, and a few weeks later Beck also paid a visit to Riga, Tallin, Copenhagen, and Oslo. Surprisingly enough, in spite of the Nazi threat hanging over Central Europe, the Poles discovered in the Baltic and Scandinavian capitals a preoccupation with "the always dangerous role played by Russia."[97] On the other hand, Moscow represented Beck's activities as an attempt on Poland's part to create a neutral bloc from the Black Sea to the Arctic Ocean and to enlist its services for the aggressive plans of Berlin and Warsaw. It was also suggested that the annexation of Lithuania and parts of Latvia would give Poland a commanding position in the Baltic area and thus provide her with a base from which an attack on Soviet territory might be launched.[98]

Meanwhile Poland's attitude toward Czechoslovakia began to

[94] Early in June the German minister in Prague mentioned in a dispatch to Berlin that some 400 Soviet aircraft had been flown into Czechoslovakia (*DGFP*, Series D, II, 490), but, according to the reports of the German chargé d'affaires in Warsaw, the actual figure was much lower. *Ibid.*, p. 499.

[95] *Ibid.*, p. 434.

[96] The whole problem of Poland's and Rumania's attitude toward the Russian threat was discussed again a few weeks later during Szembek's visit to Bucharest. See Szembek, pp. 325-26.

[97] Beck, *Final Report*, p. 151; see also *ibid.*, p. 152.   [98] *Pravda*, July 2 and 19, 1938.

assume an increasingly unfriendly character, especially after Prague failed to answer satisfactorily Warsaw's repeated protests against the anti-Polish activities of the Comintern, which allegedly enjoyed the protection and support of the Czech authorities.[99] Polish official circles had, indeed, "little sympathy . . . with the Czechoslovaks as a people, or with the Czechoslovak government,"[100] and the pressure put on Prague to give the Polish minority in the Teschen area rights equivalent to those to be granted to the Sudeten Germans clearly indicated a growing determination on the part of Beck to insist on "compensation" for any gains scored by Hitler.[101] The impression that what Ribbentrop used to describe as "la communauté d'intérêts" between Poland and Germany[102] was now developing into "la communauté de travail"[103] was evidently spreading in Western Europe, for the Polish Foreign Minister, while acting independently of Berlin, was nevertheless pursuing a course parallel to that of the Wilhelmstrasse. Thus, throughout the tragic summer of 1938, Beck's policy was never able to cast off the ominous shadow of Hitler, although most of the Polish opposition parties, from the National Democrats to the Socialists, voiced their strong support for the Czechs in their courageous resistance to the threat of Nazi aggression:

The fate of Poland depends upon the fate of Czechoslovakia. . . . The defeat of Czechoslovakia would mean the defeat of Poland. If the British say that the frontiers of England are on the Rhine, we can apply this metaphor to our own case and say with equal justification

---

[99] See *Czas*, April 6, 1938; *Osteuropa*, XIII (1937-38), 622, 762; *Bulletin of International News*, XV, No. 16 (Aug. 13, 1938), 706. The Polish government also purported to be disturbed by the reports about Prague's military cooperation with Moscow, allegedly going far beyond the terms of the mutual assistance treaty of 1935 and including the construction of Soviet air bases in Slovakia. These rumors began to circulate soon after the signature of the Russo-Czechoslovak pact and had been repeatedly and indignantly denied by Czech official spokesmen. See K. Krofta, *Czechoslovakia and the Crisis of Collective Security* (Prague, 1936), pp. 36-37.

[100] *DBFP*, 3d Series, II (London, 1949), 287; see also *ibid.*, I, 478, and Szembek, p. 324. The underlying causes of this antagonism went, of course, much deeper than the Teschen dispute, and involved, among other factors, the basic differences in Warsaw's and Prague's attitude toward Russia. See Studnicki, *Kwestia Czechosłowacji a racja stanu Polski,* and Wandycz, *France and Her Eastern Allies.*

[101] See Beck, *Final Report,* p. 154.

[102] Szembek, p. 194.   [103] Noël, p. 209.

that the frontier of Poland is on the Moldau. . . . The situation must be clear to every honest Polish citizen: Czechoslovakia today— Poland tomorrow. . . . It is our duty to defend Czechoslovakia today if we want to prevent Hitler from invading Poland tomorrow.[104]

Poland's determination to achieve political and possibly territorial gains at the expense of Czechoslovakia[105] was not weakened by Moscow's threatening words and gestures, and the Warsaw government remained silent even when the Soviet authorities abolished the remnants of "cultural autonomy" enjoyed by the Polish population in some border districts of Belorussia and deported large numbers of "undesirable elements" from that area to Siberia and Central Asia.[106] During the next few weeks the serious crisis in Polish-Soviet relations was aggravated by new developments. On July 24 the Russians claimed that the Polish police prevented normal work of their officials in Warsaw by forcibly detaining and cross-examining them, by subjecting them to close supervision whenever they left the precincts of the Soviet Embassy, and by harassing them with other acts of petty chicanery; similar conditions were allegedly impeding the work of the USSR Consulate in Lwów.[107] Poland's failure to stop these "inadmissible practices" led to Soviet repressions against the members of the Polish Embassy in Moscow and the personnel of the Polish consulates in Russia.[108] Meanwhile the campaign of bitter invective against Poland continued uninterruptedly and reached

[104] J. Swencicki, "The Defense of Czechoslovakia Is the Defense of the Independence of Poland" (quoted from World News and Views, XVIII, No. 48 [Oct. 1, 1938], 1100-1). The attitude of the Polish opposition parties and military circles toward Beck's Czechoslovak policy and the problem of the Russo-Czech alliance are discussed in detail in S. Stanisławska's study "Stosunek opozycji polskiej do polityki Becka wobec Czechosłowacji wiosną 1938 roku," Sprawy Międzynarodowe, XII, No. 11/12 (Nov.-Dec., 1959), 30-67, and in M. Boguslavskii's article "Politicheskaia bor'ba v Pol'she v sviazi s nastupleniem fashistskikh agressorov na Chekhoslovakiiu," Voprosy Istorii (May, 1948), pp. 20-39. For a representative selection of the editorial opinion of the Polish press during the period from August to October, 1938, see Ratyńska, ed., Opinia polska wobec Monachium w świetle prasy; see also her article under the same title in Sprawy Międzynarodowe, XIII, No. 1 (Jan., 1960), 86-94.
[105] The Polish plan to occupy Teschen in the event of the "disintegration" of Czechoslovakia dated back to at least 1934. Beck, Final Report, p. 78.
[106] Czas, June 5, 1938.
[107] See Izvestiia, July 23 and Aug. 14, 1938; Vneshniaia politika SSSR, IV, 368-69; Osteuropa, XIV (1938-39), 127.
[108] This dispute was finally settled by Potemkin and Grzybowski on August 16, 1938. Izvestiia, Aug. 17, 1938.

its climax during the Second Session of the Supreme Soviet of
the USSR (August 10-21, 1938), when a number of prominent
deputies made new statements openly denouncing Warsaw's domestic and foreign policies:

The Polish fascist *szlachta* are covetous of the laurels of the fascist
vandals in Germany. They are striving with might and main to outdo
their neighbors, the German fascists. More and more frequently the
shattering of glass is to be heard at night on the streets of Warsaw,
Lwów, and Kraków in the homes of poor Jews.[109] The millions of
Ukrainian peasants in Western Ukraine have been deprived of the
right to use their mother tongue. The Ukranian schools have been
raided and closed. . . . What has the Polish republic given to
the millions of Ukrainians in Western Ukraine? It has given them
poverty, hunger, disfranchisement, and the degrading title of "yokels"
(*khlop*). And this Polish fascist *szlachta,* together with German fascism,
is dreaming even today of putting the yoke on the free citizens of the
Ukrainian Soviet Socialist Republic. They are dreaming of making a
"yokel" of this republic. But . . . however the Polish fascist gentry
may rattle their tin swords to the tune of the German fascists, the
Ukrainian citizens of the Soviet Union are unperturbed. We know
that gentlemen of Warsaw will have to go back a sight further than
Berlin to find their swords again if they attack Soviet Ukraine.[110]

While the Polish press and the Polish government ignored most
of these attacks, Warsaw could obviously not afford to disregard
the ominous massing of Soviet forces along some sectors of Russia's
frontier with Poland and Rumania. A number of Polish fighters
were concentrated not far from the Rumanian border, with specific orders to attack Soviet planes attempting to cross the frontier
in that area.[111] The Poles also announced their willingness to
send a part of their air force to Rumania in order to assist their
allies in bringing down any unauthorized planes flying over Ru-

[109] A reference to a series of anti-Semitic incidents in Poland which began to
multiply especially after the pogrom in Przytyk in May, 1936. While the Polish
government officially condemned these brutal attacks, it failed to take any decisive
action to suppress them; moreover, it tolerated and even openly encouraged the so-
called economic warfare against Polish citizens of Jewish faith.

[110] Excerpts from a speech by A. E. Korneichuk quoted from USSR, Verkhovnyi
Sovet, *Second Session, Verbatim Report,* p. 208.

[111] *USFR,* 1938, I, 507. This measure was probably taken because of reports (later
proved as spurious) that Rumania was withdrawing her objections against Soviet
aircraft flying over her territory in return for Moscow's promise not to press its
claims to Bessarabia for twenty-five years. See *DGFP,* Series D, II, 710, 724, 847.

manian territory.[112] In Warsaw's opinion, these precautionary measures were sufficient to eliminate the possibility of a large-scale intervention on the part of Poland's eastern neighbor, whom Beck and his associates regarded as their country's potential enemy and whose "meddling" in European affairs was, from their point of view, "intolerable" and "inadmissible."[113]

At the same time the Kremlin intensified its offensive against Poland on the diplomatic front, accusing Warsaw of "drifting more and more towards the German camp."[114] While the Soviet ambassador to the Court of St. James's, Ivan Maiskii, complained to Lord Halifax that the relations between Russia and Poland "were not cordial, or even always correct,"[115] Litvinov expressed in his talks with the French ambassador Moscow's desire to know whether Paris would honor its alliance with Warsaw in the event of a Polish-Soviet war resulting from Poland's attack on Czechoslovakia.[116] The same question was later submitted officially to the French government, which informed the Soviet Union that, should such eventuality occur, France "would have no obligation whatsoever to support Poland."[117] These inquiries seemed to indicate that the Kremlin's sudden preoccupation with the problem of French assistance was not purely academic, and the possibility that the Soviet Union was considering an armed action against Poland became the "chief nightmare" of some Western diplomats.[118] Meanwhile the Polish Army opened its fall maneuvers in Volhynia, and the Russians apparently regarded this military demonstration close to the frontiers of the USSR as a warning not to take any rash measures in the defense of Czechoslovakia.[119] The

[112] *USFR*, 1938, I, 508.

[113] See Ambassador Raczyński's report of September 23, 1938, published in *Sprawy Międzynarodowe*, XI, No. 1 (Jan., 1958), 84, and Beck's instructions to Lipski of September 19, 1938, *ibid.*, No. 2 (Feb., 1958), p. 114.

[114] *DBFP*, 3d Series, II, 107.   [115] *Ibid.*   [116] Coulondre, p. 152.

[117] *USFR*, 1938, I, 556.

[118] *Ibid.*, p. 564. Ambassador Bullitt stressed in his alarming reports from Paris that Russia "had prepared to the last detail a plan to march to the aid of Czechoslovakia across Poland," and that the Quai d'Orsay made no secret of its apprehensions that, in the event of a German attack against Czechoslovakia, "the first additional war to start would be war between the Soviet Union and Poland." *Ibid.*, pp. 555-56.

[119] See Beck's opinion expressed in his instructions to Lipski of September 19, 1938 (*Sprawy Międzynarodowe*, XI, No. 2, 114); see also Boguslavskii, "Politicheskaia bor'ba," *Voprosy Istorii*, p. 27, and *Istoriia Pol'shi*, p. 432. A detailed account of the maneuvers is given in *Czas*, Sept. 19, 1938.

French leaders purported to believe that their whole system of alliances was jeopardized: the possibility that Rumania would support Poland had to be taken into consideration, and the final result of these developments could be, in Foreign Minister Bonnet's words, "that France's three allies would be fighting each other and France and England would be left alone to face the attack of Germany and Italy."[120]

These strongly exaggerated fears were groundless,[121] and the long-expected Soviet action, when it finally materialized, had the relatively innocuous form of a stiffly worded note handed by Deputy Commissar for Foreign Affairs Potemkin to Polish Chargé d'Affaires Jankowski on September 23.[122] It stated that the Soviet government was in possession of information to the effect that Polish troops had occupied positions on the border of Czechoslovakia and were ready to invade the territory of that country. These "widespread and alarming" reports had not been denied by the Polish government, in spite of the publicity given to them, and the Soviet Union hoped that an official denial would be issued by Warsaw without further delay. If the Poles failed to heed this suggestion and if Polish troops violated the frontiers of Czechoslovakia, the Kremlin would be "compelled" to denounce the nonaggression pact of 1932 without any formal notification, in accordance with Article Two of that treaty.[123]

The Soviet *démarche*, instead of making Beck hesitate, in real-

[120] *USFR*, 1938, I, 556.

[121] If an armed conflict broke out, Beck was prepared to change Polish foreign policy "within twenty-four hours," since in the event of a general European war Poland "could not be on the side of Germany even indirectly." *Final Report*, p. 157. The possibility that the USSR would start military operations against Poland and Rumania in order to enforce the passage of Soviet troops through their territory was discounted by Litvinov himself in his conversations with the French on September 2 and 11, 1938. Bonnet, *Défense de la paix*, pp. 199-200.

[122] The Poles suspected that there was a certain connection between the date of the Soviet *démarche* and a four-day delay in the delivery of Beneš's personal letter to President Mościcki. According to Beck, Warsaw's lack of faith in Prague's sincerity had determined to a large extent the attitude of the Polish government toward the message of the Czech President. *Final Report*, p. 158. Beneš himself was later to claim, with obvious exaggeration, that Poland's negative reply had provided him with "the last and decisive reason" for rejecting Moscow's plan to "provoke war with Germany in 1938." Quoted from Namier, *Europe in Decay*, p. 284.

[123] The text of the Soviet note is given in *Izvestiia*, Sept. 26, 1938; see also Degras, III, 305.

ity strengthened his position by arousing strong anti-Soviet sentiments in Poland.[124] The Polish answer to Moscow was delivered
with unprecedented speed on September 23 at 7 P.M. and the exchange of notes was published in the press on the following morning. Russia was informed that the measures taken in connection
with the defense of the Polish republic were the "exclusive concern" of the Warsaw government, which was "not obliged to give
explanations to anyone," and that the Polish leaders were "fully
acquainted" with the texts of international agreements concluded
by their country.[125] An oral declaration made by Chargé d'Affaires
Jankowski expressed Poland's surprise at the Soviet action since
no military measures of any kind had been taken on the Polish-
Russian frontier.

The diplomatic circles in Moscow regarded the Soviet note as
an attempt to warn and intimidate Poland; they pointed out,
however, that actually the formula used in the *démarche* put the
Russians under no obligation to act.[126] In any case, the whole incident provided the Kremlin with an opportunity to play the role
of Czechoslovakia's protector and enabled the Soviet press to
launch another series of propaganda attacks against Poland. According to *Izvestiia,* the "blatant and arrogant tone" of the Polish
note was very characteristic:

In the press of Poland's actual ally, fascist Germany, which had already
been informed by Warsaw of the "bold" Polish reply to the Soviet
government, the Polish answer was received with roars of enthusiasm
and cries of encouragement. . . . In its answer, the Polish government hastens to state that the measures which provoked the warning
of the Soviet government were only taken in defense of the Polish republic. Such a statement might perhaps be reassuring if the Polish
government used the idea of defense in the meaning universally
adopted in human relations. It is quite another matter if Poland regards defense in the same way as Japan, who only defends herself by
invading foreign territory with her armies. Future events will show
whether Poland prefers the universally adopted or the specifically
Japanese interpretation of defense.[127]

[124] *DBFP,* 3d Series, III (London, 1950), 33. For the reaction of the Polish press
see *Gazeta Polska,* Sept. 25, 1938, as quoted in *Czas,* Sept. 26, 1938.
[125] *Izvestiia,* Sept. 26, 1938; *DGFP,* Series D, II, 948-50.
[126] *DGFP,* Series D, II, 949.   [127] *Izvestiia,* Sept. 26, 1938.

This comment was, in spite of its caustic language, conspicuous by the absence of any threats, and seemed to vindicate Beck's judgment that the Soviet note was but a "meaningless piece of propaganda."[128] For the time being, Moscow limited itself to organizing what the Polish Foreign Minister called "a somewhat theatrical military demonstration" in the region of Minsk which involved units of two army corps and a considerable number of motorized and armored troops.[129] This show of force failed to impress the Poles, who knew that no mobilization had been ordered or carried out in Russia,[130] but it resulted in the increase of tension along Poland's eastern border. The period between September 23 and October 10 was especially critical: there were unconfirmed reports of incidents during which Polish troops and peasants working in the fields were allegedly fired at by the NKVD patrols, the illegal traffic through the frontier increased, and a few raids by armed gangs highlighted the general atmosphere of uneasiness and anxiety.[131] The bilateral convention for preventing frontier incidents was invoked by the Poles, but the Soviet authorities either denied the charges or refused to meet with the Polish representatives. Warsaw was still of the opinion that the Russians were not likely to take any risky steps, but Beck thought it prudent to ask the German ambassador whether the Reich would adopt "the friendly attitude of a good neighbor" in the

---

[128] *DGFP*, Series D, II, 982. There is no evidence to support the claim of Soviet historiography that Moscow's warnings prompted the Polish leaders to modify their policy toward Czechoslovakia. *Istoriia Pol'shi*, p. 427; Boguslavskii, "Politicheskaia bor'ba," *Voprosy Istorii*, p. 27.

[129] Beck, *Final Report*, p. 168.

[130] *Ibid.* According to Beck, Polish countermeasures were limited to "air patrols along the frontier," since Warsaw "did not consider it necessary to make any special arrangements to meet this demonstration." *Ibid.;* see also *DBFP*, 3d Series, V (London, 1952), 8, and the official record of Beck's conversation with Count Csáky on October 6, 1938, published in *Sprawy Międzynarodowe*, XI, No. 7/8 (July-Aug., 1958), 72-73. This statement is, however, at variance with Beck's account of the September crisis given during his interview with Hitler on January 5, 1939. *DGFP*, Series D, V, 157.

[131] See Cardwell, p. 32; *Osteuropa*, XIV (1938-39), 39. Polish newspapers refrained at that time from publishing any reports on these incidents, but Ambassador Lipski (who, of course, might have purposely exaggerated the situation) later confided to Ribbentrop that "skirmishes had frequently occurred" and "airplanes had been shot down." *DGFP*, Series D, V, 137.

event of any Polish-Soviet complications.[132] It was, indeed, probable that the USSR might try to create a "sort of Polish-Soviet 'Sudeten problem,' "[133] as was indicated by the following comment in *Pravda:*

The Polish reactionary press is raising a howl about the rights of the Sudeten Germans and the other national minorities in Czechoslovakia. However, if one wanted to count the number of Poles living in the Ukrainian and Belorussian provinces of the Polish state, the result of this count could scarcely be cited as a reason for these provinces belonging to Poland. And, if we should interest ourselves further in the ticklish question as to what right to self-determination and generally what rights the Ukrainian and Belorussian population of Poland enjoys, the result would be no less eloquent.[134]

The tension began to decrease after Prague's acceptance of the Polish ultimatum demanding the return of the Teschen area, but Poland's participation in the dismemberment of Czechoslovakia was denounced in the Soviet press as a dastardly act, perpetrated in collusion with the Nazi aggressors,[135] and Molotov publicly accused Warsaw of "drawing dividends as an ally of German fas-

[132] *DGFP*, Series D, V, 79. Göring hastened to reassure Warsaw that "in the event of involvement with Russia, Poland could count on a more effective help on the part of Germany." Lipski's report of October 1, 1938, published in *Sprawy Międzynarodowe*, XI, No. 5 (May, 1958), 91. Beck was also said to have received assurances from the Japanese ambassador that "if Prague rejected the ultimatum, Poland need have no fear of the USSR." *Bulletin of International News*, XV, No. 20 (Oct. 8, 1938), 924.

[133] *The Times* (London), Sept. 26, 1938.

[134] *Pravda*, Sept. 21, 1938. Potemkin also observed at that time that Poland would be the first power to regret its participation in the destruction of Czechoslovakia, since the Ukrainians living under Warsaw's rule "were already beginning to move." *DGFP*, Series D, II, 998.

[135] *Izvestiia*, Oct. 3, 1938. As S. Mackiewicz observes, it is incorrect and unfair to charge Beck with acting in connivance with Hitler, since the occupation of Teschen was only "a form of protest against the settling of the whole matter without consulting Poland." *Colonel Beck and His Policy*, p. 119; see also Beck, *Final Report*, pp. 160-61. Similarly, the claims of Polish Communist historians about the existence of an unwritten understanding or "gentlemen's agreement" between Poland and Germany (see J. Chudek, "Polska wobec wrześniowego kryzysu czechosłowackiego 1938 r.," *Sprawy Międzynarodowe*, XI, No. 4 [April, 1958], 75-76, 79, and K. Lapter, "Polityka Józefa Becka," *ibid.*, No. 5 [May, 1958], 56) seem rather far-fetched. Nevertheless, Beck's undeniable eagerness to profit from the ruin of Czechoslovakia not only tarnished Poland's reputation abroad but also proved to be a fatal political blunder.

cism."[136] At the same time, however, Moscow did nothing to implement its earlier threats to Poland,[137] and its belated gestures of defiance could not change the fact that the Soviet Union had suffered a diplomatic defeat of the first magnitude which considerably impaired its prestige throughout East Central Europe. It seemed that Russia's influence would become, at least for the time being, a negligible quantity as far as that part of the continent was concerned, and well-informed sources in the Polish capital reckoned with the possibility that Warsaw's main effort would be directed in the future toward achieving the position it had long sought to attain—the role of the decisive factor in Eastern Europe.[138] The Poles appeared already to be conscious of this new opportunity, and some of Beck's associates showed a tendency to regard the Soviet Union as "increasingly less dangerous" and to belittle its military potential.[139] Other, more cautious observers looked upon Russia as an "uncertain factor of fundamental importance" and thought that a change in the attitude of mistrust and suspicion toward the USSR could thoroughly transform the whole international situation.[140] In this connection, the significance of Polish-Soviet relations was, indeed, "difficult to overestimate."[141]

[136] *Pravda*, Nov. 9, 1938; Degras, III, 309.

[137] In this connection see Ambassador Bullitt's report on a conversation between Bonnet and Litvinov in *USFR*, 1938, I, 84. While some Western diplomats and statesmen blamed the Soviet Union for Czechoslovakia's debacle, it should be remembered that, according to the terms of the treaties of mutual assistance of 1935, the USSR was obliged to aid the Czechs only if France decided to honor her commitments with regard to Prague.

[138] *DGFP*, Series D, V, 87.

[139] *USFR*, 1938, I, 97; see also Germany, Auswärtiges Amt, *The German White Paper*, p. 41. Beck himself thought that the Soviet Union had been "effectively driven out of Europe, probably for a long time." Szembek, p. 370.

[140] *USFR*, 1938, I, 92. [141] *Ibid*.

VI. The Aftermath of Munich

Throughout the Czechoslovak crisis Polish-Soviet relations had been, according to Ambassador Grzybowski's euphemistic expression, "in a state of some exacerbation,"[1] but the repercussions of the Munich conference marked the beginning of their temporary improvement.

The first tentative step toward this normalization was made during a private conversation between Grzybowski and Potemkin early in October.[2] The Polish Ambassador suggested that the political situation produced by recent events indicated the desirability of a change for the better in Poland's relations with the USSR, which would certainly be in the interest of both parties. While Potemkin refrained from making any comments, he arranged a meeting between Grzybowski and Litvinov, during which the representatives of Poland and Russia seemed to agree that an understanding between their countries would adequately ensure peace in Eastern Europe.[3] Both nations had been excluded from the Munich settlement and obviously resented this rebuff, combined with the danger of a revival of the Four-Power Pact, but the most potent factor which brought them together was un-

---

[1] *Polish White Book,* p. 204.

[2] It should be remembered that only a few days earlier (on October 4) Potemkin made his famous remark to the French ambassador: "My poor friend, what have you done? As for us, I do not see any other outcome than a fourth partition of Poland." Coulondre, p. 165. This observation was by no means original; already on October 1 *Pravda* asserted that the Polish leaders were "digging, with their own hands, the grave of Poland's independence," and that the time was not far off "when fascist Germany, intoxicated by her impunity, would place the question of Poland's partition on the day's agenda."

[3] *Polish White Book,* p. 204.

doubtedly their common fear of the resurgent and triumphant might of the Third Reich. In addition to this, there were probably other motives that induced the Kremlin to seek an agreement with Warsaw. As Count Schulenburg, German ambassador to Moscow, saw it,

By flirting with Poland, the Soviet Union hopes to drive a wedge into German-Polish relations. . . . By normalizing her relations with Poland the Soviet Union hopes to be able to break Poland loose from the front of the aggressor states, which [it] imagines to exist. . . . The Soviet Union is interested in the maintenance of the status quo in the East, i.e., in the preservation of Poland and the Baltic states in their present character as buffers and insulators against Germany, and [it] believes that Poland can be assumed to have the same interest.[4]

Another important issue which prompted Poland and Russia to forget for a moment their old differences was the Ukrainian problem.[5] It began suddenly to receive a great deal of attention in the German press and in the schemes of the Wilhelmstrasse, and the major effect of this development appeared to be a *détente* between Moscow and Warsaw, since neither the Poles nor the Russians were inclined to tolerate the existence of a center of Ukrainian irredentism from which a crusade for the "liberation" of all Ukrainian ethnic territories could be launched.[6]

[4] *DGFP*, Series D, V (Washington, 1953), 139-40.

[5] In 1938-39 the Ukrainian issue resolved itself into whether there was going to be an attempt by Germany to conquer the Soviet Ukraine and to incorporate it into some greater Ukrainian state. The Ukrainian problem was further complicated by the fact that its complete solution was likely to involve the annexation of territories inhabited by the Ukrainians within the boundaries of Poland, Rumania, and Czechoslovakia. The creation by Prague of an autonomous Carpatho-Ukraine early in October, 1938, was regarded by many observers as a milestone toward the establishment of an independent Ukrainian state. The role which the Carpatho-Ukraine played in German plans was, however, comparatively modest. As Hitler and Ribbentrop explained to the Japanese ambassador in Berlin, "Ruthenia [did] not interest Germany either from the economic or the strategic point of view" and had for her only an accessory value in connection "with the organization of a campaign of the [Ukrainian] émigrés." Szembek, pp. 399-400. A detailed and well-documented report concerning Germany's attitude toward the Carpatho-Ukraine and the Ukrainian question in general is given in Ilnytzkyj, I, 127-212; see also R. Nowak, "Die Zukunft der Karpatenukraine," *Zeitschrift für Geopolitik*, XV (Nov., 1938), 889-99.

[6] In spite of Poland's apparent community of interest with the Soviet Union in the Carpatho-Ukrainian question, the Polish press described that province as a center of Communist propaganda and as a Czech "corridor" in the direction of the USSR. See *Czas*, Sept. 23 and Nov. 6, 1938; *DGFP*, Series D, V, 91. Ambassador Lipski, in his conversations with Göring on August 24 and with Hitler on September 20, 1938, also stressed "the strategic factor vis-à-vis Russia" and assured the

The course of the Moscow talks indicated that some basic difficulties had to be removed in order to restore normal relations and to create an atmosphere of mutual understanding between the two countries. In Grzybowski's opinion, a lasting improvement of the situation required the fulfillment of some essential prerequisites, including a strict observance of the existing agreements; according to his complaints,

The Soviet government had a tendency toward their one-sided modification, as in the case of the cancellation of the train running between the Polish frontier and Kiev, the endless procrastination over our admitted claims to property, and finally the frontier regulations, which were slowly becoming a dead letter, while incidents and violations of the regulations were multiplying endlessly.[7]

In addition to these fundamental preliminary requirements, Grzybowski proposed a marked increase in trade turnover between Poland and Russia, but Litvinov rejected this idea for the time being as premature and suggested instead the signature of a joint political declaration that could eventually serve as the first step toward the realization of the Polish desiderata. A draft of the proposed statement was submitted for the consideration of the Polish government toward the end of October, but Warsaw's answer was delayed for some time owing to the destruction of the Polish military cemetery in Kiev on orders of the Soviet authorities. The situation was also complicated by Russia's suspicions regarding Beck's trip to Rumania on October 19-20, during which he tried unsuccessfully to enlist King Carol's support for the annexation of the Carpatho-Ukraine by Hungary.[8] In spite of these difficulties, however, the Moscow negotiations were resumed

---

German leaders that "by creating a common Polish-Hungarian frontier . . . we would erect a wider barrier against Russia." Germany, Auswärtiges Amt, *Documents and Materials Relating to the Eve of the Second World War*, I, 180; *Sprawy Międzynarodowe*, XI, No. 2 (Feb., 1958), 114, and No. 3 (March, 1958), 84; see also the official record of Beck's discussions with Count Csáky on October 5-6, 1938, published in *Sprawy Międzynarodowe*, XI, No. 7/8 (July-Aug., 1958), 71-73.

[7] *Polish White Book*, pp. 204-5.

[8] For details see Beck, *Final Report*, pp. 165-68; Comnen, *Preludi del grande dramma*, pp. 276, 283-94; and H. Batowski, "Rumuńska podróż Becka w październiku 1938 roku," *Kwartalnik Historyczny*, LXV (1958), No. 2, 423-39. According to Comnen, the Polish Foreign Minister broached during his talks with the King the idea of a five-power bloc, able to oppose "the two enemies of peace, the Reich and the Soviets." After Beck's departure, the Soviet chargé d'affaires in Bucharest reportedly made official inquiries about the contents of the conversations. Lukacs, p. 210.

after a brief interruption, and on November 26, 1938, the text of the Polish-Soviet declaration was released simultaneously in both capitals. It stated that the relations between Poland and Russia would continue to be based on the existing agreements and that the two governments were favorably disposed to the extension of the commercial intercourse between their countries; it was also agreed to settle some "current and longstanding matters" and to "dispose" of the various frontier incidents that had recently taken place.[9] At the same time the Polish Telegraphic Agency issued an official commentary on the declaration, stressing the determination of both partners to honor their obligations and thus to contribute to the stabilization of conditions on the Polish-Soviet frontier.[10]

While some foreign observers were prone to overestimate the importance of the joint communiqué, Ambassador Schulenburg was quick to point out that the content of the declaration was not significant by itself and acquired importance only as a result of the international developments of the past few months. The provisions of the nonaggression pact, which seemed to be contradicted by the Polish-Soviet exchange of notes preceding the Munich conference, were now again in agreement with the political interests of the two countries. While two months earlier Russia had issued a thinly veiled threat to invade Poland if the latter violated the borders of Czechoslovakia, she appeared now to take no interest whatever in Warsaw's alleged intention to intervene in the Carpatho-Ukraine; there was also a noticeable change in the attitude of the Soviet press toward Poland. In discussing the reasons which prompted the Kremlin to change its policy toward Warsaw in spite of all unsettled basic differences between Poland and Russia, the German diplomat noted that the Carpatho-Ukraine under Berlin's influence was bound to be regarded by the Soviet Union as a major threat and as a "crystallizing point" for the Ukrainian independence movement. Under these circumstances, it was not surprising that the USSR believed its interests coincided with those of Poland in frustrating Germany's attempts to revitalize the Ukrainian issue.[11]

[9] *Polish White Book,* pp. 181-82.   [10] *Ibid.,* p. 182.   [11] *DGFP,* Series D, V, 138-39.

An attempt to interpret the Moscow communiqué as an indication of Poland's and Russia's common desire to curb the Nazi drive toward the East was also made by Schulenburg's British colleague:

> While . . . Poland may have some sympathy with the idea of a buffer state between her and the Soviet Union, and might, therefore, in certain circumstances welcome an independent Ukraine and White Russia, she would almost certainly now be compelled, if she supported an independence movement in the Soviet Ukraine, to contemplate the grant of wide autonomous powers to her own Ukrainian minority. This . . . she has no intention of doing. . . . Furthermore, strategically it would seem that Poland could not tolerate a Soviet Ukraine under German influence, since Poland would then be open to German pressure on three fronts. Assuming, therefore, that Poland is not willing to cooperate with Germany in the invasion of the Soviet Ukraine . . . it would seem that Poland would be forced into active support of the Soviet Union in resisting such an invasion. In this connection the recent reaffirmation by the Polish and Soviet governments of the Polish-Soviet nonaggression pact seems definitely to show which way the wind is blowing.[12]

While the leading Ukrainian newspapers in Poland attacked the November declaration,[13] the Polish press welcomed it as a timely and "absolutely urgent" warning to Berlin that its further activities in the Carpatho-Ukraine would only strengthen the ties between Warsaw and Moscow.[14] The Polish-Soviet rapprochement was undoubtedly the strongest possible measure of protection against the Greater Ukraine propaganda, and all shades of public opinion in Poland supported it without hesitation, hoping that it would have a sobering effect on the influential group in the Nazi Party which actively favored Germany's eastward expansion.[15] This continued emphasis put on the Carpatho-Ukrainian issue tended, however, to obscure the fact that the Ukrainian

[12] *DBFP*, 3d Series, III (London, 1950), 576-77.

[13] See *Osteuropa*, XIV (1938-39), 258.

[14] *Kurjer Krakowski*, Nov. 29, 1938, as quoted in *Bulletin of International News*, XV, No. 25 (Dec. 17, 1938), 1219; see also "World Opinion," *The Nineteenth Century and After*, CXXV (Jan., 1939), 125, and *Osteuropa*, XIV (1938-39), 258-59.

[15] According to an American observer, even the radical circles which had in the past advocated anti-Soviet crusades now admitted that Poland and the USSR had a common interest in the Ukrainian issue. *The New York Times*, Jan. 1, 1939.

question, important as it was, represented only a single aspect of Polish-Soviet relations. Though both Moscow and Warsaw were undoubtedly concerned about the possible developments arising out of the autonomous status granted to the Carpatho-Ukraine and Berlin's pronounced interest in this matter, they certainly could not view the manifold problem of their mutual relations solely from that angle. Sensational headlines announcing new international upheavals allegedly connected with the Ukrainian question did not give due attention to some issues which, in the long run, were no less important than the dramatic events shaping up behind the Carpathians.

The comments emanating from Moscow showed that the Kremlin regarded the November declaration as the first serious setback to Hitler's aggressive schemes. According to an *Izvestiia* editorial, certain "circles" trying to violate peace in Eastern Europe could now see for themselves that the USSR and Poland were determined to maintain the stability of their relations in spite of all malicious attempts to disrupt their normal functioning. The newspaper also mentioned the possibility of an increased trade turnover between the two countries and hinted that other current questions could be easily solved as a part of a general settlement regulating the entire complex of Polish-Soviet relations. The communiqué signed by Russia and Poland was only one of the measures of Soviet policy aimed at the creation of a system of collective security, and the USSR, as a "powerful factor of peace," was prepared to give its support to all countries "really interested in the strengthening of their security."[16]

The Polish side, while welcoming the offers of Soviet aid, largely ignored the hints that peace would be best safeguarded by Warsaw's participation in a scheme of mutual assistance which included Russia and other interested powers. In Beck's opinion, Poland had once more succeeded in reasserting her independence from Moscow and Berlin by making a necessary readjustment in her relations with the Soviet Union and restoring a normal state of affairs along her eastern frontier. Once the old system of equilibrium between Germany and Russia was reestablished, however, Warsaw was no longer interested in continuing its advances to

[16] *Izvestiia*, Nov. 28, 1938.

the Kremlin and refused to commit itself to any anti-German moves.[17] The November declaration was, according to Ambassador Grzybowski, only a "precise summary" of Poland's basic attitude toward the USSR. It had no hidden meaning and was never regarded by Warsaw as the nucleus of a future alliance:

To our eastern neighbor we guaranteed the complete loyalty of our policy, its sincere striving for improvement in neighborly relations, and the development of economic relations. In return we required respect for existing agreements and that the Soviet authorities should adapt their conduct to these agreements. At the same time we fully realized that our partner's intentions were rather more complex, that his ambitions went considerably further, and that his aim was not only to worsen relations between Poland and Germany, but also to win us over to his own political system. But we had the right to expect that we would be able to protect ourselves against that.[18]

Thus, while repairing her fences in the east, Poland meticulously avoided taking any provocative steps with regard to the Third Reich, although storm signals from the direction of Berlin were already clearly visible over the horizon. German pressure on Poland was increasing almost daily, but the Nazi leaders were still trying to win Warsaw's support against the Soviet Union.[19] Ribbentrop, when making to Lipski on October 24, 1938, his proposal for a "general settlement" of all issues dividing Poland and Germany, suggested that both nations should conduct "a joint policy toward Russia on the basis of the Anti-Comintern Pact." At the same time he stressed that, if the Polish government ac-

[17] Thus, for example, the Poles chose to ignore the hints dropped by Major Korotkikh, Soviet military attaché in Kaunas, that Moscow might be willing to conclude an alliance with Poland and the Western powers on condition that Warsaw would acquiesce in Russia's occupation of the Baltic states and permit the Red Army to march through the regions of Wilno and Lwów. L. Mitkiewicz, "Czy był możliwy front antyniemiecki" [Was an Anti-German Front Possible?], Kultura, No. 12/146 (Dec., 1959), pp. 102-7; see also T. Pełczyński's letter to the editor in Kultura, No. 4/150 (April, 1960), pp. 155-57.

[18] Polish White Book, pp. 205-6.

[19] The question of an expedition against the Soviet Union was obviously next on Hitler's agenda. Already on August 10, Göring observed during a conversation with Lipski that the Russian project would "acquire actuality" after the settlement of the Czech problem; he also suggested that Poland "might have certain direct interests in Russia, for example, in the Ukraine." Documents and Materials Relating to the Eve of the Second World War, I, 149; see also Lipski's report on his conversation with Göring on August 24, 1938, in Sprawy Międzynarodowe, XI, No. 3 (March, 1958), 85.

cepted the German proposals regarding Danzig and the motor road through the Corridor, the question of the Carpatho-Ukraine would be solved "in accordance with Poland's attitude to the matter."[20]

The Germans were not unduly concerned about the Moscow declaration, and Ambassador Moltke was inclined to believe that the unexpected improvement in Polish-Soviet relations came as a result of Warsaw's economic difficulties in the Teschen district,[21] although he admitted that its main reason was probably Poland's fear that Germany would disregard her vital interests.[22] Meanwhile Lipski did his best to persuade the Wilhelmstrasse that the communiqué contained "nothing new politically" and practically amounted only to a confirmation of the status quo in Polish-Soviet relations.[23] Ribbentrop, in a somewhat patronizing manner, accepted this explanation, but expressed his surprise at the fact that Germany had not been notified in advance about the intentions of the Polish government.[24] As far as his personal views were concerned, he took it for granted that the Poles had no desire to "initiate a pro-Bolshevik policy."[25] He returned to the same topic a fortnight later, during his conversation with Lipski on December 15, stressing that the Nazis "welcomed a strong Poland who would defend her interests against Russia," and that the Polish-Soviet agreement was, in his opinion, "not being contrary to this line."[26]

---

[20] Polish White Book, pp. 47-48.

[21] According to Moltke, some factories in that area, which had in the past delivered a substantial part of their output to the Russian market, now had difficulties in selling their goods, and a revival of the "almost dormant" Polish-Soviet economic relations appeared to be the only practicable solution. DGFP, Series D, V, 136; see also Germany, Auswärtiges Amt, The German White Paper, pp. 33-34.

[22] DGFP, Series D, V, 136.   [23] Ibid., p. 137.

[24] See also an exchange of views between Beck and Moltke on this subject. Ibid., p. 145.

[25] Ibid., p. 137.

[26] Ibid., p. 143. While Ribbentrop was invoking the old spirit of Polish-German cooperation, the war of nerves against Poland and Russia continued unabated (see France, Ministère des Affaires Étrangères, The French Yellow Book, p. 43), although Moltke advised his superiors to show more restraint in dealing with the Ukrainian issue (DGFP, Series D, V, 108). On December 16, 1938, the Polish chargé d'affaires in Prague was instructed to ask the Czechoslovak government to take immediate steps to stop the incessant flow of anti-Polish propaganda spread by "certain circles and organizations" with Berlin's support and encouragement (Czas, Dec. 18, 1938); on December 17, Soviet envoy Aleksandrovskii informed the Czech Foreign

Berlin was obviously trying to reach an agreement with Warsaw "on a very broad political plane,"[27] and Hitler, during his
last meeting with Beck on January 5, 1939, discussed again the
familiar topic of the Russian danger, observing that a strong Poland was "an absolute necessary" for Germany and that "every
Polish division engaged against Russia was a corresponding saving
of a German division."[28] He also mentioned the rumors spread in
the press in connection with the alleged Ukrainian plans of the
Reich, and then declared emphatically that Poland "did not have
the slightest thing to fear from Germany in this respect";[29] at the
same time he assured the Poles that he was interested in the
Ukraine only from the economic point of view and had "no interest in it politically," thus implying that Germany was prepared to recognize that area as Poland's sphere of influence.[30]
Beck, in his reply, maintained that his country was merely trying
to find "an acceptable *modus vivendi*" with its Russian neighbors, and that Poland would never enter into a "dependent relationship" with the Soviet Union. Regarding the Carpatho-
Ukraine, he warned Hitler that the continued existence of that
"seat of unrest" might eventually force Warsaw to intervene; he
also sought to persuade the Germans that it would be absurd to
use that province as the nucleus of a "Greater Ukraine."[31]

Beck's conversation with his German colleague, held on the
following day in Munich, also centered around the Ukrainian
question. Ribbentrop tried to be even more reassuring than Hitler and asserted that the Germans were interested in the Soviet
Ukraine only to the extent that they inflicted damage on Russia
everywhere they could, "just as she did on us." He admitted that
Berlin maintained "constant relations" with the Russian Ukraine,
but protested that the Nazis had never established any intimate contacts with the Polish Ukrainians. In order to remove the possibility of future misunderstandings, the Reich was ready to make

---

Ministry that his government would regard any campaign in favor of a "Greater
Ukraine" as an unfriendly action. Some German sources described this double
protest as an "expression of parallelism" in Moscow's and Warsaw's attitude
toward the Ukrainian question. See *Osteuropa*, XIV (1938-39), 258.
[27] *Polish White Book*, p. 51.   [28] *Ibid.*, p. 53.   [29] *DGFP*, Series D, V, 153.
[30] *Polish White Book*, p. 53; see also Szembek, pp. 375-76.
[31] *DGFP*, Series D, V, 158.

further concessions to Warsaw regarding the Ukrainian issue but this would necessarily require reciprocation on Poland's part. Germany would, indeed, regard the Ukrainian question as "covered by a special Polish prerogative" and would "support Poland in every way" in dealing with that problem if a general and "generous" settlement of all outstanding issues between Warsaw and Berlin was reached. While Hitler took a negative attitude toward the creation of a Greater Ukraine, he was willing to cooperate with the Poles in finding an acceptable solution of the Ukrainian question if Poland showed "a more and more pronounced anti-Russian attitude"; should she, however, decline this offer, there would be obviously "no question of any mutual interest."[32]

Ribbentrop's broad hint that Poland's accession to the Anti-Comintern Pact would be the first step in the right direction met with a negative response on the part of Beck, although the Polish Foreign Minister was cautious enough not to close the door to further negotiations and did not entirely exclude the possibility of an agreement with Germany on the problem of Russia at some future date. However, while admitting that Poland's aspirations as far as the Ukraine was concerned were "still alive," he refused to make any definite commitments and firmly declined the invitation to join Germany, Italy, and Japan in an "ideological" coalition against the Soviet Union, since "these questions had always been kept strictly separate from diplomatic relations with Russia." Though Poland was willing to cooperate with Germany against the subversive activities of the Comintern, she could not enter into a political treaty with Berlin to this end, since then she would be unable to maintain her neighborly relations with the USSR which were essential to her security.[33]

The last attempt to persuade the Poles to seize the "great opportunity" was made by Ribbentrop during his trip to Warsaw on January 25-27, 1939. The German Minister was visibly annoyed with the cunctatory tactics of his hosts; he "condemned the passivity of M. Beck's attitude," while attempting at the same time to convince him that Poland's adherence to the Anti-Com-

[32] *Ibid.*, p. 160.   [33] *Ibid.*, p. 161.

intern Pact would not endanger in any way her interests: "On the contrary, if Poland sat in the same boat as we, she could only gain added security."[34] He also touched in broad terms upon the subject of the policy to be pursued by Warsaw and Berlin toward Moscow, mentioning again the Ukrainian problem and proposing German-Polish cooperation in this field. Beck, in his reply, affirmed that Poland's aspirations were "directed toward the Soviet Ukraine and a connection with the Black Sea,"[35] but he pointed out that a German-Polish alliance would be a risky step, jeopardizing the whole future of Poland. Thus, the only positive result of the conversation was the fact that, in Beck's own words, "M. Ribbentrop had understood our attitude toward Russia and the impossibility of Poland joining the Anti-Comintern Pact."[36] Ribbentrop's trip finally convinced the Germans that they might as well give up all hopes for enlisting Poland's support in their eastern adventure, notwithstanding Beck's promises that he would "give further careful consideration to this question."[37] It also revealed to the Poles that their policy of equilibrium could work only so long as neither of their big neighbors demanded that they make their choice according to the principle "he who is not with me is against me." For, as Count Szembek observed to Ambassador Grzybowski on December 10, 1938, it was "exceedingly difficult" to maintain balance between Russia and Germany:

Our relations with the latter are entirely founded on the theory of the leading personalities of the Third Reich that, in the future conflict between Germany and Russia, Poland would be the natural ally of Germany. Under these circumstances, the good-neighbor policy, which has its origin in the accord of 1934, could easily appear to be but a pure and simple fiction.[38]

[34] *Ibid.*, p. 168.
[35] Ribbentrop's memorandum on his conversation with Beck is probably not entirely accurate on this point. Beck's own account stresses that he told his German colleague in no uncertain terms that the Poles "took very seriously" their nonaggression pact with Russia and regarded it as a permanent solution. *Final Report*, p. 173. According to Szembek, Beck was of the opinion that the Ukrainian problem would acquire immediate importance only if the Soviet Union broke up into national states, which was "still a remote prospect." Szembek, p. 413.
[36] *Polish White Book*, p. 56; see also *ibid.*, p. 58.
[37] *DGFP*, Series D, V, 168.
[38] Szembek, pp. 386-87.

Meanwhile Polish-Soviet relations seemed to be on their way toward a further improvement as a result of some minor conciliatory gestures made by the Kremlin. The restoration of the Polish cemetery in Kiev was progressing satisfactorily, the railroad traffic on the line Zdołbunów-Shepetovka was resumed, and most of the problems arising out of the recurring frontier incidents were solved, but the discussions concerning other issues were impeded as a result of Soviet delaying tactics.[39] This endless procrastination was especially apparent in the conduct of preliminary negotiations which were expected to lead to the conclusion of a trade agreement between the two countries.

The deterioration of political relations between Poland and Russia had been matched by a similar development in the economic field. High hopes for an expansion of Polish-Soviet trade, entertained by many Polish politicians and industrialists after the signature of the nonaggression pact, were never realized; on the contrary, the commercial intercourse between the two countries continued to decrease from year to year,[40] and Polish-Soviet business connections were in a state of progressive decline, partly as a result of Poland's inability to grant Russia long-term credits and partly because of political considerations which prompted

[39] *Polish White Book*, p. 206.

[40] For more information on Polish-Soviet economic relations in 1933-38 see Poland, Sejm, *Sprawozdanie stenograficzne*, Okres III, Posiedzenie CXXXVI, p. 18; CXXXIX, p. 26; Kadencja IV, Posiedzenie XXVII, pp. 3-5; Poland, Senat, *Sprawozdanie stenograficzne*, Okres III, Posiedzenie LXV, pp. 18-20; Kadencja IV, Posiedzenie XVI, pp. 43-45; *Kurjer Warszawski*, March 5, June 15, and Aug. 31, 1936; April 14, May 26, and Dec. 18, 1937; *Czas*, Feb. 23, 1939. The following table illustrates the development of Poland's trade with the Soviet Union since 1933 (in thousands of złotys):

Year	Imports from USSR	Exports to USSR
1933	17,697	59,945
1934	17,740	25,477
1935	14,942	11,086
1936	16,200	9,010
1937	14,499	4,415
1938	9,850	1,403

See Poland, Głowny Urząd Statystyczny, *Mały Rocznik Statystyczny, 1939* (Warsaw, 1939), pp. 166-67; *Kurjer Warszawski*, May 26, 1937; *The Economist* (London), May 20, 1939, p. 432.

Moscow to place its contracts with other countries while Poland ranked in Soviet trade behind Portugal and Greece.[41] Now it was becoming increasingly clear that, unless a more stable basis for Polish-Soviet trade was found, Poland would have to abandon any hope for establishing satisfactory economic relations with Russia.[42]

Preliminary talks were conducted in Moscow on December 16-19, 1938, by Dr. Łychowski, the director of the commercial policy department of the Polish Ministry for Industry and Trade, and by A. I. Mikoyan, the people's commissar for foreign trade, with the participation of Ambassador Grzybowski. In Mikoyan's words, the Russians had "everything to buy, but really nothing to sell";[43] their desire to obtain war materials from Poland proved, however, impracticable, and it was equally difficult to satisfy some of their other requirements. In spite of this unpromising start, both sides agreed to meet again in January and came to an understanding that the general trade turnover between their countries should reach the sum of 140-160 million złotys annually.[44] However, no further steps were taken for several weeks after the completion of the preliminary talks, and this lack of action prompted Litvinov to an unprecedented warning to Grzybowski to expedite the negotiations in order "to forestall German

---

[41] *The New York Times,* Dec. 4, 1938. The following table shows Poland's share in Soviet foreign trade:

Year	1934	1935	1936	1937
Imports (% of total)	2.2	1.1	.6	.3
Exports (% of total)	.9	.9	1.1	.8

See *Mały Rocznik Statystyczny,* p. 168. The share of the USSR in Polish exports declined from 6.7% in 1931 to 1.2% in 1935 and to .1% in 1938; at the same time the share of Germany increased from 16.8% in 1931 to 22.7% in 1938. *Czas,* Feb. 23, 1939.

[42] Up to 1938, the commercial relations between Poland and the Soviet Union had been based on the principle of barter and were regulated in accordance with a system of annual quotas. Detailed lists of goods to be exchanged and other specifications were usually included in customs agreements negotiated by the Polish Ministry of Foreign Affairs and the Soviet Embassy in Warsaw. While this system proved workable, it was obviously not as satisfactory as a full-fledged trade treaty.

[43] *Polish White Book,* p. 206.

[44] For the text of the communiqué see *Izvestiia,* Dec. 21, 1938; English translation in Degras, ed., III, 314.

intrigues."[45] Finally, the discussions reopened in Moscow on January 19. The bargaining was unusually hard, and the Poles found it especially difficult to agree to the postponement of the important transit agreement; they were also forced to make some minor concessions to the Russians.

The first general Polish-Soviet trade treaty to be based on the most-favored nation principle was signed, along with separate agreements on trade turnover and clearing operations, on February 19, 1939, and was formally ratified in May of the same year.[46] According to its provisions, Poland was to import from Russia cotton, hides and furs, apatite, tobacco, manganese ore, and asbestos, and was in turn to export to the USSR coal, iron products, zinc, textiles, textile machinery, leather, and viscose. Arrangements were made for an evenly balanced exchange of goods, with a general annual turnover of 110 million złotys; thus Russia's share in Poland's foreign trade was now expected to reach between 6 and 7 percent.[47] Further discussions concerning the fulfillment of quotas were to start immediately but, owing to the procrastination of the Soviet representatives, they were never concluded. Hence, in spite of the concessions made by the Poles, the treaty had no practical value, and Ambassador Grzybowski was prompted to make, in a letter to Count Szembek, this apt observation:

At times I have the impression that in our persistent striving for practical things we are overlooking the possibilities of this country. It looks also as if, when making any kind of agreement with this state, we have to consider only the actual fact that it is made, and not the gain which may result from its conclusion.[48]

While the Poles and the Russians were occupied with their

[45] *Polish White Book*, p. 206. This was probably a reference to the expected visit to Moscow of a German trade mission under Dr. Schnurre, which left Berlin late in January but interrupted its journey at Warsaw and later returned home without going to the Soviet capital. Russian diplomatic circles complained that it was the Poles who, through their intrigues, contrived to prevent the commercial negotiations between the Soviet Union and Germany. *DBFP*, 3d Series, IV (London, 1951), 82; *DGFP*, Series D, IV (Washington, 1951), 623; see also Kleist, pp. 20-21.

[46] For the text of the treaty see *Vneshniaia politika SSSR*, IV, 406-7, and *Polish White Book*, pp. 182-83. See also *Czas*, Feb. 23, May 17, and June 1, 1939; *Pravda*, May 18 and June 2, 1939; *Osteuropa*, XIV (1938-39), 457-58.

[47] Buell, p. 349.   [48] *Polish White Book*, p. 207.

prolonged and tedious negotiations on the subject of trade and tried to regulate some of the other issues affecting their relations, they apparently did not consider it necessary to place the Ukrainian problem on their agenda.[49] With the exception of the protest note to Czechoslovakia, the Soviet official attitude toward Pan-Ukrainian propaganda had been so far quite restrained, and on December 27, 1938, the *Journal de Moscou,* generally regarded as the mouthpiece of the Narkomindel, published an article minimizing the danger of a German attack against the Ukraine and stressing that the Soviet Union remained "fully indifferent to the commotion raised beyond its borders over the so-called 'Ukrainian problem.'" The newspaper affirmed, moreover, that the ties of friendship binding the Ukrainian people to the other peoples of the USSR were "indestructible," and that any attempt to infringe upon Soviet territory would result in the destruction of the aggressor.[50] These semiofficial utterances prompted some of the Western diplomats in Russia to reappraise the situation and to assume a rather skeptical attitude regarding Hitler's alleged Ukrainian plans.[51] It is true, the speculations that the Nazis were preparing to attack the Soviet Union continued to appear in the world press, but the big propaganda drive for the creation of a "Greater Ukraine" was definitely losing its original momentum. Even in Eastern Galicia, that hotbed of Ukrainian nationalism, the feverish excitement was gradually disappearing and the unbearable tension which had gripped both the Ukrainian and the Polish population only a few months ago was showing some signs of relaxation.[52] Polish official circles also began to play

[49] This information is based on Ambassador Grzybowski's letter to the author dated Oct. 13, 1958.

[50] Quoted from *Moscow News,* Jan. 2, 1939. [51] See *DBFP,* 3d Series, III, 579.

[52] In October and November, 1938, Polish-Ukrainian clashes occurred in Lwów and some other places. See *The New York Times,* Oct. 14 and Nov. 5, 1938. These events, as well as the developments in the Carpatho-Ukraine, produced a tense atmosphere throughout Eastern Galicia. In December, the Ukrainian representatives in the Sejm tabled a bill providing for the establishment of an autonomous "Galician-Volhynian Land," enjoying full rights of self-government except in foreign policy and in military and financial matters. After the rejection of the bill, the UNDO Party (which had already in May decided to discontinue its policy of cooperation with the Polish government) demanded in a resolution the granting of "absolute independence" to the Ukrainian national group within the framework of the Polish state; the underground OUN regarded this "minimal" program

down the significance of the Carpatho-Ukrainian issue, and Beck, the most ardent champion of the common Polish-Hungarian frontier, stated in an interview that the "Ruthenian question" was not of great importance to Poland.[53] When making this remark, he probably had some advance information that the status of the Carpatho-Ukraine would soon be settled in accordance with Poland's wishes; he also was reported to have received assurances from Grigore Gafencu, Rumania's new foreign minister, that Bucharest would not oppose Polish-Hungarian plans "if and when circumstances permitted a change" in the frontiers of Czechoslovakia.[54]

Things were certainly beginning to move faster as the fateful Ides of March approached. At the very time when Beck was dismissing the Carpatho-Ukrainian question with a disdainful gesture, the attention of the world was focused on Moscow, where Stalin was addressing the Eighteenth Congress of the All-Union Communist Party. While the Soviet dictator also displayed a nonchalant attitude toward the Carpatho-Ukrainian problem, it was striking that he devoted so much attention to this, as he put it, "absurd and foolish" issue. His remarks were meant to be witty, but their humor was rather constrained. Stalin suggested that Great Britain and France used Czechoslovakia as a bait to lure Germany in the direction of the Ukraine and accused them of trying to "poison the atmosphere" and to provoke a conflict between the Third Reich and the Soviet Union "without any visible grounds." While he ridiculed "madmen" who dreamt of "annexing the elephant, that is, the Soviet Ukraine, to the gnat, namely, the so-called Carpatho-Ukraine," he clearly indicated that he would be willing to make a deal with "normal" people in Germany who were ready to discuss matters in a reasonable way.[55]

---

as unsatisfactory and advocated the incorporation of all Ukrainian ethnic territories in Poland into an independent Ukrainian state. See Poland, Sejm, *Sprawozdanie stenograficzne*, Kadencja V, Posiedzenie III, pp. 48-51; *Sprawy Narodowościowe*, XII (1938), 285-86; Makukh, pp. 468-73; *Entsyklopediia Ukrainoznavstva*, I, Part II, 563-66.

[53] *The New York Times*, March 12, 1939.   [54] *Ibid.*, March 7, 1939.

[55] CPSU, *XVIII S"ezd VKP(b), Stenograficheskii otchët*, pp. 13-14; *Documents on International Affairs, 1939-1946*, I, 367.

Hitler's reaction to these suggestions was prompt and convincing, although some of the moves he was about to make had been certainly planned beforehand, possibly as early as the beginning of January. On March 13, only three days after Stalin's speech, the German minister to Budapest called on Regent Horthy and Premier Teleki and informed them that the Führer agreed to the occupation of the Carpatho-Ukraine by Hungary, provided that the Hungarian Army acted at once and thus coordinated its operations with those to be undertaken by German troops in Bohemia and Moravia. On March 14 Hungary sent an ultimatum to Prague, demanding an immediate withdrawal of the Czech Army from Carpatho-Ukrainian territory; on the same day, the government of the Carpatho-Ukraine issued a declaration of independence and asked the German Reich to take the new state under its protection. However, no help from Berlin was forthcoming, Ukrainian irregulars were overwhelmed after a brief, though valiant, resistance, and the Polish-Hungarian frontier was reestablished for what turned out to be a period of only six months.

The question naturally arises as to what reasons could have induced Hitler to change so suddenly his attitude and to throw the Carpatho-Ukraine to the wolves. It has been pointed out that the occupation of Bohemia, Moravia, and, partly, also Slovakia gave Germany a favorable strategic position which enabled her to control southern approaches to Poland more effectively than ever before, and that the Nazis appeased the Hungarians and secured their loyalty and gratitude without really sacrificing any important advantage.[56] At the same time, however, the fall of the Carpatho-Ukraine formed a prelude to the negotiations between Berlin and Moscow which were to open in a few weeks' time. The Ukrainian issue became irrelevant to Hitler as soon as he decided to destroy Poland with the active help of the Soviet Union, and the sacrifice of the Carpatho-Ukraine and of the greater Ukrainian project paved the way to the coming German-Russian rapprochement. While the Hungarian invasion was officially de-

[56] See H. L. Roberts, "The Diplomacy of Colonel Beck," in Craig and Gilbert, eds., *The Diplomats*, p. 605.

nounced by the USSR as a violation of the "elementary rights" of the population of the Carpatho-Ukraine,[57] the very fact that Budapest's action was condoned and even encouraged by Berlin demonstrated to the Kremlin in the most convincing way Germany's lack of interest in any Ukrainian adventure.

Thus, having enjoyed a brief but spectacular prominence in world affairs, the Ukrainian problem as an international issue was temporarily shelved in March, 1939, but its disappearance from the limelight was hardly an "important contribution to peace," as Ciano hopefully declared in his congratulatory telegram to the Hungarian foreign minister.[58] Rejoicing in Budapest was sincere, but the celebrations in Warsaw were tinged with bitterness and frustration, and Beck's triumph was marred by a foreboding of coming disaster. His apprehensions were well founded, for the fall of the Carpatho-Ukraine eventually proved to have been merely the first step toward the fourth partition of Poland.

[57] *Izvestiia,* March 20, 1939; *Documents on International Affairs, 1939-1946,* I, 76.
[58] *The New York Times,* March 18, 1939.

VII. Toward the Fourth Partition

In addressing the Foreign Affairs Committee of the Senate on March 11, 1939, Beck declared that Polish policy toward the Soviet Union was "absolutely consistent" and not subject to any changes or fluctuations. While the attempts to establish this relationship on the basis of sound neighborliness and reciprocal respect had been impaired to some extent by the tension resulting "not from a Polish-Soviet dispute, but from attitude toward other states and problems," the aftereffects of that temporary crisis had been eliminated and the mutual dealings between Warsaw and Moscow were now characterized by a return to normalcy.[1]

Beck's statement was published in the Soviet press without any editorial comment, but the absence of usual personal attacks against the Polish Foreign Minister seemed to indicate that the Kremlin was prepared to let bygones be bygones and to reappraise the whole complex of Polish-Soviet relations in the light of recent international developments. Soon afterwards Litvinov invited Grzybowski to a confidential conference, in the course of which he proposed to the Ambassador a deal involving a partition of the Baltic states between Poland and Russia, with the Dvina as the boundary between the Polish and Soviet zones of influence, but Grzybowski left no doubt in the Foreign Commissar's mind about Warsaw's negative attitude toward this offer.[2]

[1] Beck, *Przemówienia*, p. 417.

[2] This information is contained in Ambassador Grzybowski's letter to the author dated March 18, 1959; a similar account included in the French edition of Beck's memoirs erroneously states that the Soviet proposal was made at the time of the Lithuanian crisis of March, 1938. Beck, *Dernier rapport,* p. 157; see also Szembek, p. 443.

These diplomatic contacts led to speculations that the Soviet Union was about to offer the Poles and the Rumanians its assistance in the event of German aggression, but all such rumors were officially denied by the Tass communiqué of March 21:

Poland and Rumania did not apply to the Soviet government for help, nor did they inform that government of any danger threatening them. What actually happened was that on March 18 the British government informed the Soviet government of the existence of weighty reasons to fear an act of violence over Rumania and inquired about the possible position of the Soviet government in such an eventuality. In reply to this inquiry, the Soviet government put forward a proposal for a calling of a conference of the states most interested—namely Great Britain, France, Poland, Rumania, Turkey, and the Soviet Union. In the opinion of the Soviet government such a conference would give the maximum possibilities for the elucidation of the real situation and the position of all the participants at the conference. The British government, however, found this proposal premature.[3]

According to London's views, it was dangerous to convene the conference proposed by Moscow without a certainty that it would succeed;[4] instead, Lord Halifax proposed that Great Britain, France, Poland, and the USSR issue a vaguely worded declaration promising to consult with each other in the event of an action constituting a threat to the independence of any European country.[5] One of the reasons for this vacillation displayed by the British was their desire "not to frighten" Warsaw and Bucharest.[6] While Polish public opinion was now more friendly toward the Soviet Union than in the past,[7] it was also certain that the governments of Poland and Rumania continued to regard Russia with uneasiness and distrust and that a Soviet offer of assistance could be, in these circumstances, "almost as unwelcome as a threat of invasion."[8] This became apparent as soon as the text of the proposed declaration had been communicated to Beck, who at once objected strongly to the USSR's acting as one of the signatory powers:

Hitherto Poland had kept balance between Germany and Soviet

---

[3] *Izvestiia*, March 22, 1939; English translation quoted from Beloff, II, 230.
[4] *DBFP*, 3d Series, IV (London, 1951), 392.   [5] *Ibid.*, p. 400.   [6] *Ibid.*, p. 423.
[7] *Ibid.*, p. 428.   [8] *Ibid.*, p. 450.

Russia and avoided coming down on one side or the other. The proposed declaration would definitely place Poland in the Soviet camp and the reaction of Germany, especially given the Führer's mentality, would undoubtedly be serious. . . . M. Beck implied that the participation of the Soviet government in any such declaration might lead to difficulties but that Poland might be able to associate herself with England and France if Soviet Russia were omitted.[9]

Poland's mistrustful attitude toward Russia was discussed at length during the Anglo-French conversations in London on March 22, 1939. While Prime Minister Chamberlain showed some understanding for the Polish point of view,[10] the French delegation thought it important not to give the Poles an excuse for disrupting the negotiations with Russia. In the opinion of the Quai d'Orsay, it was possible that Beck could be persuaded to accept indirect assistance from Moscow, if only the Western powers succeeded in keeping things quiet and avoided any public agreement with the USSR.[11] Meanwhile the British government found itself in an embarrassing situation when Litvinov informed Ambassador Seeds that the Kremlin was ready to sign the proposed declaration and waited only for its acceptance by France and Poland; at the same time Beck made his counterproposal of a confidential bilateral understanding between Warsaw and London as a means of avoiding Poland's open association with Russia.[12] British acceptance of the Polish proposal and Chamberlain's famous guarantee to Poland of March 31 implied the dropping of the abortive project of a four-power declaration, originally sponsored by Whitehall. Since these steps were taken after Moscow's tentative approval of the British plan, they looked like a studied snub to the Soviet government, and Moscow could hardly be reproached for viewing with skepticism any new suggestions emanating from London; as Ambassador Seeds put it, the Russians "had had enough and would henceforward stand apart free from any commitments."[13]

[9] *Ibid.*, p. 453.

[10] A few days later Chamberlain confessed in a private letter to "the most profound distrust of Russia," whose motives seemed to him to have little in common with the West's ideas of liberty and to be aimed only at "getting everyone else by the ears." K. Feiling, *The Life of Neville Chamberlain* (London, 1946), p. 403.

[11] *DBFP*, 3d Series, IV, 458-59.   [12] *Ibid.*, p. 500.   [13] *Ibid.*, p. 574.

The possibility of Russia's assistance to Poland and the related problem of Polish-Soviet relations were examined again by the British statesmen and Beck during his visit to London on April 4-6, 1939. The Polish Foreign Minister reiterated his view that it would be risky to bring Russia into any discussions because of the acute state of tension existing between Germany and the Soviet Union.[14] While Poland was anxious to preserve correct relations with the USSR, she realized that the establishment of close treaty connections between Warsaw and Moscow was almost certain to provoke Berlin's wrath and could conceivably lead to an outbreak of hostilities.[15] Besides, Poland could not make her policy dependent upon either of her two powerful neighbors; if she failed to maintain her independence, "she would no longer be an element of peace, but an element likely to provoke war."[16] If the British tried to improve their relations with Russia, the Poles would raise no objections; they could not help, however, remaining skeptical about the results of any discussions with Moscow. For the time being, Warsaw would not join in the conversations between Britain and the USSR; it would also refuse to give its assent to any agreement which would have the effect of linking it with the Soviet Union,[17] but would welcome an understanding which would permit the Poles to obtain war equipment from the West over Soviet territory and to receive supplies of Russian raw materials and goods required for military purposes.[18]

Beck's wary attitude toward Moscow was regarded by some British leaders as understandable in view of his country's past relations with Russia,[19] and even Ambassador Maiskii admitted that the Kremlin was fully aware of Poland's "groundless" apprehensions that the presence of the Red Army might exert a disturbing influence on Polish society.[20] At the same time, however, he accused Beck of formulating Polish foreign policy in accordance with his allegedly pro-German sympathies, and suggested that Britain and France make their assistance to Poland and Rumania conditional on their adopting a "reasonable" attitude toward the Soviet Union.[21] Meanwhile Tass issued an official de-

[14] *Ibid.*, 3d Series, V (London, 1952), 2.   [15] *Ibid.*, p. 6; see also *ibid.*, IV, 502.
[16] *Ibid.*, V, 13.   [17] *Ibid.*, p. 12.   [18] Beck, *Final Report*, p. 178.
[19] *DBFP*, 3d Series, V, 36.   [20] *Ibid.*, p. 20.   [21] *Ibid.*, p. 83.

nial of the reports published in the French press to the effect
that the USSR would, in the event of war, supply Poland with
war material and close its raw materials market to the Germans.[22]
It is doubtful whether the Kremlin's statement was intended to
pacify the apprehensions of the Nazis. It merely made it clear that
the Russian rulers were not willing to allow the prestige of their
country to be used as a counter in the political game between
Germany and the Western powers.[23] Besides, the communiqué
did not exclude the possibility of Russia's military assistance to
Poland. It only indicated that the Poles would have to fulfill
certain conditions before they became eligible for Moscow's help.

Since Polish public opinion and especially the Polish government were considered "not ripe" for any alliance with the Soviet
Union and since any pressure exercised on Warsaw was likely to
backfire against its originators,[24] the British government decided
to concentrate its efforts on Russia. The beginning of this prolonged and tortuous bargaining was inauspicious, and it was
hard to see how the USSR could make an effective contribution
to any defensive scheme when its neighbors, supposedly menaced
by Germany, were steadfastly refusing to consider all plans of
action which involved cooperation or even consultation with
Moscow. In order to find a way out of this predicament, London
suggested that the Soviet Union issue a general declaration that
it would be prepared to assist, "in such manner as would be
found most convenient," any of its European neighbors attacked
by an aggressor and resisting this invasion.[25] While the British
proposal was being submitted to the Soviet government, however,
Gafencu was about to begin his famous "diplomatic journey" to
Berlin and other capitals of Europe, and Litvinov thought it unwise to assume vague commitments at a time when the Rumanian
Foreign Minister "might be willingly signing away something at
Germany's command."[26]

On April 18 Moscow's counterproposal was communicated to
London and Paris, revealing at once the basic differences in the

[22] *Izvestiia*, April 4, 1939; *Vneshniaia politika SSSR*, IV, 416. For English translation see *DGFP*, Series D, VI (Washington, 1956), 197.
[23] See *DGFP*, Series D, VI, 197.   [24] *DBFP*, 3d Series, V, 204-5.   [25] *Ibid.*, p. 206.
[26] *Ibid.*, pp. 221-22.

Western and the Soviet approach to the problem of mutual assistance. According to this plan, Britain, France, and Russia were to pledge themselves to give all necessary assistance, including military aid, to the nations of Eastern Europe situated between the Baltic and the Black Sea and bordering on the USSR. The extent and the form of this assistance were to be discussed and settled by the three great powers, without any consultation with the state attacked by the aggressor and regardless of whether it desired such help. Any doubts as to the true intentions of the Kremlin were removed by two additional conditions requiring that the British government explain that its guarantees offered to Poland referred exclusively to an act of aggression committed by Germany, and that Warsaw and Bucharest declare their alliance to be operative in the event of aggression from any quarter or else denounce it altogether as being directed against the Soviet Union.[27]

It was obvious that the Russian plan was objectionable from the Polish viewpoint, and some Western diplomats openly expressed their conviction that the very fact that such proposals had been advanced by Russia was likely to prejudice the possibility of Polish-Soviet cooperation.[28] This point was emphasized in the official British reply to Moscow:

The Soviet government are well aware of the hesitation of the Polish government to be too closely associated with the Soviet Union in political arrangements. The Soviet government may well consider that this hesitation is unjustified, but it undoubtedly exists and must be taken into account. . . . It is undesirable to do anything to disturb Polish confidence at the present time and it is important that Polish self-reliance should be maintained. To enter into an arrangement with the Soviet government at this stage by which Soviet assistance would be afforded whether Poland likes it or not, would have a most disturbing influence in Warsaw.[29]

Meanwhile the Polish press tried to minimize the significance and the possible value of Anglo-Soviet contacts by arguing that Russia was hardly a factor capable of influencing international events. It was also stressed that Moscow's attitude made it ex-

[27] *Ibid.*, pp. 228-29.   [28] *Ibid.*, p. 231.   [29] *Ibid.*, p. 268.

ceedingly difficult, if not entirely impossible, to achieve the main
objective of London's policy, namely to secure Soviet assistance
in the event of Nazi aggression while paying at the same time all
due attention to the sensibilities of the Poles and the Rumanians.[30] In spite of these difficulties, however, Warsaw seemed to be
satisfied with the "propitious" development of Polish-Soviet relations and reacted favorably to Litvinov's dismissal from the
post of People's Commissar for Foreign Affairs.[31] The events of
the next few weeks could indeed be interpreted as an indication
that the prospects for a new rapprochement between Poland and
Russia were brighter than ever, especially since Molotov adopted
a "most courteous attitude" toward the Poles and intervened personally in the settlement of some outstanding issues disputed by
the two countries.[32] Beck, in his famous address to the Sejm on
May 5, referred quite openly to far-reaching "hints" made by the
Nazi leaders to Poland, thus implying that Warsaw had remained
loyal to her obligations regarding the Soviet Union in spite of
German promises of territorial gains.[33] This declaration undoubtedly found an interested audience in Moscow; in any case, Molotov invited Grzybowski to call on him on May 7 and opened the
conversation with gracious compliments on Beck's speech, emphasizing his admiration for his Polish colleague's words on national honor.[34] The Ambassador stressed on his part that his
country intended to maintain a friendly and loyal attitude
toward all its neighbors and that it regarded "sympathetically"
the projected cooperation between the Western powers and the
Soviet Union.[35]

A few days later Potemkin, who was on his way back to Mos-

---

[30] *Ibid.*, p. 357; see also *Ilustrowany Kurjer Codzienny* as quoted in *Czas*, May 2,
1939, and *The Times* (London), April 22, 1939.

[31] According to a theory developed in Warsaw, Litvinov's resignation could be
attributed to his negative attitude toward bilateral Anglo-Soviet negotiations and
his preference for multilateral treaties within the framework of the League of
Nations. *Czas*, May 5, 1939. This opinion was not shared, however, by Western
observers, who interpreted Molotov's appointment as a warning to Poland and
feared that the sudden change in Moscow might signify Russia's abandonment of
the policy of collective security and her decision to embark on a policy of isolation. *DBFP*, 3d Series, V, 413.

[32] Beck, *Final Report*, p. 190.

[33] Beck, *Przemówienia*, p. 431; English translation in *Polish White Book*, p. 87.

[34] *Polish White Book*, p. 208.   [35] *Ibid.*; see also *DBFP*, 3d Series, V, 476.

cow from a trip to Ankara, Bucharest, and Sofia, was instructed
by the Kremlin to accept Beck's unofficial invitation to interrupt
his journey at Warsaw.[36] Even before reaching the Polish capital,
Potemkin praised Poland's "active influence" in the struggle for
peace.[37] During his brief stopover in Warsaw, his personal charm
and diplomatic skill disarmed and subdued the Polish Foreign
Minister, who was deeply impressed with his "sincerity" and later
confided to Ambassador Noël that, for the first time since 1932,
he "had a conversation free from mistrust with a representative
of the Soviet Union."[38] Both sides agreed that recent events had
shown the falsity of rumors about the existence of a Polish-
German understanding directed against the USSR. The Polish
government was unwilling to ally itself with either one of Poland's big neighbors against the other, and this attitude was undoubtedly to the advantage of Russia, since no large-scale military action against the Soviet Union could be undertaken without Warsaw's participation.[39] Potemkin was apparently completely satisfied with these explanations and assured the Poles on
behalf of his government and in accordance with Moscow's "special instructions" that, if they became the victims of aggression,
they could expect the Kremlin to assume a "benevolent" attitude
toward Poland.[40]

While Beck congratulated himself for having successfully removed all Soviet doubts and suspicions,[41] he also did his best to
clarify Poland's views regarding the current negotiations between
the Western powers and Russia[42] and to eliminate in advance
any speculations that the Poles might be willing to agree to some
form of closer association with Moscow for the purpose of mutual
assistance. As Grzybowski stated to Molotov at the time of Potemkin's visit to Warsaw, Poland was reluctant to enter into any political or military agreement with the USSR:

[36] See Beck, *Final Report,* p. 191.   [37] *Czas,* May 11, 1939.
[38] Gafencu, p. 187; see also Noël, p. 377.   [39] *Polish White Book,* p. 183.
[40] Beck, *Final Report,* pp. 191-92. According to Ambassador Moltke, Potemkin
proposed at the same time the abrogation of the Polish-Rumanian treaty, which,
in his words, was directed against the Soviet Union. When Beck explained that
the latest version of this treaty contained no specific mention of the USSR, Potemkin
refrained from making any further claims. *DGFP,* Series D, VI, 510.
[41] Gafencu, p. 187.
[42] For a detailed account of these negotiations see *DBFP,* 3d Series, VI (London,
1953), 780-82.

We could not accept a one-sided Soviet guarantee. Nor could we accept a mutual guarantee, because in the event of a conflict with Germany our forces would be completely engaged, and so we would not be in any position to give help to the Soviets. Also we could not accept collective negotiations, and made our adoption of a definite attitude conditional on the result of the Anglo-Franco-Soviet negotiations. We rejected all discussion of matters affecting us other than by the bilateral method. . . . In the event of conflict we by no means rejected specified forms of Soviet aid, but considered it premature to determine them definitely. We considered it premature to open bilateral negotiations with the Soviets before the Anglo-Franco-Soviet negotiations had achieved a result.[43]

The Polish Ambassador tried to sweeten this bitter pill by emphasizing Poland's loyalty toward the Soviet Union and her continued interest in the three-power negotiations, but while Molotov "made no objection whatever" to Grzybowski's lengthy discourse, he undoubtedly realized that it was useless to hope for any basic change in Warsaw's "policy of independence."[44] For the time being, Moscow thought it prudent not to appear overanxious in offering its assistance to those who were reluctant to accept it; in fact, the Soviet press began to complain that the Western powers wanted Russia to defend Poland and Rumania but were not willing to offer her any help in the event of a direct aggression against the USSR.[45] These accusations were repeated in the Soviet note to the British government of May 15[46] and in Molotov's speech to the Supreme Soviet on May 31, in which he also made several references to Poland and stated that "a certain improvement" was noticeable in the relations between Moscow and Warsaw.[47]

These rather reserved but not unfriendly remarks were made only a week after the arrival in the Polish capital of Nikolai K. Sharonov, former minister of the USSR to Greece, who was to take over the post of Soviet ambassador to Poland that had remained vacant since the fall of 1937. The Poles welcomed Rus-

---

[43] *Polish White Book*, p. 208.   [44] See *DBFP*, 3d Series, V, 571.
[45] *Izvestiia*, May 10, 1939.   [46] *DBFP*, 3d Series, V, 558-59.
[47] USSR, Verkhovnyi Sovet, *Sozyv I, Sessiia III, Stenograficheskii otchët* (Moscow, 1939), p. 467; English translation in Degras, ed., III, 337. For Polish editorial comment see *Czas*, June 2, 1939.

sia's new representative with cordiality and courtesy, regarding his appointment as another friendly gesture on the part of Moscow.[48] On June 2 Sharonov presented his credentials to President Mościcki and pledged himself to uphold and develop neighborly relations between the two countries.[49] The President, in a brief reply, stated that Poland appreciated the importance of direct and friendly cooperation with the Soviet Union and expressed his conviction that the development of normal trade relations could be regarded as the best example to be followed by both nations in their striving toward mutual amity and understanding.[50] A few days later, Sharonov discussed in detail Polish-Soviet relations in his conversation with Szembek, putting a special emphasis on their satisfactory state and on the necessity for their further improvement. He pointed out that the two countries should work toward a "complete fulfillment" of the trade treaty and expressed his hopes that the remaining difficulties in this field would be overcome. As far as the international situation was concerned, the Ambassador thought that it would develop satisfactorily and that there would be no war in Europe in the foreseeable future.[51]

While Sharonov was trying to appease the apprehensions of the Poles with assurances of good will, the Soviet government extended to Warsaw an offer to supply the Polish Army with necessary military equipment.[52] At the same time, however, Poland was asked to agree to certain unacceptable conditions,[53] and Grzybowski's request to speed up the transit negotiations was put off with assurances that, in the event of war, this question would be decided in Poland's favor.[54] Then, on June 29, Moscow suddenly increased its pressure on Warsaw with the publication of Zhdanov's article in *Pravda,* in which the Soviet leader criticized Beck for his declaration that Poland was not interested in receiving any guarantees from the USSR and charged that the Western powers were conducting their talks with Russia only to make it

---

[48] See *Osteuropa,* XIV (1938-39), 669. [49] *Polish White Book,* p. 184.
[50] *Czas,* June 3, 1939. [51] *Polish White Book,* p. 185. [52] *Ibid.,* p. 208.
[53] According to Ambassador Grzybowski's letter to the author (Oct. 13, 1958), these proposals were made directly to the Polish authorities in Warsaw; they included, among other things, a provision that Soviet army officers should be attached to the Polish General Staff.
[54] *Polish White Book,* p. 208; see also *USFR,* 1939, I (Washington, 1956), 196.

easier for themselves to strike a bargain with the aggressors. The ambiguous attitude of the Kremlin strengthened Warsaw's determination to avoid involvement in any multilateral alliance with the participation of the Soviet Union which could be expected to supersede the British guarantees given to Poland and to put her entirely at Russia's mercy. Poland's position with regard to the negotiations between the Western powers and the USSR was summarized by one of Beck's closest associates as follows:

(a) . . . the Polish government could not agree that the name of Poland should be mentioned in any arrangement between the Western powers and the Soviet Union;

(b) . . . the idea that assistance should be rendered by the Soviet Union to an attacked country without the latter's consent was not acceptable in regard to Poland. So far as other countries are concerned, the Polish government regards it as dangerous interference with security in Eastern Europe.[55]

In accordance with Warsaw's wishes, the British government informed Russia that it would be inadvisable to enumerate in the text of the treaty all the nations in whose defense France, the Soviet Union, and the United Kingdom were to cooperate, the more so since some of them were opposed to any guarantees imposed upon them against their will.[56] Moscow agreed to defer the final settlement of this question but continued to express its dissatisfaction with the alleged unwillingness of London and Paris to join the USSR in an agreement based on the principles of equality and reciprocity.[57] It also saw sinister implications in the fact that, while the British government did not propose to defend Poland against Russia, it was equally reluctant to guarantee the Soviet Union against Poland and tried to exclude any pledge to this effect from the draft of the treaty.[58]

The next serious difficulty which developed in the course of the Moscow negotiations resulted from the Kremlin's insistence that Britain, France, and the USSR should render their assistance to Poland and nine other states mentioned in the preliminary out-

---

[55] *DBFP*, 3d Series, VI, 24. For the attitude of the Polish press toward these problems see *Czas*, May 26, 1939.

[56] *DBFP*, 3d Series, VI, 35.   [57] *Ibid.*, p. 219.   [58] *Ibid.*, pp. 38-39, 90.

line of the treaty[59] in the event of "indirect aggression." According to Molotov's vague definition, this phrase covered

action accepted by any of the above-mentioned states under threat of force by another power, or without any such threat, involving the use of territory and forces of the state in question for purposes of aggression against that state or against one of the contracting parties, and consequently involving the loss of, by that state, its independence or violation of its neutrality.[60]

Various obscure and ambiguous terms used in this definition served only to confirm the impression that the Soviet Union was interested chiefly in providing itself with a plausible excuse for intervening in the internal affairs of its neighbors, especially the Baltic states. It was also obvious that, as the British government maintained, the adoption of the Kremlin's formula by the Western powers would fill the countries concerned with mistrust and apprehensions;[61] the Quai d'Orsay insisted, however, that it was vitally important to reach an agreement with Russia and that, therefore, an acceptance of the Soviet definition of indirect aggression was preferable to a breakdown of negotiations.[62] Under these circumstances Britain was forced to yield to the pressure of her ally and the conversations continued, although even a veteran representative of the Foreign Office described them as a "humiliating experience": "Time after time we have taken up a position and a week later we have abandoned it; and we have had the feeling that Molotov was convinced from the beginning that we should be forced to abandon it."[63]

Meanwhile Warsaw preserved an attitude of detachment with regard to the Moscow talks,[64] and the Polish press refrained carefully from any comments that might be interpreted as an attempt

[59] They included Belgium, Estonia, Finland, Greece, Latvia, the Netherlands, Rumania, Switzerland, and Turkey. The Netherlands and Switzerland were subsequently dropped from the list.

[60] DBFP, 3d Series, VI, 313.　　[61] Ibid., p. 333.

[62] Ibid., pp. 396-97.　　[63] Ibid., p. 422.

[64] In Warsaw's opinion, Poland "stood to gain, or, at any rate, not to lose" regardless of the result of the negotiations. Ibid., p. 440. According to Grzybowski, the conclusion of an agreement between the Western powers and the USSR, while diminishing Poland's importance in international affairs, would nevertheless bring her certain advantages; on the other hand, a breakdown of the negotiations would tend to strengthen Warsaw's position. Szembek, p. 470.

to interfere with the negotiations. A few sympathetic references to the plight of the Baltic states were published, but there was hardly any direct criticism of Soviet attempts to impose "guarantees" on Poland's small neighbors.[65] The Poles were now anxious to avoid anything that could conceivably lead to a misunderstanding with the USSR and assured Moscow that they would sincerely respect its rights and interests, the Polish motto being "Russia for the Russians and Poland for the Poles."[66] According to a British diplomat, Warsaw's entire policy toward the Soviet Union could be described as one of "cautious but detached rapprochement":

There are now very few frontier incidents. The Soviet Ambassador and his staff are presentable and, stranger still, are well spoken of and well received. The new commercial treaty . . . is in provisional force and works well. . . . The Soviet commercial mission are now allowed to work here.[67] . . . Nothing is now heard of trials of Communists. The Polish government are doing all they can quietly to improve their relations with Soviet Russia.[68]

Beck himself characterized at that time the state of Polish-Soviet relations as "quite satisfactory" and revealed his intention of sending to Moscow an agricultural mission in response to a Russian invitation; he also seemed not averse to Grzybowski's suggestion to invite Mikoyan to Poland in order to impress him with the country's industrial development.[69] While Warsaw was still reluctant to initiate any political or military talks with the USSR, it continued to count on Russia's assistance in munitions and raw materials. The hopes that Moscow would be willing to grant economic help to Poland were apparently based on the supposition

[65] See the editorial "Pakt Trzech a państwa bałtyckie" [The Three-Power Pact and the Baltic States] in Czas, June 5, 1939, and Gazeta Polska as quoted in Czas, June 6, 1939.

[66] A. Romer, "Polska a Rosja" [Poland and Russia], Czas, July 17, 1939.

[67] This mission arrived in Warsaw on June 21, 1939. Its negotiations with the Polish government gave rise to reports that Polish-Soviet trade turnover might be increased to 500 million złotys annually, thus compensating the Poles for a marked decline in their trade with Germany. Osteuropa, XIV (1938-39), 668-69.

[68] C. J. Norton to Lord Halifax, July 21, 1939. DBFP, 3d Series, VI, 441.

[69] See DBFP, 3d Series, VI, 545, and Szembek, p. 443. According to Ambassador Biddle, Beck purported to be gratified and encouraged by a considerable increase in Poland's trade with Russia. USFR, 1939, I, 332.

that the Kremlin was vitally interested in the survival of the border states and had no desire to face victorious German troops deployed along the western frontier of the Soviet Union.[70] This seemingly logical appraisal of the situation had to be drastically revised as a result of new developments which were already shaping up during the first days of August and which radically changed the whole international configuration before the end of that month.

On August 11 the British and French military missions, headed by Admiral Drax and General Doumenc, arrived in Moscow to start "technical" negotiations with the Soviet delegation, led by Marshal Voroshilov.[71] After a general discussion of the Western and Soviet plans of action in the event of hostilities in Europe, the talks took a sudden dramatic turn on August 14 when the Russians asked for a "definite answer" to the question whether the Red Army would be allowed to operate through Poland and Rumania; specifically, Voroshilov wanted to know whether Soviet troops would be permitted to march through the Wilno gap against East Prussia and to move through Galicia in order to "make contact" with the enemy.[72] When Doumenc assured the Soviet delegation that the Poles and Rumanians would "implore" the Russians to assist them, Voroshilov remained unmoved and demanded a precise answer to his question, insisting that "this was a cardinal point to the Soviet Union to which all other points were subordinate" and that it would be unfortunate if the Germans were allowed to destroy the Polish and Rumanian armies merely because the governments of those two countries were reluctant to ask for Soviet help.[73] The continuation of military discussions without a clear and conclusive solution of this problem appeared to the Russians as sheer waste of time.

After the contents of this discouraging conversation had been

[70] *DBFP*, 3d Series, VI, 767; see also *Czas*, June 2, 1939, and Szembek, p. 470.
[71] Semiofficial British record of these talks may be found in *DBFP*, 3d Series, VII (London, 1954), 561-93; for the Soviet version see "Negotiations between the Military Missions of the USSR, Britain and France in August 1939," *International Affairs* (Moscow), V, No. 2 (Feb., 1959), 110-23; No. 3 (March, 1959), 106-22.
[72] *DBFP*, 3d Series, VII, 573.
[73] *Ibid.*, pp. 572-73; see also the official statement of the Soviet military mission of August 14, 1939, as quoted in *International Affairs*, V, No. 2. 122-23.

duly communicated to London and Paris, the British and French governments decided to do everything in their power to enforce Warsaw's compliance. The Foreign Office considered it essential that Soviet troops should be permitted to throw their full force against the enemy:

Without early and effective Soviet assistance, neither Poland nor (still less) Rumania can hope to stand up to a German attack on land or in the air for more than a short time. The supply of arms and war material is not enough. The Soviet forces can only collaborate effectively on Polish or Rumanian soil. . . . To defer a decision until war breaks out will be too late. . . . Unless the required cooperation of Poland and Rumania is secured, negotiations . . . will break down. The effect of this on Soviet policy cannot be foreseen, but the possibility of a policy of accommodation with Germany should not be excluded. In that event Russia might either share the spoils with Germany at the expense of Poland and Rumania, or remain neutral and constitute the chief menace when the war was over.[74]

In the face of the mounting French and British pressure,[75] Beck tried at first to use evasive tactics, availing himself of all customary diplomatic subterfuges. While assuring the Quai d'Orsay that he would reconsider the whole matter,[76] he warned Poland's allies that the Russians were untrustworthy partners, that the value of their potential military contribution was extremely dubious,[77] and that Warsaw's agreement to the entry of Soviet troops could well result in an immediate declaration of war by Germany.[78] As time went on, however, Beck made no further attempt to dodge the issue by procrastination and imparted to the British ambassador his apprehensions that the Russians' insistence on marching through the Wilno gap and Eastern Galicia showed they were merely trying to isolate Poland by separating her from her Rumanian allies and from the Baltic countries.[79] The arguments that the breakdown of the negotiations could prompt Moscow to an agreement with Hitler and that it might be essential for Poland to

[74] *DBFP*, 3d Series, VII, 39.
[75] For a chronological account of all approaches made by the French and British ambassadors and military attachés to the Polish leaders during the second half of August see *ibid.*, pp. 558-60.
[76] *Ibid.*, p. 53.   [77] *Ibid.*, p. 54.   [78] *Ibid.*, p. 53.   [79] *Ibid.*, p. 70.

get supplies from the Soviet Union failed to dispel Beck's "innate mistrust of Russian intrigue" and seemed only to strengthen his determination to oppose the entry of the Red Army into Poland under whatever pretext.[80] While he postponed his answer and agreed to confer in the meantime with the highest state authorities, it was by now evident that only a negative reply could be expected. It was communicated to the ambassadors of the Western powers orally on August 19,[81] after extensive consultations with military leaders, including Marshal Śmigły-Rydz.[82] At the same time Beck tried to soothe the resentment of London and Paris with the assurances that he was prepared to do everything possible to facilitate the task of the British and French missions in Moscow; he also consented to treat the exchange of views between Poland and her allies as unofficial and to preserve secrecy as to its contents.[83]

While the Polish answer came as something of a shock to the Western powers, it was not entirely unexpected; indeed, some foreign observers were freely admitting that the Poles had valid political reasons for their attitude.[84] In Warsaw's opinion, to allow Soviet troops to occupy eastern Poland was tantamount to ceding it to Russia,[85] and there was a large amount of truth in Beck's statement that Marshal Voroshilov was trying to achieve by peaceful means what he had failed to win by force of arms in 1920.[86] Nevertheless the warnings voiced by Lord Halifax and disregarded by the Polish leaders were also based on some irrefutable arguments:

[80] *Ibid.;* see also Gafencu, p. 217.

[81] Beck declared on this occasion: "We are asked to endorse a new partition; if we are to be partitioned, we will at least defend ourselves. There is no guarantee . . . that the Russians, once they have established themselves in the eastern part of our country, would effectively participate in the war." Noël, p. 423; see also Beck, *Final Report,* pp. 193-94. The Polish chief of the General Staff shared these apprehensions. *DBFP,* 3d Series, VII, 61.

[82] General Musse, French military attaché in Warsaw, was unsuccessful in his personal attempt to persuade Śmigły-Rydz to accept military collaboration with the USSR. Noël, pp. 422-23.

[83] *DBFP,* 3d Series, VII, 86. According to Beck, he and the Allied ambassadors decided at that time that the text of the official reply to Voroshilov should stress the possibility of a friendly understanding between Poland and the Soviet Union in the event of an armed conflict with Germany. *Final Report,* p. 194.

[84] *DBFP,* 3d Series, VII, 87; see also *ibid.,* p. 112.

[85] See D. J. Dallin, p. 4.   [86] *DBFP,* 3d Series, VII, 86.

We may be on the brink of war in which within the next few weeks or even within the next few days Poland may be the victim of a crushing attack. If M. Beck thinks that he can avert or reduce the probability of such an attack merely by refraining from agreeing to accept assistance from the Soviet Union, I think that he is deluding himself. . . . I fully appreciate the disadvantages and risks of allowing Soviet troops on Polish soil; but these risks would seem to be preferable to the risk of the destruction of Polish independence for lack of their assistance, however unwelcome this may be; and the best way to avoid having to accept such assistance in fact is to promote the conclusion of an Anglo-Franco-Soviet agreement by assenting to the elaboration of plans for such assistance to be given in case of need.[87]

Meanwhile the Russians set the record straight by issuing an official denial of reports in some Polish newspapers that the deadlock in the Moscow negotiations had been reached as a result of the Kremlin's demands for British and French military assistance in the event of war in the Far East.[88] While describing these rumors as "sheer invention," the Tass communiqué of August 19 stressed that "differences of opinion which in fact exist are concerned with a completely different subject," thus suggesting indirectly that the real bone of contention lay in Warsaw's own backyard. On August 21 the Soviet press disclosed that a commercial credit agreement between Germany and the USSR had been signed in Berlin two days earlier, and *Pravda* commented editorially that this accord might prove "a serious step in the question of further improving not only economic but also political relations" between the two countries.[89] The time for an understanding between the Western powers and the Soviet Union was apparently running out, and Poland's allies found it harder than ever to conceal their irritation over Beck's "folly" and "recalcitrance."[90] Ambassador Noël was instructed to make a final attempt to get from the Polish government an authorization for General Doumenc to give a conditional pledge to the Russians that their troops would be permitted to enter Polish soil;[91] simultaneously Doumenc sent to Warsaw one of his assistants, Captain Beaufre, with the mission to

[87] *Ibid.*, pp. 88-89.
[88] *Pravda*, Aug. 19, 1939; see also *DBFP*, 3d Series, VII, 74.
[89] *Pravda*, Aug. 21, 1939.
[90] *DBFP*, 3d Series, VII, 102.   [91] *Ibid.*, p. 130.

"agir sur les Polonais."[92] However, while the French and the British left no stone unturned to persuade the Poles "to see reason," Warsaw remained adamant to their entreaties.[93]

In spite of the Polish objections, the French government instructed Doumenc to give the Russians an affirmative answer in principle to their query,[94] and the General requested Voroshilov to reopen the negotiations which had been adjourned since August 17. When the Marshal was informed that the French mission had now full authority to sign a military convention giving the right of passage to Soviet troops at the points specified by the Russians,[95] he saw at once through this rather awkward strategem and refused to be impressed by Doumenc's apparent compliance with the Kremlin's demands:

I ask whether there is a reply approved by the Polish and Rumanian governments, or merely a reply from the French government on the following lines: "We have put the question to Poland and we hope to receive a reply in the affirmative, etc." That is no reply for us. It is a useless waste of time. . . . We must have a definite reply from the governments of these countries, showing that they agree to the passage of our troops. . . . If the Poles had given an affirmative reply, they would have insisted on being present at our talks. As they have not done this, it means that they know nothing of the matter or that they do not agree.[96]

Thus the abortive plan of the Quai d'Orsay to save the situation by resorting to diplomatic subterfuges proved of no avail. At the same time Voroshilov informed Doumenc that it would be advisable to postpone any further meetings of the military missions until the political conditions were "clearer";[97] and, indeed, the next few days were to remove all remaining doubts and uncertainties. On August 22 it was officially announced that Ribbentrop was coming to Moscow to negotiate a nonaggression pact with the Soviet Union, and "the sinister news broke upon the world like an explosion."[98] All hopes and illusions born out of naïveté and wishful thinking were crumbling into dust, and the future seemed darker and more forbidding than ever.

---

[92] Reynaud, *Au coeur de la mêlée*, p. 308.
[93] *DBFP*, 3d Series, VII, 112.   [94] *Ibid.*, p. 107.
[95] *Ibid.*, p. 609.   [96] *Ibid.*, pp. 612-13.
[97] *Ibid.*, p. 141.   [98] Churchill, *The Gathering Storm*, p. 394.

This latest development in the war of nerves against Poland was, of course, not at all surprising to those who had seen the handwriting on the wall as early as October, 1938, and who realized the full significance of Hitler's Carpatho-Ukrainian gambit. After a few promising informal contacts between the German and Soviet representatives during the early spring of 1939, Ambassador Schulenburg was instructed by Ribbentrop to call on Molotov and to inform him that, in the event of a war between Poland and the Third Reich, the Nazis were prepared to make far-reaching concessions to the Russians:

If . . . it should come to hostilities with Poland, we are firmly convinced that even this need not in any way lead to a clash of interests with Soviet Russia. We can, even today, go so far as to say that when settling the German-Polish question—in whatever way this is done—we would take Russian interests into account as far as possible.[99]

The first moves made by Berlin were necessarily cautious and circumspect. The Germans were aware of the fact that the normalization of their relations with Moscow was "obstructed by a lot of rubble,"[100] which could be removed only gradually. Thus, during the conversations between State Secretary Weizsäcker and Soviet Chargé d'Affaires Astakhov an attempt was made to dispel the Kremlin's suspicions with regard to Hitler's Ukrainian plans and to persuade the Russians that "Beck's interpretation of [that] policy could . . . be best refuted by Germany's conduct over the Carpatho-Ukraine."[101] These approaches were apparently successful, for already on June 14 Astakhov reportedly told the Bulgarian minister to Berlin that, if Germany concluded a nonaggression pact with Russia, Moscow would very likely refrain from signing a treaty with Britain.[102] Ribbentrop considered, however, that "enough had been said" in the political field and that the talks should be temporarily suspended.[103]

It was only on July 26 that Dr. Schnurre mentioned, in a conversation with Astakhov, the possibility of a full-fledged agreement between the two countries; the Soviet Chargé d'Affaires responded to this suggestion with great interest and was especially

---

[99] DGFP, Series D, VI, 591.
[100] Ibid., p. 606.   [101] Ibid., p. 609.
[102] Ibid., p. 729.   [103] Ibid., p. 813.

anxious to know "whether the territories which once belonged to Austria were not . . . tending towards Germany, particularly the Galician and Ukrainian territories."[104] Schnurre's assurances that no German-Soviet clash of interests need result from this question seemed to pave the way for a "realistic" solution of the basic differences between Berlin and Moscow, and Schulenburg was instructed on July 29 to sound out Molotov. If the latter abandoned his reserve, he was to be told that the Germans were willing to reach an understanding with the Russians to respect their interests in Poland and in the Baltic countries.[105]

Ribbentrop was now tackling the whole problem with a sense of persistence and urgency.[106] On August 2 he had a personal meeting with Astakhov and reaffirmed Weizsäcker's and Schnurre's statements that there was no issue "from the Baltic to the Black Sea" that could not be settled by Germany and the Soviet Union to their mutual satisfaction; he also expressed his conviction that, in the event of a "Polish provocation," the Poles would be overwhelmed within a week, and in this connection hinted that the Nazis were willing to reach an understanding with Moscow on Poland's fate.[107] Schulenburg made a similar suggestion in his conversation with Molotov, but while the Soviet Premier appeared unusually frank and showed "evident interest," he still remained rather cautious in responding to German overtures.[108] It was obvious that the Kremlin preferred to adopt a wait-and-see attitude and to let the Western powers and Germany outbid each other in their concessions to the Soviet Union; indeed, it seemed to Schulenburg that the Russians were still seriously thinking of an agreement with Britain and France.[109] Moscow's reluctance to commit itself was also evident during Schnurre's meeting with Astakhov

---

[104] *Ibid.*, p. 1008. For a detailed account of the Soviet-German negotiations preceding the conclusion of the nonaggression pact see A. Dallin, "The Month of Decision: German-Soviet Diplomacy, July 22–August 22, 1939," *Journal of Central European Affairs*, IX (April, 1949), 1-31, and Rossi, *Le pacte germano-soviétique;* see also W. Basler, "Zur Vorgeschichte des deutsch-sowjetischen Nichtangriffspaktes 1939," Beiträge zur Geschichte der Beziehungen zwischen dem deutschen Volk und den Völkern der Sowjetunion, *Zeitschrift für Geschichtswissenschaft*, Band II (1954), Beiheft 1.

[105] *DGFP*, Series D, VI, 1016.   [106] See *ibid.*, p. 1047.

[107] *Ibid.*, p. 1050.   [108] *Ibid.*, pp. 1060-61.

[109] *Ibid.*, p. 1062.

on August 10; when asked about Russia's interests in Poland, the
Soviet diplomat answered that he had no instructions to discuss
this subject and that he doubted whether he would receive any
specific directives from his government regarding that complex
problem.[110] Only four days later, however, Astakhov was authorized by Molotov to inform the Germans that the USSR was willing to discuss all the questions that had been raised during the
preliminary talks, including the Polish issue.[111]

This general "declaration of intention" set the stage for the
decisive phase of German-Russian negotiations, based on the
premise that the "living spaces" of the USSR and the Third Reich
"touch each other, but . . . do not overlap."[112] The feverish activity of the next few days centered in Moscow, where Schulenburg was busy submitting to Molotov far-reaching proposals from
the Wilhelmstrasse, aimed at achieving a "basic and rapid" German-Russian rapprochement.[113] The Kremlin insisted that the
signature of a nonaggression pact could take place only a week
after the conclusion of the economic agreement, but Hitler's personal letter to Stalin[114] succeeded in changing the Soviet dictator's
mind, and Ribbentrop's arrival in Moscow was scheduled for August 23.

While Poland was hardly mentioned in the exchange of messages between Berlin and Moscow, it was obviously the acute crisis
in German-Polish relations that prompted the Nazis to conduct
the negotiations with Molotov at a breath-taking tempo. In any
case, the Polish problem occupied a prominent place in Ribbentrop's conversations with the Soviet leaders. According to the account of the German Foreign Minister,

we . . . discussed what should be done on the part of the Germans and on the part of the Russians in the case of an armed conflict. A line of demarcation was agreed upon . . . in order that in
the event of intolerable Polish provocation, or in the event of war,
there should be a boundary, so that the German and Russian interests in the Polish theater could and would not collide.[115]

[110] *Ibid.,* Series D, VII (Washington, 1956), 19.
[111] *Ibid.,* p. 59.   [112] *Ibid.,* p. 63.
[113] *Ibid.,* p. 84.   [114] For the text of this message see *ibid.,* p. 157.
[115] International Military Tribunal, *Trial of the Major War Criminals,* X, 268;
see also Ribbentrop, p. 112, and Kleist, pp. 54-63.

There was, of course, no reference to Poland in the text of the German-Soviet nonaggression pact of August 23, but her fate was settled in a secret additional protocol, which was to be regarded as an integral part of the treaty and was to come into effect "in the event of a territorial and political transformation of the territories belonging to the Polish state."[116] In accordance with this document, the "spheres of interest" of Germany and the Soviet Union were to be bounded "approximately by the line of the rivers Narew, Vistula, and San,"[117] and the question whether an independent Poland should be allowed to exist was to be decided at a later date by means of an understanding between the Nazis and the Russians. It was also agreed to recognize the interest of the Soviet Union in Bessarabia and that of Lithuania in the Wilno area; the northern frontier of Lithuania was to divide the "spheres of interest" of Germany and the USSR in the Baltic region.

The signature of the German-Soviet pact could not fail to produce a tremendous impression throughout the world. The event was generally recognized as one of the landmarks in the history of our times, and its importance for Poland's relations with both Berlin and Moscow could not be overestimated. Surprisingly enough, Beck was one of the few statesmen who professed to believe that this development, which actually destroyed the very foundation of his policy of balance, did not really change the situation, since the Russians had been evidently "playing a double game" for some time; in any case, he asserted, it would not affect Poland's attitude, and she would continue to support her allies in the defense of the principles of justice and integrity in international relations.[118] Apparently the only thing that worried the Polish

[116] For the text of the secret protocol see *DGFP*, Series D, VII, 246-47, and Degras, III, 360-61. The authenticity of the protocol is disputed by J. Bouvier and J. Gacon in their book *La vérité sur 1939*, pp. 195-97.

[117] As Molotov informed Schulenburg on August 25, the inadequacy of the maps used during the negotiations created a mistaken impression among the German and Soviet delegations that the upper course of the Narew extended to the frontier of East Prussia. *DGFP*, Series D, VII, 295-96. This mistake was later corrected by inserting into the text of the protocol the name of the river Pissa, a tributary of the Narew.

[118] *DBFP*, 3d Series, VII, 115-16. Beck apparently hoped that the German-Soviet treaty would contain an "escape clause," which would automatically void it if one of the contrahents attacked a third power (*USFR*, 1939, I, 301); at the same time, however, he did not exclude the possibility that Ribbentrop and Molotov might agree on a partition of Poland. *DBFP*, 3d Series, VII, 150.

Foreign Minister was the possible impact of the news from Moscow on French and British public opinion, which in the past had been inclined to rely too much upon the efficacy of Russian help.[119] Beck's views were shared by some of his associates, who regarded the Soviet-German treaty as the "counterpart of the Polish-Soviet nonaggression pact" and believed that Warsaw had no reason to expect an anti-Polish turn in Russian foreign policy;[120] far from being dismayed by the Soviet "betrayal," they felt that it vindicated Poland's wary attitude toward the USSR.[121]

In spite of the news about Ribbentrop's journey, the Western missions in Moscow refused to believe that further talks with the Soviet leaders were useless and pinned their hopes on the assurances of "competent Russian quarters" that the conclusion of the German-Soviet pact was "in no way incompatible" with the continuation of the Anglo-Franco-Russian negotiations.[122] The British and French ambassadors in Warsaw continued to persuade Beck to agree, at least in principle, to the passage of Soviet troops through Polish territory,[123] but received from him only a vague statement to the effect that, in the event of German aggression, collaboration between Poland and the USSR, "under technical conditions to be settled subsequently," was "not excluded."[124] This minor concession gave rise to rumors that the Poles had actually agreed to the entry of Russian troops,[125] and this misleading information was apparently communicated to General Doumenc in Moscow, thus adding to the confusion and uncertainty prevailing among the members of the Western delegations;[126] meanwhile Molotov, waiting for the results of his negotiations with Ribbentrop, accused Britain and France of "lack of sincerity" and of

[119] *DBFP*, 3d Series, VII, 116. The reaction of Polish public opinion to the pact was "surprisingly calm." *Ibid.*, pp. 204-5. The Polish press tended to discount the importance of the German-Russian rapprochement, emphasizing that it would not change the existing relationship of forces in Europe and describing it as a sign of weakness of both partners. See *Czas*, Aug. 23-25, 1939.

[120] *DBFP*, 3d Series, VII, 116; see also Szembek, p. 490.

[121] See the statement of the Polish Embassy in Washington in *The New York Times*, Aug. 22, 1939, and Beck's instructions to Polish diplomatic missions abroad quoted in Pobóg-Malinowski, III, 26.

[122] *DGFP*, Series D, VII, 208-9.   [123] Noël, p. 425.

[124] *DBFP*, 3d Series, VII, 150. Beck had told the British ambassador as early as August 18 that, if war should break out, Poland might modify her attitude with regard to the problem of Russian help. *Ibid.*, p. 70.

[125] *USFR*, 1939, I, 357.   [126] See Beloff, II, 271.

"playing" with the Soviet Union.[127] Finally, on August 25, Drax
and Doumenc were summoned to the Kremlin and told by Voroshilov that, in view of changed circumstances, it would be pointless to continue their conversations.[128] In a vehement diatribe, the
Marshal placed the blame for the failure of the talks squarely on
Warsaw's shoulders:

During the whole time of our conversations the Polish press and Polish
people were continuously saying that they did not want the help of
the Soviets, and from Rumania there was no answer at all. Were we
to have to conquer Poland in order to offer her our help, or were we
to go on our knees, and offer our help to Poland? The position was
impossible for us.[129]

Similar charges were repeated in Voroshilov's widely publicized
interview which appeared in the Soviet press two days later:

The Soviet military mission thought that the USSR, having no common frontier with the aggressor, could come to the help of France,
England, or Poland only if its troops were allowed to pass through
Polish territory, for there is no other way to come into contact with
the troops of the aggressor. . . .   Although it is completely obvious
that this attitude was correct, the French and English military missions did not agree with the Soviet mission in this, while the Polish
government openly stated that it did not need and would not accept
military aid from the USSR. This circumstance made military cooperation between the USSR and these countries impossible. This was
the basis of disagreement. It was on this that negotiations were broken
off.[130]

This line of argumentation was also followed by Molotov in his
speech to the Supreme Soviet on August 31, 1939; moreover, he
blamed the British for not attempting to remove the Polish objections and for actually "supporting" them.[131]

[127] *DBFP*, 3d Series, VII, 142.
[128] *Ibid.*, p. 225.   [129] *Ibid.*, p. 614.
[130] *Pravda*, Aug. 27, 1939; English translation quoted from Degras, III, 361-62.
Voroshilov hinted in the same interview that, in spite of this disappointing experience, the Soviet Union would be willing to assist Poland with raw materials
and military supplies.
[131] USSR, Verkhovnyi Sovet, *Sozyv I, Sessiia IV, Stenograficheskii otchët* (Moscow,
1939), pp. 197-98; English translation in *DBFP*, 3d Series, VII, 616.

The failure of the Moscow discussions prompted the Western statesmen to some sober afterthoughts; indeed, a few of them were wondering by now how their diplomats and negotiators could have been so "deceived" by the Russians.[132] While the evidence of Soviet-German contacts during the spring and summer of 1939 was still only circumstantial, there could be no doubt that the Russians had been conducting simultaneously two mutually contradictory sets of negotiations, carefully weighing the advantages offered them by the Western powers and balancing them against the gains promised by Germany. The proofs of Soviet duplicity were too obvious to be obscured by Voroshilov's ranting discourses or by Molotov's "hearty simplicity" in deploring the collapse of the talks.[133] Accusations of "perfidy" and "treachery" were liberally applied to the men in the Kremlin by their disgruntled would-be partners,[134] and Ambassador Seeds made this revealing statement in his report to Lord Halifax:

If I may be permitted a human touch at this serious moment I beg to be allowed to express my personal gratification at Your Lordship's instructions which enabled me, after months of patience and self-control, to accuse the Soviet Prime Minister to his face of "bad faith," a charge which an accuser cannot usually make and survive. That the accusation had to be made through a subservient and very frightened M. Potemkin as interpreter and witness was particularly galling to the recipient, who savagely asked whether those words figured textually in my instructions.[135]

[132] *USFR*, 1939, I, 302.

[133] *DBFP*, 3d Series, VII, 237.

[134] *Ibid.*, p. 244. The Western diplomats tended, of course, to overlook the fact that the decision to come to terms with Germany was, from Moscow's point of view, no less logical and justified than their own dismay and frustration about the failure to reach any agreement with the Soviet Union.

[135] *Ibid.*, p. 385.

VIII. The Catastrophe

The beginning of the German aggression against Poland in the morning hours of September 1, 1939, did not bring any immediate change in Polish-Soviet relations. On September 2 Grzybowski was instructed to see Molotov and to inform him officially about the state of war between Warsaw and Berlin. During the interview, which took place on September 3, the Soviet Premier never challenged the Ambassador's statement that the Third Reich was guilty of an unprovoked attack, and apparently "agreed in recognizing Germany as the aggressor."[1] He wanted to know, however, whether the Poles expected London and Paris to honor their treaty obligations with regard to Poland, and when Grzybowski replied that he anticipated a declaration of war by both Britain and France in the course of the next day, Molotov appeared to smile skeptically.

For the time being the Soviet Union was maintaining an attitude of outward friendliness toward Poland, and Sharonov even urged Beck to take advantage of the opportunity offered by Voroshilov in his interview of August 27 and to initiate without further delay negotiations with Moscow regarding the supply of raw materials and war equipment.[2] In accordance with this suggestion, a

[1] *Polish White Book,* p. 209; see also Beck, *Final Report,* p. 210. Later, an official publication of the Comintern charged that it was "the Polish capitalists and big landlords, inspired by England and France," who unleashed the conflict and "drove the peoples of Poland into war." *Kommunisticheskii Internatsional,* XXI, No. 8/9 (Aug.-Sept., 1939), 45; *The Communist International* (New York ed.), XVI, No. 10 (Oct., 1939), 1077.

[2] Ambassador Steinhardt reported from Moscow on August 28 that Grzybowski received instructions to act on the assumption that the Soviet government would give Poland economic assistance in the event of a Polish-German war and thus

special Polish courier was dispatched to the Soviet capital, but did
not arrive there before September 6; in the meantime, as Molotov
told Grzybowski during their next meeting, the entry of Britain
and France into the war had "created an entirely new situation,"[3]
radically different from that at the time of Voroshilov's interview.
Poland was now, from the Soviet point of view, "synonymous"
with her Western allies, and the USSR, anxious to preserve its
neutrality, had to direct its undivided attention to safeguarding its
own interests.[4] Russia was still willing to supply the Poles with
raw materials as stipulated by the terms of the trade agreement
between the two countries, but subsequent promises of additional
deliveries could not be fulfilled and the quotas for the current
year could not be increased. It was also impossible to grant the
Poles any transit facilities, since this would constitute a violation
of the German-Soviet nonaggression pact.[5] The situation might
change, however, and then, as Molotov intimated, a modification
of Moscow's attitude toward Poland could be expected.

While these fruitless conversations were going on and while the
Soviet press restricted its reporting of hostilities in Poland to
strictly factual and objective accounts, the Kremlin was engaged
in a lively exchange of secret messages with the Wilhelmstrasse,
most of them concerned with the various aspects of the Polish
question. As early as August 27 Schulenburg was instructed to
find out, in a discreet way, whether the reports about the withdrawal of Soviet troops from the Polish frontier were true and, if
necessary, ask Moscow to revoke such orders, since any appearance
of threat to Poland from the side of the USSR was bound to
weaken her defensive posture with regard to Germany and could
also influence Britain and France in their decision whether or not
to come to her assistance.[6] Although it was well known to all observers in the Soviet capital that the Red Army units on Russia's
western frontier were permanently maintained in a state of full
war strength,[7] Berlin was not satisfied with Molotov's oral assur-

---

make good the promises made on various occasions to the Poles by Molotov,
Potemkin, and Mikoyan. Warsaw also intended to ask the Russians to permit
Poland to import a certain amount of "essential materials" by the way of
Murmansk. *USFR*, 1939, I (Washington, 1956), 344-45.
   [3] *Polish White Book*, p. 188.   [4] *Ibid.*, p. 210.   [5] *Ibid.*, p. 188.
   [6] *DGFP*, Series D, VII (Washington, 1956), 362-63.   [7] *Ibid.*, p. 408.

ances and insisted that the Soviet government issue a special *démenti*. After some hesitation, the Kremlin yielded to the entreaties of the Nazis, and Tass was authorized to publish a statement to the effect that, "in view of the increasing gravity of the situation in the eastern territories of Europe and of the possibility of surprises," the Soviet high command decided to strengthen the garrisons on the western frontier of the USSR.[8]

As soon as the Western powers declared war on Germany, Ribbentrop began to urge Moscow to invade and occupy eastern Poland.[9] In order to prompt the Soviet leaders to make up their minds as soon as possible, the German Foreign Minister warned them that military considerations could compel the Wehrmacht to take action against Polish forces in the Russian "sphere of interest."[10] Molotov's answer, delivered to Schulenburg on September 5, was, however, full of caution and hesitation:

We agree with you that at a suitable time it will be absolutely necessary for us to start concrete action. We are of the view, however, that this time has not yet come. It is possible that we are mistaken, but it seems to us that through excessive haste we might injure our cause and promote unity among our opponents. We understand that as the operations proceed, one of the parties or both parties might be forced temporarily to cross the line of demarcation between the spheres of interest of the two parties; but such cases must not prevent the strict execution of the plan adopted.[11]

The guarded, restrained tone of this reply reflected to a certain extent the widespread apprehensions, apparently prevalent among the ruling circles of Russia, that the fluidity of the international situation increased the vulnerability of the USSR and that the Soviet Union could be drawn into the war even against its own will.[12] Nevertheless, while Ribbentrop agreed with Moscow's view that the extension of German military operations beyond the demarcation line should in no way affect the validity of the secret protocol of August 23, he directed Schulenburg to resume at once

[8] *Izvestiia*, Aug. 30, 1939.
[9] *DGFP*, Series D, VII, 541. At the same time special broadcasts from Germany tried to weaken the morale of the Polish Army by predicting Russia's imminent intervention in the war.
[10] *Ibid.* [11] *Ibid.*, Series D, VIII (Washington, 1954), 4. [12] *Ibid.*, p. 13.

his discussions with the Kremlin concerning Soviet intervention in Poland. Finally, the Russians appeared to give way, and Molotov, probably impressed by premature news about Warsaw's fall,[13] promised the German Ambassador on September 9 that Soviet action against Poland would commence "within the next few days."[14] Meanwhile the signs that a large-scale operation was being prepared by the Red Army began to multiply: a considerable number of reservists received mobilization orders,[15] some schools were converted into hospitals, and various goods, including foodstuffs and gasoline, became scarce or vanished from the market.[16]

On September 10 Molotov informed Schulenburg that, though over three million men had been mobilized, the Red Army needed a fortnight or possibly three weeks to complete its preparations, this delay being due to the fact that Soviet military authorities had expected a prolonged campaign in Poland and were "taken completely by surprise" by its rapid development. Moscow's original plan had been to wait for a further advance of the German Army, which would have enabled the Kremlin to declare that, since Poland was falling apart, it was the duty of the Soviet Union to come to the rescue of the Ukrainians and Belorussians "threatened" by the Wehrmacht.[17] This argument would have made Soviet intervention "plausible to the masses," without making the USSR appear as an aggressor; an official German report issued on the previous day indicated, however, that an armistice in Poland was imminent, and Russia could obviously not risk starting a "new war."[18]

While Molotov's apprehensions were based on an erroneous interpretation of a radio dispatch, they showed that the suspicion with which the Russians regarded their Nazi partners was still very much alive. It took several more days before German entreaties and persuasions convinced the Soviet rulers that it was no longer

[13] This spurious report prompted the Soviet Premier to send his congratulations to the German government. *Ibid.*, p. 34.

[14] *Ibid.*, p. 35.

[15] This partial mobilization was limited to the Ukraine, Belorussia, and the Leningrad, Moscow, Kalinin, and Orel military districts; according to an official statement published in the Soviet press, it was ordered because the Polish-German war was taking on "a broader and more threatening character." *Izvestiia*, Sept. 10, 1939; English translation in Degras, ed., III, 372.

[16] *DGFP*, Series D, VIII, 36.   [17] *Ibid.*, p. 44.   [18] *Ibid.*, p. 45.

possible to delay their intervention.[19] On September 14 Schulenburg was told that Russian troops were all but ready to strike
against Poland and that the operation would begin "sooner than
anticipated"; it was, however, impossible to start any action before
the fall of Warsaw, which alone could give weight to the argument
that the Polish state was about to disintegrate.[20] The Germans
assured the Kremlin that the Polish capital would be occupied in
a few days' time[21] and warmly welcomed Moscow's decision to intervene:

The Soviet government thus relieves us of the necessity of annihilating
the remainder of the Polish Army by pursuing it as far as the Russian
boundary. Also the question is disposed of whether, in the absence of
a Russian intervention, a political vacuum might not occur in the
area lying to the east of the German zone of influence.[22]

In order to clarify the situation, Ribbentrop proposed the publication of a German-Soviet communiqué which would stress the
anxiety of the two governments to put an end to the "intolerable
political and economic conditions" existing in Poland and to restore "peace and order" in their respective spheres of influence;
this joint statement would obviate the necessity of using the alleged "threat" to the Ukrainians and Belorussians by Germany as
an excuse for Soviet intervention. He also suggested that a mixed
military commission be established with the purpose of coordinating the operations of the Wehrmacht and the Red Army.[23]

The Germans were apparently concerned over a considerable
stiffening of the Polish resistance, especially in the regions of Warsaw and Lwów,[24] and wanted to complete their eastern campaign
before the coming of the rainy season brought the operations of
their armored and motorized divisions to a standstill.[25] For the
time being, however, nothing was happening at the Polish-Russian
border. Ambassador Sharonov, during his meeting with Beck at

[19] Ibid., p. 44.   [20] Ibid., pp. 60-61.
[21] Ibid., p. 68. Actually German troops did not enter Warsaw until September 30.
[22] Ibid., p. 69.   [23] Ibid., p. 70.
[24] Marshal Śmigły-Rydz informed Beck at the same time that the German pressure was weakening as a result of the wearing out of the enemy's troops and
equipment. Beck, Final Report, p. 225.
[25] DGFP, Series D, VIII, 69.

Krzemieniec (where the diplomatic corps had been evacuated from Warsaw) on September 11, discounted rumors about an impending Soviet attack on Poland and attributed partial mobilization in Russia to the fact that the Germans were bombing some targets on the western frontier of the USSR, thus forcing Moscow to take precautionary measures.[26] In spite of his rather optimistic appraisal of the situation on the Polish-German front,[27] Sharonov decided to leave Poland temporarily in order to get in touch with the Narkomindel by telephone, but promised to return in two days' time or, should he be ordered to report in person to his superiors in Moscow, within a week.[28] Before his departure for Shepetovka on September 12, he granted visas to two Polish officials who were being sent to Russia to negotiate about the purchase of medical supplies, and also expressed his hope that Poland would be able to secure delivery of other goods from the USSR.[29]

The reassuring attitude displayed by the Soviet Ambassador failed to allay Beck's fears that the Russians might try to take advantage of Poland's serious situation;[30] in fact, Communist agitators were already busy spreading rumors that Berlin and Moscow had reached an agreement concerning a new partition of Poland, and that the Red Army was only waiting for an opportune moment to occupy the eastern borderlands.[31] The local population received the news about these impending changes rather passively, with a curious mixture of apathy and disbelief; the war with Germany was still going on and continued to monopolize the undivided attention of the whole country.

Meanwhile the tension along the Polish-Russian frontier began

[26] Polish White Book, p. 189; see also F. Sławoj-Składkowski, "Prace i czynności Rządu Polskiego we wrześniu 1939 r." [The Activities of the Polish Government in September, 1939], Kultura, 1948, No. 5, p. 113.

[27] It is noteworthy that a few days earlier Sharonov assured one of the foreign diplomats that the Germans would stop their advance before reaching Krzemieniec, and that Lwów, too, would escape the Nazi occupation; this would seem to indicate that he was already informed about the terms of the Soviet-German secret protocol of August 23. See Noël, p. 498.

[28] Polish White Book, p. 188.

[29] Sharonov left Krzemieniec accompanied by his military attaché and some other members of the personnel of the Soviet Embassy; the remaining officials, headed by the second secretary, stayed in Poland. Beck, Final Report, p. 220; Polish White Book, p. 188.

[30] Beck, Final Report, p. 220.   [31] Noël, p. 497; Beck, Final Report, p. 221.

suddenly to increase. On September 14 Tass reported that Polish
planes were violating with a disturbing frequency the borders of the
USSR, endeavoring to penetrate far into Soviet territory.[32] On the
same day, *Pravda* published an editorial "On the Internal Causes
of Poland's Military Defeat," obviously written with the specific
purpose of providing the necessary justification for the approaching intervention.[33] According to that article, the complete rout of
the Polish Army was caused not only by Germany's superior might
or by the absence of any effective help from Great Britain and
France but also by Poland's internal weaknesses and contradictions:

Polish ruling circles . . . did everything possible to worsen their
relations with national minorities and to bring them to a state of
extreme tension. The national policy of the ruling circles of Poland
is characterized by the oppression and humiliation of national minorities, especially of the Ukrainians and Belorussians . . . who
are subject to the crudest, most shameless exploitation by Polish landowners. . . . The ruling circles of Poland did everything to transform the Western Ukraine and Western Belorussia into a lawless
colony, handed over to the Polish gentry for pillage.[34]

The ominous significance of this editorial could not escape the
attention of foreign observers in Moscow, and it was generally expected that it would be followed by a diplomatic action on the
part of the Soviet government, such as the denunciation of the
nonaggression pact of 1932.[35] In any case, it was obvious that fateful decisions regarding Poland were about to be made. On September 15 the Russians secured themselves a free hand in the west by
signing an agreement with Japan to end the conflict on the Mon-
golian-Manchurian frontier.[36] On September 16 Molotov received
Schulenburg at 6 P.M. and informed him that the Red Army would
begin its action shortly—"perhaps even tomorrow or the day

---

[32] *Izvestiia*, Sept. 14, 1939; *Vneshniaia politika SSSR*, IV, 445. Some Polish aircraft were allegedly chased back over the border; four planes were forced to land
in the Soviet Union, and their crews were detained by the Russian authorities.
[33] *DGFP*, Series D, VIII, 61.   [34] *Pravda*, Sept. 14, 1939.
[35] *Polish White Book*, p. 211; see also Italy, Ministero degli Affari Esteri, *I documenti diplomatici italiani*, 9th Series, I (Rome, 1954), 128, and *USFR*, 1939, I, 432.
[36] See *Izvestiia*, Sept. 16, 1939, and Degras, III, 373-74.

after."[37] Stalin was conferring at that very time with the military leaders and would himself communicate to the Ambassador the results of this consultation. The reasons and objectives of Moscow's intervention were to be explained in the press and radio and in official notes to all diplomatic missions accredited to the Kremlin. While the argument about the protection of national minorities against the Nazi threat was perhaps obnoxious to the Germans, the Russians were unable to use any other motivation, for, as Molotov admitted with brutal frankness, "the Soviet Union had heretofore not bothered about the plight of its minorities in Poland and had to justify abroad, in some way or other, its present intervention."[38]

At 8 P.M. Schulenburg was finally summoned to the presence of Stalin who, flanked by Molotov and Voroshilov, informed him that Soviet troops would cross the Polish frontier at 6 A.M. on September 17 along the line Polotsk–Kamenets-Podolsk.[39] The Soviet air force would immediately open its operations against the targets east of Lwów, and it was advisable that German planes should stay clear of the territory situated eastward of the line Białystok–Brest Litovsk–Lwów. A Soviet mission would be dispatched forthwith to Białystok to establish contact with the Wehrmacht and to prevent any possible incidents between the two advancing armies. At Schulenburg's request, Stalin agreed to change some points in the note to Poland explaining reasons for Moscow's action, but thought it necessary to postpone the publication of a joint Soviet-German communiqué for two or three days.[40]

The great tragedy was now moving toward its denouement. At 2:15 A.M. Ambassador Grzybowski was asked by telephone to come to Potemkin's office at three o'clock. The Deputy Commissar for Foreign Affairs, obviously deeply stirred by the dramatic qualities of the situation, read to him the text of the note which was intended to justify the imminent violation of the Polish-Soviet nonaggression pact:

[37] *DGFP*, Series D, VIII, 76. For an account of Soviet plans and preparations for the invasion see Pospelov, ed., I, 248.
[38] *DGFP*, Series D, VIII, 77.   [39] *Ibid.*, p. 79.   [40] *Ibid.*, p. 80.

The Polish-German war has revealed the internal bankruptcy of the Polish state. In ten days of hostilities Poland has lost all her industrial regions and cultural centers. Warsaw as the capital of Poland no longer exists. The Polish government has collapsed and shows no signs of life. This means that the Polish state and its government have virtually ceased to exist. Treaties concluded between the USSR and Poland have thereby ceased to operate. Abandoned to her fate and left without leadership, Poland has become a fertile field for any accidental and unexpected contingency, which may create a menace to the USSR. Hence, while it was neutral hitherto, the Soviet government can no longer maintain a neutral attitude toward these facts. Nor can the Soviet government remain indifferent when its blood brothers, the Ukrainians and Belorussians living on Polish territory, having been abandoned to their fate, are left without protection. In view of this state of affairs, the Soviet government has instructed the high command of the Red Army to order troops to cross the frontier and to take under their protection the lives and property of the population of the Western Ukraine and Western Belorussia. At the same time the Soviet government intends to take every step to deliver the Polish people from the disastrous war into which they have been plunged by their unwise leaders and to give them an opportunity to live a peaceful life.[41]

It would be futile to dwell on the problem whether the Soviet invasion was justified from the legal point of view, though it is obvious that no country "ceases to exist" as a result of military occupation.[42] Ambassador Grzybowski at once described Moscow's note as a unilateral abrogation of existing and binding international agreements; while protesting against its contents and form, he refused to accept it or to transmit its text to his government.

[41] *Pravda*, Sept. 18, 1939; Degras, III, 374.
[42] For a comprehensive discussion of this question from the point of view of international law see G. Ginsburgs, "The Soviet Union as a Neutral, 1939-1941," *Soviet Studies*, X, No. 1 (July, 1958), 24-27; see also Montanus, p. 23. As Grzybowski observed, the occupation of Serbia and Belgium in 1914-18 had not affected the legal status of those countries (*Polish White Book*, p. 211); similarly, a declaration made by Secretary of State Cordell Hull on October 2, 1939, stressed that "mere seizure of territory . . . does not extinguish the legal existence of a government" (quoted from *The New York Times*, Oct. 3, 1939). It should be added, however, that Poland had dropped sanctions against Italy in June, 1936, because, in Beck's words, "unfortunate Abyssinia had already ceased, *de facto*, to exist as an independent country." Beck, *Dernier rapport*, pp. 107-8; deleted from the English translation.

At the same time he pointed out that the President of Poland and the duly constituted authorities of the country were still performing their functions on Polish soil[43] and that Polish troops continued to fight the enemy, thus defending the sovereign rights of the state.[44]

After this brief legalistic discourse, Grzybowski made a pathetic appeal to "Slavonic solidarity" (which had been so contemptuously disregarded by Poland at the time of Munich), but his emotional plea failed to call forth a sympathetic response. Finally, after fruitless attempts to convince the Ambassador that he should take the contents of the note into cognizance and that in any case the Poles would have been unable to stop the German onslaught before it reached the frontiers of Russia, Potemkin agreed to refer the matter to his superiors and to convey to them Grzybowski's entreaties to stop the invasion and to desist from stabbing Poland in the back.[45] However, the Soviet rulers, apparently oblivious of Stalin's pledge to support "nations which are the victims of aggression and are fighting for the independence of their country,"[46] refused to change their decision,[47] and the Ambassador also persisted in his determination not to accept the fateful document, promising only to inform his government of the fact of the aggression.[48]

[43] President Mościcki resided at that time at Załucze, a village near the Rumanian frontier. Most of the government departments were located at Kuty and Kosów (well-known resorts in the Carpathians), while Marshal Śmigły-Rydz and his headquarters operated at Kołomyja.

[44] When the Red Army crossed the Polish-Soviet border, the great battle around Kutno and the fighting in the region between the Vistula and the Bug were still in progress. The Poles had succeeded in throwing back the *Panzer* units approaching Lwów, and the defenders of Warsaw, Oksywie, and the Hel peninsula continued to resist enemy attacks. Most military experts seem to agree, however, that the campaign in Poland was lost even before the entry of Soviet troops, although the Russian invasion undoubtedly hastened the collapse of the Polish Army. See Kirchmayer, p. 8.

[45] *Polish White Book*, p. 212.

[46] CPSU, *XVIII S"ezd VKP(b), Stenograficheskii otchët*, p. 15; Degras, III, 321.

[47] *Polish White Book*, p. 212.

[48] The dramatic night interview with Potemkin was only the beginning of Grzybowski's troubles. When he, in accordance with Beck's instructions, demanded his passports on September 19, the Deputy Commissar refused to acknowledge the diplomatic privileges of the personnel of the Polish Embassy and the consulates in the USSR on the ground that the Soviet government no longer recognized the existence of the Polish state. Only after the intervention of the doyen of the diplomatic corps in Moscow did Molotov agree to reconsider Potemkin's ruling, but the

The news about the Soviet invasion caught the Polish high command completely by surprise; it disrupted all defensive plans prepared by the General Staff and put an end to any hopes that an effective resistance might be organized in southeastern Poland.[49] Soviet armored divisions and motorized troops quickly overwhelmed sparse detachments of the frontier guards and a few depleted units of the regular Polish Army, and rapidly advanced westward, trying to intercept the refugees and evacuees moving toward the Rumanian frontier;[50] at the same time millions of leaflets were dropped over eastern Poland, inciting the local population to start an uprising against their "eternal enemies, the Polish landlords."[51] Marshal Śmigły-Rydz considered it necessary that the Polish government leave the country as soon as the Russians had crossed the line of the Dniester, in order to escape capture with all its unforeseeable consequences,[52] and the Rumanian ambassador offered on behalf of King Carol "hospitality or the right of transit" to the Poles.[53] Beck, in accepting this proposal, informed Ambassador Grigorcea that, in view of the difficult international situation, he would not demand that Rumania honor her treaty obli-

permission for the departure of the Poles was withheld until the staff of the Soviet Embassy in Warsaw left the besieged city and arrived in Königsberg. In the meantime, the acting consul-general in Kiev, Matusiński, "disappeared" on his way to see a plenipotentiary of the Narkomindel, and the Soviet authorities refused to give any information about his fate. After fruitless attempts to obtain his release, the Polish Ambassador and his staff left Russia on October 11, 1939. *Ibid.,* pp. 212-14. According to Mr. Grzybowski's letter to the author of October 13, 1958, Matusiński spent the winter of 1939-40 in a Moscow prison, and probably died there in 1940 or 1941.

[49] According to these plans, a bridgehead was to be established in Eastern Galicia between the Dniester and Stryj rivers, but the Soviet onslaught prevented its completion and made impossible the withdrawal of some 200-300,000 Polish soldiers into Rumania and Hungary. The Red Army alone captured about 60,000 prisoners in that area, while some 90,000 surrendered to the Germans; 32,000 succeeded in escaping to Rumania and 35,000 to Hungary. See Anders, p. 11; Norwid-Neugebauer, pp. 105-6, 131, 134; Poland, Polskie Siły Zbrojne, Komisja Historyczna, *Polskie Siły Zbrojne w drugiej wojnie światowej,* I, Part I, 281; see also the last order of the day issued by Marshal Śmigły-Rydz on September 20, 1939, as quoted by Sławoj-Składkowski in "Prace i czynności Rządu Polskiego," *Kultura,* 1948, No. 6, pp. 119-20.

[50] See G. I. Antonov, "The March into Poland, September 1939," in Liddell Hart, pp. 73-78.

[51] H. Vashchenko, " 'Vyzvolennia' Zakhidn'oi Ukrainy bol'shevykamy: Ofitsiini dokumenty i diisnist'," *Ukrains'kyi Zbirnyk* (Munich), I (Dec., 1954), 67-68; see also A. Claire, "The Workers and Peasants Draw New Boundaries," *The Communist International* (New York ed.), XVI, No. 11 (Nov., 1939), 1139.

[52] Beck, *Final Report,* p. 229.   [53] *Ibid.,* p. 228.

gations with regard to Poland;[54] he hoped, however, that the question of transit of the Polish authorities through Rumanian territory would be approached by Bucharest "with a maximum of goodwill."[55] Before leaving the country in the morning hours of September 18, Beck notified the Polish embassies in London and Paris that the legal government of Poland, while still functioning within the territory of the Republic, had protested to Moscow against the Soviet invasion and expected its allies to take similar steps; it also reserved the right to call upon Britain and France to fulfill their treaty obligations with regard to Poland.[56]

While Red troops were pouring into Poland and the Soviet press was full of reports about the jubilation and indescribable joy allegedly displayed by the local population in welcoming their "liberators,"[57] the Nazis and the Russians were still filled with

[54] As Beck explains in his memoirs, he did not ask the Rumanian government to regard the Soviet invasion as *casus foederis* because of his conviction that this appeal would remain unheeded. *Ibid.*, p. 226; see also *USFR*, 1939, I, 430.

[55] Beck, *Final Report*, p. 228. These hopes were not fulfilled: in Beck's own words, the attitude of the Rumanian authorities toward President Mościcki and the former members of the Polish government "could not be justified by any international conventions or any customs based on tradition." *Ibid.*, p. 233; see also W. Pobóg-Malinowski, "Na rumuńskim rozdrożu" [At the Rumanian Crossroads], *Kultura*, 1948, No. 7, pp. 116-33; No. 8, pp. 80-116; No. 9/10, pp. 130-78, and A. Cretzianu, "Rumunia a wrzesień 1939" [Rumania and September of 1939], *Kultura*, No. 3/77 (March, 1954), pp. 106-15.

[56] *Polish White Book*, p. 190; Beck, *Final Report*, p. 226. The Western reaction to the Soviet aggression showed a conspicuous lack of unanimity. Most of the leading newspapers had only contempt for Moscow's "base and despicable" conduct (*The Times* [London], Sept. 18, 1939), but there were some notable exceptions (such as Lloyd George's article, "What Is Stalin Up To?" in *The Sunday Express*, Sept. 24, 1939). The official statement of the British Ministry of Information of September 18 was necessarily restrained in its tone and only asserted that the invasion could not be justified by the arguments put forward by Russia. *The New York Times*, Sept. 19, 1939. While Prime Minister Chamberlain deplored the "cynical attack" and sympathized with its "unhappy victim" (Great Britain, *Parliamentary Debates*, House of Commons, 5th Series, CCCLI, 977), Churchill considered that the Soviet action "was clearly necessary for the safety of Russia against the Nazi menace" and publicly welcomed the creation of a new "Eastern Front." In a paper submitted to the War Cabinet on September 25, he wrote: "Russia has occupied the same line and positions as the enemy of Poland, which possibly she might have occupied as a very doubtful and suspected friend. The difference in fact is not so great as might seem." Churchill, *The Gathering Storm*, pp. 448-49. The British and French embassies in Moscow shared this view and advised their governments against any drastic anti-Soviet measures which "could only benefit Germany without helping Poland." *USFR*, 1939, I, 433.

[57] In some places Soviet troops were accorded a friendly reception owing to the rumors that they were coming to help the Polish Army against the Germans. Noël, p. 504, and Beck, *Dernier rapport*, p. 325. For a firsthand account of the

mutual suspicions, and Stalin was reluctant to believe that the German Army would withdraw to the demarcation line as stipulated by the secret protocol.[58] On September 18 a joint Soviet-German communiqué, drafted by Stalin himself, was published in both capitals. It stated that the German and Soviet forces did not pursue any objectives contrary to the interests of Moscow and Berlin, and intended only to "restore peace and order in Poland" and to help the Poles in establishing "new conditions" for their political life.[59] Only two days later, however, Molotov imparted to Schulenburg the Kremlin's apprehensions that the Germans were planning to leave Lwów on their side of the boundary, and asked him to clarify this matter without delay.[60] Another controversy settled amicably at the same time was also concerned with the delimitation of the two "spheres of interest." The Nazis proposed that the demarcation line should, instead of following the upper San, leave the city of Przemyśl to Germany and then run southward through Turka to the Użok Pass, but this modification, quite sensible from the strategic point of view, was unacceptable to the Russians.[61] A joint communiqué issued on September 22 defined the provisional demarcation line between the two armies in accordance with the stipulations of the secret protocol.[62] Meanwhile, the Red Army was moving with a considerable speed toward the "four-river line." On September 19 it took Wilno, and Lwów surrendered on the following day; Białystok and Brest Litovsk were reached on September 22, and within the next four days Soviet troops occupied Chełm, Zamość, Augustów, and Suwałki, thus penetrating into the very heart of the Polish state and approaching the southeastern fringe of East Prussia.[63]

Soviet invasion see Makukh, pp. 484-86, and Z. Sobieski, "Reminiscenes from Lwów, 1939-1946," *Journal of Central European Affairs*, VI (Jan., 1947), 351-53.

[58] *DGFP*, Series D, VIII, 92.   [59] *Izvestiia*, Sept. 20, 1939; *DGFP*, Series D, VIII, 97.

[60] *DGFP*, Series D, VIII, 104. Some spurious reports credited Hitler at that time with plans to make Lwów the capital of a Western Ukrainian puppet state, which he "might some day use as a stepping stone to the Russian Ukraine." *The New York Times*, Sept. 15, 1939.

[61] *DGFP*, Series D, VIII, 109-10, 113.

[62] *Pravda*, Sept. 23, 1939; *DGFP*, Series D, VIII, 122.

[63] On their westward march, Russian troops had to fight what Molotov later described as "serious encounters" with scattered and disarrayed units of the Polish Army in the regions of Kowel, Wilno, Orany, Grodno, and Białystok, and espe-

In order to put an end to all uncertainties and to remove all causes that could conceivably lead to friction in the future, the Russians were now ready to "establish definitively, jointly with the German government, the structure of the Polish area," and to partition the whole of Poland between the two powers, while abandoning at the same time the project providing for the creation of a residual Polish state;[64] they also proposed that Germany give up her claim to Lithuania in exchange for the whole of the province of Lublin and a part of the province of Warsaw.[65] The negotiations concerning this subject and other pending issues were to take place in Moscow. On September 23 Ribbentrop declared his readiness to go once more to the Soviet capital, and his talks with the Russian leaders were tentatively scheduled for the end of the month.[66]

The Moscow discussions, which took place on September 27 and 28, were concerned chiefly with the problem of final frontier settlement. The Germans were offered a choice of two alternatives: they could either retain Lithuania in their sphere of influence, with the boundary in Poland following the course of the Pissa, Narew, Vistula, and San rivers, or surrender their "rights" to Lithuania in return for additional Polish teritory between the Bug and the Vistula and the tip around Suwałki. The Russians quite obviously favored the latter proposal, and Stalin contended that it would be unwise to split the territory inhabited by a purely Polish population:

History has proved that the Polish people continually struggle for unification. To partition the Polish population would therefore easily create sources of unrest from which discord between Germany and the Soviet Union might possibly arise.[67]

---

cially in the Polesie area, where resistance continued until October 5. Norwid-Neugebauer, pp. 135-36. While these engagements had only a local importance, the casualties suffered by the Red Army reached a total of 2,599, including 737 killed. These losses were counterbalanced by a war booty which consisted of some 900 guns, 10,000 machine guns, 300,000 rifles, and 300 airplanes. USSR, Verkhovnyi Sovet, *Sozyv I, Sessiia V, Stenograficheskii otchët* (Moscow, 1939), p. 13; Degras, III, 392-93.

[64] *DGFP*, Series D, VIII, 105; see also *ibid.*, p. 130.

[65] *Ibid.*, p. 130.   [66] *Ibid.*, pp. 123-24.

[67] *Ibid.*, p. 160. Stalin found it convenient to ignore the fact that the boundary proposed by him left some purely Polish areas under Soviet rule.

The arguments used by the Soviet dictator seemed to impress Ribbentrop, who was also anxious to eliminate the possibility of "Polish intrigues for disturbing German-Russian relations," and hoped that the solution along the lines proposed by Moscow would enable the Nazis to deal with the Polish question at their discretion.[68] At the same time he made an attempt to enlarge the German share of the spoils by suggesting that the new boundary should run in a straight line from Brest Litovsk past Grodno to the Niemen river, and then west of Kaunas to the Latvian frontier, but Stalin was not willing to make any further concessions; the Soviet rulers also resisted successfully Ribbentrop's claim to the oil district of Drohobycz and Borysław, promising only to supply Germany with the whole annual production of petroleum from that area.[69] The final decision was referred to Hitler, who agreed, "with some misgivings," to barter Lithuania for additional slices of Poland.[70]

Having thus solved the territorial issue, the two parties agreed to recognize the frontier settlement as final and proclaimed their readiness to "eliminate any interference by third powers with this decision."[71] The "reorganization" of Polish territory was to become "a reliable foundation for the further development of friendly relations" between Germany and Russia. In a secret protocol, both partitioning powers stressed their determination not to tolerate "Polish agitation which affects the territories of the other party," and pledged themselves to "suppress in their territories all beginnings of such agitation and inform each other concerning suitable measures for this purpose."[72] A declaration bearing the signatures of Ribbentrop and Molotov claimed that the Soviet Union and the Third Reich had created "a firm founda-

[68] *Ibid.*, p. 161.   [69] *Ibid.*, p. 160.

[70] Ribbentrop, p. 129. Lithuania, before losing her own independence, also received territorial gains at the expense of Poland. By an agreement signed in Moscow on October 10, 1939, the Soviet Union transferred to Lithuania the city and the district of Wilno "for the purpose of consolidating the friendship" between the two nations. *Pravda*, Oct. 11, 1939; Degras, III, 381.

[71] *Pravda*, Sept. 29, 1939; Degras, III, 377. There is a certain analogy between this declaration and the convention signed by Russia, Prussia, and Austria on January 26, 1797, which also asserted that a "complete, final, and irrevocable" partition of Poland had been accomplished.

[72] *DGFP*, Series D, VIII, 166.

THE FOURTH PARTITION OF POLAND

Based on Brown and Herlin, *The War in Maps*

tion for a lasting peace in Eastern Europe" and suggested that it would be in the general interest of humanity to put an end to the war between Germany and Poland's Western allies.[73]

The "Friendship and Frontier Treaty" of September 28, 1939, was welcomed by the Soviet press as a great triumph of Moscow's foreign policy;[74] this reaction showed that the Kremlin regarded its understanding with Germany as a profitable deal.[75] The new boundary was much more advantageous to the Soviet Union than the Curzon line; it left to Russia not only the provinces acquired by her as a result of the third partition of Poland but also the region of Białystok (first annexed in 1807) and the whole of Eastern Galicia, which (with the exception of the district of Tarnopol) had never belonged to the Tsarist Empire.[76] These territories were officially incorporated into the USSR only after elaborate attempts to "legalize" the annexation. Early in October the "Provisional City Council" of Lwów (appointed by Soviet military authorities) called upon "the population of the Western Ukraine" to elect, by means of a "general, equal, direct, and secret vote," a "National Assembly," which would decide the question "of the state existence of the Western Ukraine"; this proposal was duly supported by the provisional city councils of Stanisławów, Tarnopol, and Łuck.[77] At the same time, a similar appeal to "the population of Western Belorussia" was issued by the "Provisional City

[73] *Ibid.*, p. 167. While the Soviet Union was apparently interested in the continuation of the war in Western Europe, its active participation in the "peace offensive" initiated by Hitler after the conquest of Poland was undoubtedly a useful propaganda move, designed to vindicate the tarnished reputation of the USSR as an "unselfish" and "persistent" champion of peace. See *Izvestiia*, Sept. 30, 1939.

[74] *Pravda*, Sept. 30, 1939.

[75] See Ribbentrop, p. 131, and Hilger and Meyer, p. 307.

[76] The total area taken over by the USSR covered some 196,000 square kilometers with a population of about 13 million, including, according to official Polish statistics, 5,274,000 Poles, 4,529,000 Ukrainians, 1,123,000 Belorussians, 1,109,000 Jews, 134,000 Russians, and 711,000 persons described in the census of 1931 as "speaking local language." See O. Halecki, "Polish-Russian Relations—Past and Present," *The Review of Politics*, V (July, 1943), 334; *Poland and the USSR, 1921-1941*, p. 135, gives slightly different figures. Molotov claimed, in his speech of October 31, 1939, that in the territory which had passed to the USSR there were "more than 7 million Ukrainians, more than 3 million Belorussians, over 1 million Poles, and over 1 million Jews." USSR, Verkhovnyi Sovet, *Sozyv I, Sessiia V, Stenograficheskii otchët*, p. 14; Degras, III, 393.

[77] *Pravda*, Oct. 11, 1939. For details see Babii, pp. 81-116.

Council" of Białystok.[78] The elections, which took place on October 22, were supervised by special committees, including the representatives of the Supreme Soviets of the Ukrainian and Belorussian Soviet Socialist Republics; the voters had to cast their ballots for or against a single slate of candidates. The "National Assemblies," meeting at Lwów (October 26-27) and Białystok (October 28-29), resolved "unanimously" to request the Supreme Soviet of the USSR to "accept the peoples of the Western Ukraine and Western Belorussia into the great family of Soviet peoples"; the Fifth Extraordinary Session of the Supreme Soviet (October 31–November 2, 1939) decided to "comply" with these petitions.[79]

The Nazi-Soviet rapprochement and its aftermath proved to the world that hostility toward Poland remained one of the strongest bonds between Germany and Russia; it also had, at least temporarily, a sobering influence upon public opinion in the Western countries. An editorial in *The New York Times* commented:

The most immediate effect is the complete moral and "ideological" change which this working alliance must bring. It clears the air. It will sweep illusions from millions of minds. . . . The world will now understand that the only real "ideological" issue is one between democracy, liberty and peace on the one hand and despotism, terror and war on the other.[80]

[78] *Pravda*, Oct. 12, 1939.
[79] See USSR, Verkhovnyi Sovet, *Sozyv I, Sessiia V, Stenograficheskii otchët*, pp. 29-102, and Babii, pp. 172-84.
[80] *The New York Times*, Sept. 18, 1939.

Conclusion

The ancient conflict dividing the Russians and the Poles has for centuries exerted a decisive influence on the destinies of Eastern and East Central Europe. The long and bitter struggle between Warsaw and Moscow for political and cultural hegemony over the vast area extending from the Baltic to the Black Sea and from the Bug to the eastern fringes of the Ukraine mobilized and arrayed against each other the forces of the two leading Slavic nations and of two different civilizations which they represented. During the interval between the world wars, this age-old antagonism assumed new and even more momentous significance, with the reborn Polish state facing a threat which transcended national and cultural dimensions and seemed to imperil, directly or indirectly, the political and social systems of all non-Communist countries. The danger of what Winston Churchill called "a poisoned Russia, an infected Russia, a plague-bearing Russia," spreading "doctrines which destroyed the health and even the soul of nations,"[1] was especially real to the next-door neighbors of the USSR. It forced their leaders to be constantly mindful of the double nature of the Soviet regime as the ruling authority of a territorial state and as the center of a world-wide revolutionary movement, whose attitude toward other countries was motivated both by the requirements of *raison d'état* and by the sense of a universal ideological mission.[2]

[1] Churchill, *The Aftermath*, p. 263.
[2] For a discussion of the problem of ideology and national interest in Soviet diplomacy see V. Aspaturian, "Soviet Foreign Policy," in R. C. Macridis, ed., *Foreign Policy in World Politics*, pp. 137-56, and several contributions in A. Dallin, ed., *Soviet Conduct in World Affairs*.

The series of agreements concluded between Warsaw and Moscow, culminating in the nonaggression pact of 1932, contributed to the stabilization of conditions along Poland's eastern frontier and enabled both sides to regulate their mutual dealings in a normal and businesslike way, but the exchange of polite statements and gestures of good will did not and could not remove the basic causes of tension. The nature of this precarious relationship was largely determined by the interplay of various factors, some of them deeply rooted in history and some of a more recent origin. The differences in national temperaments, institutions, and ideals, the burdensome heritage of the past, the diametrically opposed concepts of the future, and the incompatibility of political interests helped to separate the Poles and the Russians with a curtain of mistrust and prejudice.[3] The Kremlin obviously resented the existence of an independent Polish state— the "tool and vanguard of Western imperialism" in its alleged plans of a new intervention against the USSR[4]—which separated Russia from Central Europe and formed both a barrier to the realization of her ambitions and a potential bridge to the heart of the continent. Moreover, while the Soviet government did not formally revive its claims to the areas ceded to Poland by the Riga Treaty, it never reconciled itself to this loss and only waited for an opportune moment to rectify the frontier in its favor.[5] Moscow's position with regard to this question was strengthened by Poland's failure to arrive at a satisfactory solution of the problem of national minorities in the eastern borderlands.[6] Piłsudski's federal idea, having failed as an instrument of Polish foreign policy, suffered another and perhaps even more painful defeat in the field of internal policy, and the Polish leaders proved unable to devise a modern and realistic program with which to replace it.

[3] It should be noted, however, that Polish public opinion was, on the whole, favorably disposed toward Russia. Szembek, p. 172. According to a prominent French observer, even some influential persons in Poland felt that their country and the USSR were kept apart only "by questions of a sentimental and historical character." See Molotov's interview with Jacques Chastenet in Molotov, p. 231; English translation in Degras, ed., III, 183.

[4] See CPSU, *XVII S"ezd VKP(b), Stenograficheskii otchët*, p. 13.

[5] See Litvinov's conversation with Bullitt as reported in Szembek, p. 251.

[6] For a detailed discussion of this question see S. J. Paprocki, ed., *Minority Affairs and Poland*, and Horak, pp. 141-84.

On the broader international arena, Polish and Soviet interests clashed most conspicuously in the Baltic area, where the tug of war between the two countries continued almost uninterruptedly, with various degrees of success for both sides. Brief skirmishes between Warsaw and Moscow were also fought in Bucharest, and the rapid increase of the Kremlin's influence in Prague after 1934 prompted the Poles to safeguard their southern flank by a series of countermeasures, which ended in Poland's Pyrrhic victory in 1938. The supreme effort of Polish diplomacy was directed toward "keeping Russia away from Europe," stopping her at her frontiers and preventing her from participating in any system of international security. There were, in Warsaw's opinion, "certain definite limits . . . imposed upon Polish policy and upon the possibility of Polish collaboration with the Soviets," and to exceed them "would have been to destroy all that Poland had stood for for centuries in the east of Europe."[7] In spite of all well-meaning efforts on the part of their Western friends, the Poles could not be persuaded to bind themselves to a power which, as they suspected, was plotting their destruction and whose expansionism was, in their opinion, directed primarily against their own country. Eventually, almost all political parties in Poland (with the obvious exception of the Communists) came to accept Russia's hostility toward Warsaw as a permanent condition and resigned themselves to a state of fruitless frigidity in Polish-Soviet relations.[8] It seems, indeed, that this almost instinctive and deep-seated mistrust of the USSR was the dominant feature of Polish foreign

[7] *Polish White Book*, p. 203. According to the Polish government circles, one of the most important obstacles in the way of Polish-Soviet cooperation was the role of the Communist Party of Poland as a militant agency of the Comintern and Moscow's support of its activities. See *USFR*, 1937, I (Washington, 1954), 190, and Szembek, p. 260. On the other hand, Władysław Gomułka, the first secretary of the Central Committee of the Polish United Workers' Party, attributes Warsaw's hostile attitude toward the USSR during the interwar period not to any "mythical 'anti-Russian complex'" of the Polish leaders but to their "class hatred" for the Soviet Union. *Pravda*, July 22, 1959; see also Załuski, pp. 31-32.

[8] To be sure, Roman Dmowski, one of Poland's foremost political thinkers, warned his countrymen that the USSR was coming closer to playing a role of first-rate importance in world affairs, and that Poland had, accordingly, to define precisely her own objectives with regard to Russia (Dmowski, *Świat powojenny i Polska*, p. 141), but even he failed to develop any constructive program of a Polish-Soviet rapprochement.

policy between the wars: it led to the underestimation of the German danger, was instrumental in determining Poland's attitude toward Czechoslovakia, and alienated her temporarily from her French ally. It was, however, not free from some inconsistencies: on the one hand, there was the feeling that the Soviet state and the Red Army represented a deadly danger to Poland and her smaller neighbors; on the other hand, there was, at times, an inclination to ignore Russia's dynamism and tremendous power potential and to disregard the military and ideological challenge from that direction.

While the Polish leaders rejected all schemes of international cooperation which involved a passive acquiescence in Moscow's hegemony in Eastern Europe or acceptance of closer ties with the USSR, they also did not allow their country to become the jumping-off place for an anti-Soviet crusade and consistently refused to join any political or ideological alliance directed against Russia, although this attitude was almost bound to precipitate, sooner or later, a Nazi assault against Poland herself. Most of the German and Russian speculations as to the territorial aspirations of Poland and her possible conduct in the event of a Nazi-Soviet conflict were based on a mistaken appraisal of the intentions and ambitions of Marshal Piłsudski and his successors. The passing years had mitigated the warlike disposition of the victor of the Vistula,[9] and the failure of his Ukrainian plans had taught him to beware of any risky adventures. Piłsudski's belief that Poland was called upon to play a decisive part in the east of Europe and that her future greatness depended upon her ability to harmonize her own aspirations with those of other non-Russian peoples of that area[10] did not necessarily imply that he had any personal plans of re-

[9] Shortly after the coup d'état of 1926, Piłsudski assured the Rumanian minister to Warsaw that he "did not wish to alarm" the Soviet Union, but wanted to "live in peace with the whole world" and to be contented "with the already over-extended frontiers" which he had to guard. Laroche, p. 60; see also Piłsudska, p. 314.

[10] In Piłsudski's opinion, Poland had been for centuries drawn eastward, in the general direction of the Black Sea. While her western frontier remained closed by the living wall of the German race, which the Poles were unable to penetrate, the triumphs and defeats in the eastern borderlands were a reliable yardstick for measuring the nation's strength and vitality. See W. Jędrzejewicz, "Piłsudski i Kemal," *Wiadomości* (London), May 23, 1954, and M. Sokolnicki, "Polityka Piłsudskiego a Turcja," *Niepodległość*, VI (1958), 19-21.

viving the bitter fighting of 1920. In his conversation with Rauschning, the old Marshal quoted Goethe's famous saying about the
art of self-restraint;[11] he was reluctant to "compromettre ma vic-
toire,"[12] and his failing health scarcely enabled him to play the
role of a conquering hero.

There were, moreover, other, no less important considerations.
While Piłsudski and his heirs might have hoped that the Soviet
regime would eventually be overthrown and that far-reaching territorial and social changes would take place in the regions which
had once shared the historical destinies of the Polish Common-
wealth, they were undoubtedly bitterly opposed to the notion that
this process of transformation should take place under the auspices of the German Reich, with its long and consistent anti-
Polish record; they realized, too, that to "aller en Ukraine serait
littéralement travailler pour le roi de Prusse."[13] The best that
Poland could hope for, if she decided to ally herself with the
Nazis, was a prominent position in the circle of Hitler's satellites.
A joint expedition against the USSR would have forced her to
rely completely on German assistance and would have reduced her
to a mere outpost of the militant Reich. In the event of a victory
over Russia, she would have been encircled by the Germans and
their eastern colonies and dependencies, while an abortive campaign could have easily resulted in Berlin and Moscow making a
bargain at her expense. Thus success and failure seemed almost
equally dangerous, and any German action planned against the
Soviet Union appeared primarily as a threat to Poland herself.[14]
There were also psychological imponderables which precluded
any possibility of an alliance with Berlin. The vast majority of the
Polish people regarded the Nazi regime with distaste and abhor-
rence, and their profound anti-German sentiments were certainly
strong enough to thwart any plans of a Hitler-inspired anti-
Russian coalition.

Thus, although in the opinion of some scholars Warsaw should
have thrown in its lot with Moscow or Berlin,[15] neither of these

[11] See Breyer, p. 176.   [12] Laroche, p. 194; see also *ibid.*, p. 202.   [13] *Ibid.*, p. 194.
[14] See Piłsudski's opinion on this subject as stated in his conversation with Moltke
on November 28, 1933. *DGFP*, Series C, II (Washington, 1959), 157.
[15] See Sharp, p. 150.

possibilities was really acceptable to the Poles. Both were fraught
with deadly perils and both could only lead to a partial or total
loss of Poland's independence and to the subordination of her
interests to those of Russia or Germany. Consequently, the most
challenging issue confronting Piłsudski and his successors was the
problem of alternatives open to Polish diplomacy in a situation
which was characterized by four factors: the growth of the German
threat, the increase of the military might of the USSR, the passivity of the West, and Poland's own limited strength and resources.[16] It seems, indeed, that the most striking peculiarity of
Poland's whole international position was the conspicuous dis-
proportion between the magnitude of problems with which she
had to cope and the measure of her actual possibilities. As the
old Marshal himself used to admit, he "had ideas for five Polands
—but they could be fulfilled to measure one only";[17] hence he had
to shape Polish policy in accordance with what was feasible and
practicable, so as not to overtax the endurance and capacity of
the instrument in his hands.[18] He realized that Poland's advantageous bargaining position in 1932-34 was due to a favorable combination of events and circumstances; he was also aware of the
fact that this political configuration "could not last forever" and
that any serious upheavals in Europe would inevitably bring
Poland "once again face to face with armed conflicts."[19]

While the Poles could exercise only a marginal control over
their own destiny and were obviously unable to prevent Germany
and the Soviet Union from reaching an agreement at their ex-

[16] For a discussion of the problem of alternatives see Giertych, pp. 83-85, and his
letter to the editor of *Wiadomości*, Oct. 7, 1951; Mackiewicz, *Historia Polski od 11
listopada 1918 r. do 17 września 1939 r.*, pp. 281-85, and his article "Co Beck po-
winien był robić" [What Beck Should Have Done], *Wiadomości*, June 1, 1952; see
also H. L. Roberts, "International Relations between the Wars," in C. E. Black,
ed., *Challenge in Eastern Europe*, p. 191, and Roos, *Polen und Europa*, pp. 399-
400. Polish Communist historians claim that the only alternative open to Poland
was a policy of alliance and cooperation with the USSR. See J. Kowalewski, "Nie-
miecki historyk o polskiej polityce zagranicznej w latach 1931-1939" [A German
Historian on Polish Foreign Policy in 1931-1939], *Sprawy Międzynarodowe*, X, No.
5 (May, 1957), 52-53; K. Lapter, "Polityka Józefa Becka," *ibid.*, XI, No. 5 (May,
1958), 52-53, 56, 59, 63-67; S. Stanisławska, "Stosunek opozycji polskiej do polityki
Becka wobec Czechosłowacji," *ibid.*, XII, No. 7/8 (July-Aug., 1959), 15.
[17] Beck, *Final Report*, p. 91.   [18] See Beck, *Przemówienia*, p. 324.
[19] Beck, *Final Report*, p. 57.

pense, they believed in the possibility of preserving their freedom of action through a policy of balancing between their two dangerous neighbors. This policy of equilibrium was based on the erroneous assumption that the ideological differences between the USSR and the Third Reich were too fundamental to permit any real cooperation of these two powers against Poland. For, although the Nazi rulers failed to secure Warsaw's support for their anti-Russian schemes, they succeeded in convincing the Polish leaders that the enmity toward Moscow was a basic and permanent feature of German foreign policy. Beck, in spite of his alleged sophistication and notwithstanding all appearances, lacked the cynicism of his German partners and failed to realize that to build a nation's policy on their words and promises was to play games with phantoms.

Beck's references to the concept of balance, which he regarded as the keystone of his policy, are too vague to indicate the precise meaning of this term in his interpretation.[20] It would seem, however, that the system of equilibrium between Germany and Russia, as envisaged by him, was of a much more limited nature than most of his critics are prone to assume; in fact, the Polish Foreign Minister himself complained more than once that "this most simple principle was understood with difficulty in other countries where people were used to trifling and complicated diplomatic moves and games."[21] It had little in common with the classical balance-of-power theory. It meant, first and foremost, that Poland refused to join any political combinations which were likely to involve her in a conflict with one of her big neighbors as an ally of the other[22] and that the improvement of her relations with Germany and Russia had to be "limited by the impossibility of making [Polish] policy dependent on any of these dangerous partners."[23] It also required that the basic political agreements concluded by Warsaw with Berlin or Moscow be counterbalanced by identical or similar understandings with the other party.

Whatever Beck's doubts and apprehensions about the Soviet intentions, he adhered meticulously to this somewhat rigid and

[20] See Beck, *Przemówienia*, p. 402, and Gafencu, p. 29. [21] Beck, *Final Report*, p. 34. [22] Beck, *Przemówienia*, p. 402. [23] Beck, *Final Report*, p. 51.

artificial "symmetry" and "synchronization" of pacts in the East and the West. On the other hand, however, the policy of balance, as understood by him, did not necessarily imply that Poland's relations with the USSR and the Third Reich had to be equally good at all times[24] or that Warsaw had to maintain an equal distance from Moscow and Berlin in all possible situations. Since he believed firmly in Piłsudski's dogma that the chief threat to Poland's independence would come from the side of Russia, it was only natural that his attitude toward the Soviet Union was characterized by the utmost caution and reserve—qualities which he did not always display in an equal measure in his dealings with Germany. Beck's "static" equilibrium did not call for any continuous oscillating and maneuvering on his part. Once established, it demanded no essential changes in accordance with the exigencies of the moment and required only certain minor readjustments, such as the November declaration of 1938 reaffirming the principles of the Polish-Soviet nonaggression pact of 1932. There is no denying, however, that this policy of immobility, based on Piłsudski's advice to "stay idle and wait to see what all the others [were] going to do,"[25] could not possibly endure in a dynamic situation, when the period of transformations anticipated by the Marshal finally arrived, and when the "conventional forms of international life" began to crumble in accordance with his predictions.[26] What Beck had planned as the relatively simple expedient of sitting on two stools eventually turned into riding two horses at once—something that indeed "can lead to some exceptionally strenuous acrobatics."[27]

In pursuing his policy, Beck overestimated the length of the prospective period of security on Poland's western frontier and displayed a casual and lighthearted attitude toward the grave issues of the day, combined with a marked coolness toward all international endeavors aimed at containing Nazi aggression before

[24] See K. Smogorzewski, "Poland and Her Neighbors," *The Slavonic and East European Review*, XVII (July, 1938), 116.

[25] Beck, *Final Report*, p. 88.

[26] See Beck, *Przemówienia*, p. 324.

[27] H. L. Roberts, "The Diplomacy of Colonel Beck," in Craig and Gilbert, eds., *The Diplomats*, p. 599.

it reached dangerous proportions. It was especially his failure to adopt a more self-assertive attitude toward Germany and his sudden predilection for the methods of totalitarian diplomacy that tended to associate his policy with that of the Wilhelmstrasse. To be sure, when sending his ultimatums to Kaunas and Prague, Beck was probably thinking not about drawing closer to Berlin but rather about strengthening Warsaw's position vis-à-vis Germany in accordance with the principle of "compensation."[28] Nevertheless, it was during the period from the *Anschluss* to Munich, when the power of the Third Reich increased most dangerously, that Poland's apparent support for Hitler's policy made a material, though indirect and unintended, contribution to the helplessness of the general European situation.

It must be admitted, of course, that the fatal years 1932-34 and their aftermath had prejudiced very strongly the possibility of bringing the developing crisis to a halt. If the catastrophe was to be averted or at least delayed, some decisive measures had to be taken at a much earlier date. With Germany defeated and disarmed and with Russia only slowly emerging from the revolutionary chaos, the nations of East Central Europe had a unique opportunity to create and consolidate a bloc of middle and small powers able to resist the encroachments of both Berlin and Moscow and thus to restore the system of equilibrium in that part of Europe which became unbalanced as a result of the dissolution of the Austro-Hungarian Empire. By uniting their forces and establishing a community of interest, they could play a role in international affairs that went far beyond their individual possibilities and afforded invaluable advantages for each and all of the partners. Unfortunately, Poland and her neighbors failed to grasp this great historical chance and let it pass—perhaps for ever. In this connection, one is also tempted to raise the question whether Poland's adherence to the Eastern Locarno would not have paved the way for the eventual triumph of the idea of collective security. It is, of course, difficult to speculate to what extent the conclusion of the Eastern Pact would have changed the course of events in Europe; it seems reasonably certain, however,

[28] See Beck, *Final Report*, pp. 154 and 160-61.

that it would have considerably reduced the possibilities of Germany's territorial expansion and that any military conflict that might have resulted would have taken place in a combination of circumstances which was definitely favorable to the cause of an anti-Nazi coalition.

By 1938 irreparable damage had already been done and it was obviously too late to save the rapidly deteriorating international situation without resorting to some drastic measures. Thus, while it may be argued that the mistakes and errors of judgment made by the Polish leaders helped to precipitate the final disaster, it is also true that there was no simple solution to the fatal dilemma which Marshal Śmigły-Rydz summed up in a high-sounding but empty phrase: "With the Germans, we risk the loss of our liberty; with the Russians—of our soul."[29] It seems, nevertheless, that Poland's reconciliation with Czechoslovakia and her determined stand in her neighbor's defense could have induced the Western powers to embark upon a more resolute policy and faced Hitler with the possibility of an all-out war when he was not yet ready to challenge the united forces of his potential adversaries. While it is highly questionable whether the key to the international situation was at that time really in Poland's hands,[30] it would appear that an armed conflict with Germany before Munich was, from the Polish point of view, more advantageous than the war which was to follow a year later, though the odds were still heavily weighted in the Wehrmacht's favor and the attitude of Russia was even less predictable than during the September days of 1939.

As a result of the fourth partition of Poland and the subsequent Soviet occupation of the Baltic countries, the belt of East European buffer states disappeared, and Beck's belated plan to create a "third force" between Germany and Russia came to a dismal

[29] There seems to be some doubt as to the actual wording of this famous remark. In Reynaud, *La France a sauvé l'Europe*, I, 587, Śmigły-Rydz is quoted as saying: "Avec les Allemands, nous risquons de perdre notre liberté; avec les Russes, nous perdons notre âme." In the revised edition of this book, the Marshal's comment is given in a slightly modified form: "Pour la Pologne, tomber sous le joug des Allemands, c'est perdre son corps; tomber sous celui des Russes, c'est perdre son âme." *Au coeur de la mêlée*, p. 308. One feels tempted to observe in this connection that the corruptive influence of Nazism was no less dangerous to the Polish "soul" than the possible impact of Communist ideology.

[30] See Giertych, p. 83.

end. The refusal of the Poles to barter their independence for illusory advantages offered at various times by Berlin and Moscow resulted in a disaster which seemed to dwarf all calamities and misfortunes recorded in the tragic annals of the Republic. Molotov, rejoicing at the demise of the "ugly offspring of the Versailles treaty," could now vent his long-suppressed feelings and openly condemn Warsaw's policy of "unprincipled maneuvering," which "proved unsound and suffered complete bankruptcy."[31] Thus, though the "Miracle on the Vistula" had secured for the people of Poland almost two decades of a relatively tranquil existence, it did not settle or terminate the ancient controversy between the Poles and the Russians. On the contrary, old fears and suspicions were intensified rather than eliminated. And, viewed from the historical perspective of the early 1960's, the melancholy story of Polish-Soviet relations during the interwar period appears only as an episode in the beginning struggle between East and West over the shape of the world's future.

[31] USSR, Verkhovnyi Sovet, *Sozyv I, Sessiia V, Stenograficheskii otchët*, p. 8; English translation in Degras, III, 388. Recent Soviet historiography criticizes Molotov's bitterly anti-Polish speech, repudiates some of his offensive statements, and stresses the positive and "progressive" significance of the reemergence of Poland as an independent state after World War I. At the same time, an effort is being made to minimize the role played by the Red Army in Poland's defeat in September, 1939. See Pospelov, ed., I, 249.

Bibliography

I. DOCUMENTS

Beck, J. *Przemówienia, deklaracje, wywiady (1931-1939)* [Speeches, Declarations, Interviews]. 2d ed. revised. Warsaw, 1939.

Communist International. *Kommunisticheskii Internatsional v dokumentakh: Resheniia, tezisy i vozzvaniia kongressov Kominterna i plenumov IKKI, 1919-1932* [The Communist International in Documents: Resolutions, Theses, and Proclamations of the Congresses of the Comintern and the Plenums of the ECCI]. Moscow, 1933.

—— Executive Committee. *Otchët Ispolkoma Kominterna* [Report of the Executive Committee of the Comintern]. Moscow, 1926.

—— Executive Committee. Plenum (VI, X-XIII). *Stenograficheskii otchët* [Stenographic Minutes]. Moscow, 1927-34.

—— 6th World Congress, 1928. *Stenograficheskii otchët*. Moscow, 1929.

—— 7th World Congress, 1935. *Report*. London, 1936.

Communist Party of Poland. *KPP: Uchwały i rezolucje* [CPP: Decisions and Resolutions]. 3 vols. Warsaw, 1954-56.

—— *KPP w obronie niepodległości Polski: Matariały i dokumenty* [CPP in Defense of Poland's Independence: Materials and Documents]. Warsaw, 1954.

Communist Party of the Soviet Union. *XVII S"ezd VKP(b), 26 ianvaria–10 fevralia 1934 g.* [17th Congress, January 26–February 10, 1934]. *Stenograficheskii otchët*. Moscow, 1934.

—— *XVIII S"ezd, 10-21 marta 1939 g.* [18th Congress, March 10-21, 1939]. *Stenograficheskii otchët*. Moscow, 1939.

Degras, J., ed. *Soviet Documents on Foreign Policy*. 3 vols. London, 1951-53.

Documents on International Affairs. 1928-46. London, 1929-51.

Eudin, X. J., et al. *Soviet Russia and the West, 1920-1927: A Documentary Survey*. Stanford, 1957.

France. Ministère des Affaires Étrangères. *The French Yellow Book: Diplomatic Documents, 1938-1939.* New York, 1940.

General Sikorski Historical Institute. *Documents on Polish-Soviet Relations, 1939-1945.* Vol. I. London, 1961.

Germany, Auswärtiges Amt. *Documents and Materials Relating to the Eve of the Second World War.* 2 vols. Moscow, 1948.

—— *Documents on German Foreign Policy, 1918-1945.* Series C, Vols. I-III; Series D, Vols. I-VIII. Washington, 1949-59.

—— *The German White Paper.* New York, 1940.

Great Britain. Foreign Office. *Documents on British Foreign Policy, 1919-1939.* 2d Series, Vols. III-VII; 3d Series, Vols. I-VIII. London, 1948-58.

International Military Tribunal. *Nazi Conspiracy and Aggression.* 10 vols. Washington, 1946-48.

—— *Trial of the Major War Criminals.* 42 vols. Nuremberg, 1947-49.

Italy. Ministero degli Affari Esteri. Commissione per la pubblicazione dei documenti diplomatici. *I documenti diplomatici italiani.* 8th Series, Vols. XII-XIII; 9th Series, Vol. I. Rome, 1952-54.

Jędrzejewicz, W., ed. *Poland in the British Parliament, 1939-1945.* Vol. I. New York, 1946.

Keith, A. B., ed. *Speeches and Documents on International Affairs.* 2 vols. London, 1938.

Kliuchnikov, Iu. V., and A. V. Sabanin, eds. *Mezhdunarodnaia politika noveishego vremeni v dogovorakh, notakh i deklaratsiiakh* [International Politics of Recent Time in Treaties, Notes, and Declarations]. Part III, Vols. I-II. Moscow, 1928.

Laserson, M. M., ed. *Development of Soviet Foreign Policy in Europe, 1917-1942: A Selection of Documents.* New York, 1943.

League of Nations. *Official Journal.* Geneva, 1932-39.

—— *Treaty Series.* Vols. CXXXVI, CXLVII, and CLVII. Geneva, 1933-35.

Litvinov, M. M. *Against Aggression.* New York, 1939.

—— *Vneshniaia politika SSSR: Rechi i zaiavleniia* [Foreign Policy of the USSR: Speeches and Declarations]. 2d ed. revised. Moscow, 1937.

Molotov, V. M. *Stat'i i rechi, 1935-1936* [Articles and Speeches, 1935-1936]. Moscow, 1937.

Piłsudski, J. *Pisma zbiorowe* [Collected Works]. 10 vols. Warsaw, 1937-38.

Poland. Ambasada. U.S. *Polish-Soviet Relations, 1918-1943: Official Documents.* Washington, 1943.

—— Ministerstwo Spraw Zagranicznych. *Official Documents Concerning Polish-German and Polish-Soviet Relations, 1933-1939.* London, 1940.

—— *Wrześniowy kryzys czechosłowacki 1938 r. w raportach Ambasadora Lipskiego* [The Czechoslovak Crisis of September, 1938, in Ambassador Lipski's Reports]. Warsaw, 1958.

—— *Z raportów ambasadorskich Wieniawy-Długoszowskiego* [Ambassadorial Reports of Wieniawa-Długoszowski: A Selection]. Warsaw, 1957.

—— Sejm. *Sprawozdanie stenograficzne* [Stenographic Minutes]. Warsaw, 1931-39.

—— Senat. *Sprawozdanie stenograficzne.* Warsaw, 1931-39.

Polska Akademia Nauk. Instytut Historii. *Dokumenty i materiały do historii stosunków polsko-radzieckich* [Documents and Materials on the History of Polish-Soviet Relations]. Vols. I-II. Warsaw, 1957-61.

Ratyńska, B., ed. *Opinia polska wobec Monachium w świetle prasy* [The Polish View of Munich in the Light of the Press]. Warsaw, 1959.

Sabanin, A. V., ed. *Mezhdunarodnaia politika v 1929 godu* [International Politics in 1929]. Moscow, 1931.

Sbornik dokumentov po mezhdunarodnoi politike i mezhdunarodnomu pravu [Collection of Documents on International Politics and International Law]. Vols. I-III, VI. Moscow, 1932-34.

Sontag, R. J., and J. S. Beddie, eds. *Nazi-Soviet Relations, 1939-1941.* Washington, 1948.

Stalin, I. V. *Works.* Vols. I-XIII. Moscow, 1953-55.

Union of Soviet Socialist Republics. Ministerstvo Inostrannykh Del. *Dokumenty vneshnei politiki SSSR* [Documents on Foreign Policy of the USSR]. Vols. I-VI. Moscow, 1957-62.

—— Narodnyi Komissariat Iustitsii. *Report of Court Proceedings in the Case of the Anti-Soviet "Bloc of Rights and Trotskyites," Heard before the Military Collegium of the Supreme Court of the USSR, Moscow, March 2-13, 1938.* Moscow, 1938.

—— S"ezd Sovetov. *Stenograficheskii otchët* [Stenographic Minutes]. Moscow, 1922-35.

—— Tsentral'nyi Ispolnitel'nyi Komitet. *Stenograficheskii otchët.* Moscow, 1925-36.

—— Verkhovnyi Sovet. *Stenograficheskii otchët.* Moscow, 1938-39.

—— Verkhovnyi Sovet. *Verbatim Report.* Moscow, 1938.

United States. Department of State. *Foreign Relations of the United States.* 1931-39. Washington, 1946-56.

Vneshniaia politika SSSR: Sbornik dokumentov [Foreign Policy of the USSR: A Collection of Documents]. Vol. IV. Moscow, 1946.

Zaleski, A. *Przemowy i deklaracje* [Speeches and Declarations]. Warsaw, 1929.

II. OTHER SOURCES

Akademiia Nauk SSSR. Institut Slavianovedeniia. *Istoriia Pol'shi* [A History of Poland]. Vol. III. Moscow, 1958.

Anders, W. *An Army in Exile*. London, 1949.

Arciszewski, F. "Some Remarks about the Strategical Significance of the New and the Old Soviet-Polish Border," *The Polish Review*, I, No. 2/3 (Spring-Summer, 1956), 89-96.

Arsen'ev, E. *Podzhigateli voiny* [The Warmongers]. Moscow, 1931.

Arski, S. *Przeklęte lata* [The Accursed Years]. 2d ed. revised. Warsaw, 1953.

Aspaturian, V. V. "Soviet Foreign Policy," in R. C. Macridis, ed., *Foreign Policy in World Politics*. Englewood Cliffs, N.J., 1958. Pp. 132-210.

Augur [pseud]. "The Foreign Policy of Poland," *The Slavonic and East European Review*, XV (Jan., 1937), 350-56.

Babii, B. M. *Vozz'iednannia Zakhidnoi Ukrainy z Ukrains'koiu RSR* [The Reunion of the Western Ukraine with the Ukrainian SSR]. Kiev, 1954.

Bączkowski, W. *Grunwald czy Piławce?* [Grunwald or Piławce?] Warsaw, 1938.

—— *Rosja wczoraj i dziś* [Russia Yesterday and Today]. Jerusalem, 1946.

—— *Towards an Understanding of Russia: A Study in Policy and Strategy*. Jerusalem, 1947.

—— *Wschód a Polska* [The East and Poland]. Warsaw, 1935.

Bainville, J. *La Russie et la barrière de l'Est*. Paris, 1937.

Basler, W. "Die britisch-französisch-sowjetischen Militärbesprechungen im August 1939," *Zeitschrift für Geschichtswissenschaft*, V (1957), Heft 1, 18-56.

—— "Zur Vorgeschichte des deutsch-sowjetischen Nichtangriffspaktes 1939," Beiträge zur Geschichte der Beziehungen zwischen dem deutschen Volk und den Völkern der Sowjetunion (*Zeitschrift für Geschichtswissenschaft*, Band II [1954], Beiheft 1).

Batowski, H. Rumuńska podróż Becka w październiku 1938 roku" [Beck's Rumanian Journey in October, 1938], *Kwartalnik Historyczny* [The Historical Quarterly], LXV (1958), No. 2, 423-39.

Beazley, R. "Poland and Russia Yesterday and Today," *The Quarterly Review*, CCLXXXV (Oct., 1947), 541-53.

Beck, J. *Dernier rapport: Politique polonaise, 1926-1939*. Neuchâtel, 1951.

—— *Final Report*. New York, 1957.

—— *Pamiętniki* [Memoirs]. Warsaw, 1955.

Beloff, M. *The Foreign Policy of Soviet Russia, 1929-1941*. 2 vols. London, 1947-49.

Beneš, E. *Memoirs*. Boston, 1953.

Bocheński, A. *Między Niemcami a Rosją* [Between Germany and Russia]. Warsaw, 1937.

Boguslavskii, M. "Politicheskaia bor'ba v Pol'she po voprosam vneshnei politiki nakanune vtoroi mirovoi voiny" [Political Struggle in Poland over the Questions of Foreign Policy on the Eve of the Second World War], *Voprosy Istorii* [Problems of History], 1949, No. 10, pp. 61-81.

—— "Politicheskaia bor'ba v Pol'she v sviazi s nastupleniem fashistskikh agressorov na Chekhoslovakiiu" [Political Struggle in Poland in Connection with the Attack of Fascist Aggressors against Czechoslovakia], *Voprosy Istorii*, 1948, No. 5, pp. 20-39.

Bonnet, G. *Défense de la paix*. 2 vols. Geneva, 1948.

—— "Les négociations franco-russes de 1938 et de 1939," *La Revue de Paris*, LIV, No. 11 (Nov., 1947), 93-101.

Boswell, A. B. *The Eastern Boundaries of Poland*. Birkenhead, 1943.

Bouvier, J., and J. Gacon. *La vérité sur 1939: La politique extérieure de l'U.R.S.S. d'octobre 1938 à juin 1941*. Paris, 1953.

Bratkowski, J. *Poland on the Road to Revolutionary Crisis*. London, 1933.

—— *Pol'skii fashizm—forpost interventsii* [Polish Fascism: An Outpost of Intervention]. Moscow, 1932.

Brauns, G. "Die Grundsätze der Beckschen Politik," *Deutsche Forschung im Osten, I* (June, 1941), 28-38.

Bregman, A. *Najlepszy sojusznik Hitlera* [Hitler's Best Ally]. London, 1958.

—— *La politique de la Pologne dans la Société des Nations*. Paris, 1952.

Breyer, R. *Das Deutsche Reich und Polen, 1932-1937: Aussenpolitik und Volksgruppenfragen*. Würzburg, 1955.

Broszat, M. *Nationalsozialistische Polenpolitik, 1939-1945*. Stuttgart, 1961.

Brunot, L. *Pologne d'hier et d'aujourd'hui*. Paris, 1947.

Budurowycz, B. B. "The Ukrainian Problem in International Politics, October 1938 to March 1939," *Canadian Slavonic Papers*, III (1958), 59-75.

Buell, R. L. *Poland: Key to Europe.* New York, 1939.

The Cambridge History of Poland. Vol. II. Cambridge, 1941.

Cardwell, A. S. *Poland and Russia: The Last Quarter Century.* New York, 1944.

Carr, E. H. *German-Soviet Relations between the Two World Wars, 1919-1939.* Baltimore, 1951.

Čelovsky, B. *Das Münchener Abkommen, 1938.* Stuttgart, 1958.

Chudek, J. "Polska wobec wrześniowego kryzysu czechosłowackiego 1938 r." [Poland and the Czechoslovak Crisis of September, 1938], *Sprawy Międzynarodowe* [International Affairs], XI, No. 4 (April, 1958), 72-79.

Churchill, W. S. *The Gathering Storm.* London, 1948.

—— *The World Crisis.* Vol. IV: *The Aftermath.* London, 1929.

Ciano, G. *Diaries, 1939-1943.* New York, 1946.

—— *Diplomatic Papers.* London, 1948.

—— *Hidden Diary, 1937-1938.* New York, 1953.

Cleinow, G. "Polen und die UdSSR seit dem Rigaischen Vertrage," *Volk und Reich,* X (1934), 490-508.

Coates, W. P., and Z. K. Coates. *Six Centuries of Russo-Polish Relations.* London, 1948.

Communist Party of the Soviet Union. Vysshaia Partiinaia Shkola. Kafedra Mezhdunarodnykh Otnoshenii. *Istoriia mezhdunarodnykh otnoshenii i vneshnei politiki SSSR, 1870-1957 gg.* [History of International Relations and Foreign Policy of the USSR, 1870-1957]. Moscow, 1957.

Comnen, N. P. *Luci e ombre sull'Europa, 1914-1950.* Milan, 1957.

—— *Preludi del grande dramma.* Rome, 1947.

Coselschi, E. *Il ministro Beck e la politica estera della Polonia.* Rome, 1939.

Coulondre, R. *De Staline à Hitler: Souvenirs de deux ambassades, 1936-1939.* Paris, 1950.

Czarnecki, B. "Gdy Niemcy chciały z Polską pokoju" [When Germany Wanted Peace with Poland], *Sprawy Międzynarodowe,* XI, No. 12 (Dec., 1958), 69-82.

—— "Od 'Monachium' do kryzysu kwietniowego 1939 r." [From "Munich" to the April Crisis of 1939], *Sprawy Międzynarodowe,* XI, No. 10/11 (Oct.-Nov., 1958), 55-69.

Czubatyj, N. D. "Ukraine between Poland and Russia," *Review of Politics,* VIII (July, 1946), 331-53.

D'Abernon, E. V. *The Eighteenth Decisive Battle of the World: Warsaw, 1920.* London, 1931.

Dąbski, J. *Pokój ryski* [The Riga Treaty]. Warsaw, 1931.

Dallin, A. "The Month of Decision: German-Soviet Diplomacy, July 22–August 22, 1939," *Journal of Central European Affairs,* IX (April, 1949), 1-31.

Dallin, A., ed. *Soviet Conduct in World Affairs: A Selection of Readings.* New York, 1960.

Dallin, D. J. *Soviet Russia's Foreign Policy, 1939-1942.* New Haven, 1942.

Davies, J. E. *Mission to Moscow.* New York, 1941.

Dean, V. M. *Europe in Retreat.* 2d ed. revised. New York, 1939.

Dennis, A. L. P. *The Foreign Policies of Soviet Russia.* New York, 1924.

Deutscher, I. *Stalin: A Political Biography.* New York, 1949.

Dmowski, R. *Niemcy, Rosja i kwestia polska* [Germany, Russia, and the Polish Question]. Lwów, 1908.

—— *Polityka polska i odbudowanie państwa* [Polish Policy and the Reconstruction of the State]. 2 vols. 3d ed. Hannover, 1947.

—— *Problems of Central and Eastern Europe.* London, 1917.

—— *Świat powojenny i Polska* [The Postwar World and Poland]. 3d ed. Warsaw, 1932.

Dodd, W. E. *Diary, 1933-1938.* New York, 1941.

Donnadieu, J. *La lutte des aigles aux marches orientales.* Paris, 1939.

Drunin, V. P. *Pol'sha, Rossiia i SSSR* [Poland, Russia, and the USSR]. Moscow, 1928.

Duroselle, J. B., ed. *Les frontières européennes de l'U.R.S.S., 1917-1941.* Paris, 1957.

Dyboski, R. "Polish-Soviet Relations," *International Affairs,* XIII (1934), 226-44.

—— "Two Neighbors of Russia and Their Policies," *The Nineteenth Century and After,* XCV (June, 1924), 804-14.

Dziewanowski, M. K. *The Communist Party of Poland: An Outline of History.* Cambridge, Mass., 1959.

—— "Piłsudski's Federal Policy, 1919-1921," *Journal of Central European Affairs,* X (July-Oct., 1950), 113-28, 271-87.

Elmer, B. *Winowajcy klęski wrześniowej* [The Culprits of the September Defeat]. Warsaw, 1946.

Feliński, W. *The Ukrainians in Poland.* London, 1931.

Fiala, V. *La Pologne d'aujourd'hui.* Paris, 1936.

Filichowski, W. *Cierpkie pobratymstwo* [A Sour Brotherhood]. Warsaw, 1938.

Filipowicz, J. "The Permanent Elements in Polish Foreign Policy," *The English Review,* XLIV (June, 1928), 672-84.

Fischer, L. *The Soviets in World Affairs: A History of Relations between the Soviet Union and the Rest of the World, 1917-1929.* 2 vols. 2d ed. Princeton, 1951.

Flandin, P. E. *Politique française, 1919-1940.* Paris, 1947.

Fleming, D. F. *The Cold War and Its Origins, 1917-1960.* Vol. I. London, 1961.

Fomin, V. G. *Imperialisticheskaia agressiia protiv Pol'shi v 1939 g.* [Imperialist Aggression against Poland in 1939]. Moscow, 1952.

François-Poncet, A. *The Fateful Years: Memoirs of a French Ambassador in Berlin, 1931-1938.* London, 1949.

Frateili, A. *Polonia, frontiera d'Europa.* Milan, 1938.

Freytagh-Loringhoven, A. *Deutschlands Aussenpolitik, 1933-1941.* Berlin, 1942.

Gafencu, G. *Last Days of Europe: A Diplomatic Journey in 1939.* New Haven, 1948.

Gamelin, M. G. *Servir.* Vol. II: *Le prologue du drama.* Paris, 1946.

Gąsiorowski, Z. J. "Did Piłsudski Attempt to Initiate a Preventive War in 1933?" *Journal of Modern History,* XXVII (June, 1955), 135-51.

—— "The German-Polish Nonaggression Pact of 1934," *Journal of Central European Affairs,* XV, No. 1 (April, 1955), 3-29.

—— "Polish-Czechoslovak Relations, 1918-1922," *The Slavonic and East European Review,* XXXV (Dec., 1956), 172-93.

—— "Polish-Czechoslovak Relations, 1922-1926," *The Slavonic and East European Review,* XXXV (June, 1957), 473-504.

—— "The Russian Overture to Germany of December 1924," *Journal of Modern History,* XXX, No. 2 (June, 1958), 99-117.

—— "Stresemann and Poland after Locarno," *Journal of Central European Affairs,* XVIII, No. 3 (Oct., 1958), 292-317.

—— "Stresemann and Poland before Locarno," *Journal of Central European Affairs,* XVIII, No. 1 (April, 1958), 25-47.

Giertych, J. *Pół wieku polskiej polityki* [Half Century of Polish Policy]. London, 1947.

Ginsburgs, G. "The Soviet Union as a Neutral, 1939-1941," *Soviet Studies,* X, No. 1 (July, 1958), 12-35.

Golsztyn, K. *Polsko-sowiecki pakt przeciwwojenny* [The Polish-Soviet Antiwar Pact]. Warsaw, 1932.

Grabowsky, A. "Der polnisch-russische Nichtangriffspakt," *Zeitschrift für Politik,* XXI (1932), 681-88.

Grabski, S. *The Polish-Soviet Frontier.* New York, n.d.

Grosz, W. *The Polish Defeat, September 1939.* Warsaw, 1950.

Grzybowski, W. *Polska w walce o pokój* [Poland in the Struggle for Peace]. Grenoble, 1941.

—— *Z.S.S.R.: Notatki ze wspomnień* [USSR: Notes from a Journal]. Paris, 1940.

Grzymała-Grabowiecki, J. *Polityka zagraniczna Polski w roku 1924* [Poland's Foreign Policy in 1924]. Warsaw, 1925.

—— *Polityka zagraniczna Polski w roku 1925.* Warsaw, 1926.

—— *Polityka zagraniczna Polski w roku 1926.* Warsaw, 1928.

Halecki, O. "Poland's Eastern Frontiers, 981-1939," *Journal of Central European Affairs,* I (July-Oct., 1941), 191-207, 325-38.

—— "Polish-Russian Relations—Past and Present," *The Review of Politics,* V (July, 1943), 322-38.

Harley, J. H. *The Authentic Biography of Colonel Beck.* London, 1939.

—— "Poland's Foreign Policy," *The Contemporary Review,* CXLVIII (Aug., 1935), 164-72.

Hartlieb, W. W. *Das politische Vertragssystem der Sowjetunion, 1920-1935.* Leipzig, 1936.

Heike, O. "Die Erinnerungen des Grafen Szembek," *Aussenpolitik,* IV (Sept., 1953), 561-67.

Henderson, H. W. *An Outline of Polish-Soviet Relations.* Glasgow, n.d.

Henderson, N. *Failure of a Mission: Berlin, 1937-1939.* London, 1940.

Herasymenko, M. P., and B. K. Dudykevych. *Borot'ba trudiashchykh Zakhidnoi Ukrainy za vozz'iednannia z Radians'koiu Ukrainoiu, 1921-1939 rr.* [The Struggle of the Workers of the Western Ukraine for Reunion with the Soviet Ukraine, 1921-1939]. Kiev, 1955.

Herriot, E. *Jadis.* Vol. II: *D'une guerre à l'autre, 1914-1936.* Paris, 1952.

Hilger, G., and A. G. Meyer. *The Incompatible Allies: A Memoir-History of German-Soviet Relations, 1918-1941.* New York, 1953.

Hofer, W. *War Premeditated, 1939.* London, 1955.

Höltje, C. *Die Weimarer Republik und das Ostlocarno-Problem, 1919-1934.* Würzburg, 1958.

Horak, S. *Poland and Her National Minorities, 1919-39: A Case Study.* New York, 1961.

Horthy, N. *Memoirs.* London, 1956.

Ilnytzkyj, R. *Deutschland und die Ukraine, 1934-1945.* Vol. I. Munich, 1955.

Ipohorski-Lenkiewicz, W. *Minister z pałacu Brühla* [The Minister from the Brühl Palace]. Buenos Aires, 1943.

Janta, A. *Patrzę na Moskwę* [I Am Looking at Moscow]. Poznań, 1933.

Jaworznicki, B. "Pakt Wschodni" [The Eastern Pact), *Sprawy Międzynarodowe,* II, No. 3/4 (July-Dec., 1949), 91-109.

—— "Polsko-radziecki pakt o nieagresji z r. 1932" [The Polish-Soviet Nonaggression Pact of 1932], *Sprawy Międzynarodowe,* V, No. 5 (Sept.-Oct., 1952), 70-82.

Johnson, G. E. W. "Poland Plays a Dangerous Game," *The North American Review,* CCXXXVIII (Sept., 1934), 268-78.

Jones, G. "Poland's Foreign Relations," *The Contemporary Review,* CXL (July, 1931), 44-52.

Jóźwiak, F. *Polska Partia Robotnicza w walce o wyzwolenie narodowe i społeczne* [The Polish Workers' Party in the Struggle for National and Social Liberation]. Warsaw, 1952.

Jurkiewicz, J. "Polska wobec planów Paktu Wschodniego w latach 1934-1935" [Poland and the Plans for the Eastern Pact in 1934-1935], *Sprawy Międzynarodowe,* XII, No. 3 (March, 1959), 18-51.

Kahanek, F. *Beneš contra Beck.* Prague, 1939.

Keeton, G. W., and R. Schlesinger. *Russia and Her Western Neighbors.* London, 1942.

Kennan, G. F. *Russia and the West under Lenin and Stalin.* Boston, 1961.

—— *Soviet Foreign Policy, 1917-1941.* Princeton, 1960.

Kirchmayer, J. *Kampania wrześniowa* [The September Campaign]. Warsaw, 1946.

Kirkien, L. *Między Wisłą a ujściem Dunaju* [Between the Vistula and the Mouth of the Danube]. Warsaw, 1932.

—— *Russia, Poland and the Curzon Line.* 2d ed. Edinburgh, 1945.

Kleist, P. *Zwischen Hitler und Stalin.* Bonn, 1950.

Kluke, P. "Deutschland und Russland zwischen den Weltkriegen," *Historische Zeitschrift,* CLXXI (1951), 519-52.

Knoll, R. *Uwagi o polskiej polityce w r. 1939* [Comments on Polish Policy in 1939]. Warsaw, 1939.

Kochan, L. *Russia and the Weimar Republic.* London, 1954.

Koitz, H. *Männer um Piłsudski: Profile der polnischen Politik.* Breslau, 1934.

Komarnicki, T. *Piłsudski a polityka wielkich mocarstw zachodnich* [Piłsudski and the Policy of the Western Great Powers]. London, 1952.

—— *Rebirth of the Polish Republic: A Study in the Diplomatic History of Europe, 1914-1920.* London, 1957.

Konovalov, S. *Russo-Polish Relations.* Princeton, 1944.

Kordt, E. *Nicht aus den Akten.* Stuttgart, 1950.

—— *Wahn und Wirklichkeit.* Stuttgart, 1947.

Kostiuk, H. *Stalinist Rule in the Ukraine: A Study of the Decade of Mass Terror, 1929-39.* Munich, 1961.

Kozhevnikov, F. I. *Sovetskoe gosudarstvo i mezhdunarodnoe pravo, 1917-1947 gg.* [The Soviet State and International Law, 1917-1947]. Moscow, 1948.

Krakowski, E. *Pologne et Russie.* 8th ed. Paris, 1946.

Kundiuba, I. D. *Istoricheskie predposylki krakha panskoi Pol'shi 1939 g.* [Historical Antecedents of the Downfall of the Landowners' Poland in 1939]. Kiev, 1959.

Kutrzeba, S. *Nasza polityka zagraniczna* [Our Foreign Policy]. Kraków, 1923.

Kwasiehorski, W. *Nad Odrą i Dnieprem: Przeszłość i przyszłość polskiej myśli imperialnej* [On the Oder and the Dnieper: The Past and the Future of Polish Imperial Thought]. Warsaw, 1939.

Laeuen, H. *Polnische Tragödie.* 2d ed. Stuttgart, 1956.

—— *Polnisches Zwischenspiel: Eine Episode der Ostpolitik.* Berlin, 1940.

Lapter, K. *Zarys stosunków polsko-radzieckich w latach 1917-1960* [An Outline of Polish-Soviet Relations, 1917-1960]. Part I. Warsaw, 1961.

—— "Polityka Józefa Becka" [The Policy of Józef Beck], *Sprawy Międzynarodowe,* XI, No. 5 (May, 1958), 47-69.

Laroche, J. A. *La Pologne de Piłsudski: Souvenirs d'une ambassade, 1926-1935.* Paris, 1953.

Lawton, L. "Ukraina: Europe's Greatest Problem," *East Europe,* III (Spring, 1939), 28-45.

Lednicki, W. *Russia, Poland and the West: Essays in Literary and Cultural History.* New York, 1954.

—— *Russo-Polish Relations: Their Historical, Cultural and Political Background.* Chicago, 1944.

Liddell Hart, B. H., ed. *The Red Army.* New York, 1956.

Litauer, S. "Role of Poland between Germany and Russia," *International Affairs*, XIV (1935), 654-73.

Lloyd George, D. *The Truth about the Peace Treaties.* 2 vols. London, 1938.

Loessner, A. "Polen und die sowjetrussisch-französische Verständigung," *Volk und Reich*, XI (1935), 712-18.

Ludat, H. *Polens Stellung in Ostmitteleuropa in Geschichte und Gegenwart.* Berlin, 1939.

Lukacs, J. A. *The Great Powers & Eastern Europe.* New York, 1953.

Łukasiewicz, J. *Polska jest mocarstwem* [Poland Is a Great Power]. Warsaw, 1938.

—— *Polska w Europie w polityce Józefa Piłsudskiego* [Poland in Europe in Józef Piłsudski's Policy]. London, 1944.

—— *Z doświadczeń przeszłości* [From the Experiences of the Past]. Jerusalem, 1943.

Lukasik, S. *Pologne et Roumanie.* Paris, 1938.

Macartney, C. A., and A. W. Palmer. *Independent Eastern Europe: A History.* London, 1962.

Machray, R. *The Poland of Piłsudski.* London, 1936.

—— "Europe's Anti-Soviet Barrier," *Contemporary History*, XXXVII (Dec., 1932), 314-18.

—— "The Policy of Poland," *The Nineteenth Century and After*, CXII (Nov., 1932), 562-72.

Mackiewicz, S. *Colonel Beck and His Policy.* London, 1944.

—— *Historia Polski od 11 listopada 1918 r. do 17 września 1939 r.* [A History of Poland: November 11, 1918, to September 17, 1939]. London, 1941.

—— *Klucz do Piłsudskiego* [The Key to Piłsudski]. London, 1943.

Mainz, K. *Der polnische Aussenhandel.* Berlin, 1935.

Makar, V. "Stril v oboroni mil'ioniv" [A Shot in the Defense of Millions], in *Al'manakh-Kalendar Homonu Ukrainy na 1956 rik* [The Almanac and Calendar of *The Ukrainian Echo* for 1956]. Toronto, 1956. Pp. 145-54.

Makowski, J. *Umowy międzynarodowe Polski, 1919-1934* [Poland's International Agreements, 1919-1934]. Warsaw, 1935.

Makukh, I. *Na narodnii sluzhbi* [In the People's Service]. Detroit, 1958.

Malynski, E. *La Pologne nouvelle.* Paris, 1930.

—— *Les problèmes de l'Est et la Petite-Entente.* Paris, 1931.

Markert, W., ed. *Polen.* Cologne, 1959.

Martynets', V. *Ukrains'ke pidpillia: Vid UVO do OUN* [The Ukrainian Underground: From UVO to OUN]. N.p., 1949.

Matthews, H. P. S. "Poland's Foreign Relations," *The Fortnightly,* CXLIV (Aug., 1938), 162-71.

Montanus, B. *Polish-Soviet Relations in the Light of International Law.* New York, 1944.

Muggeridge, M. "Germany, Russia, and Japan," *The Nineteenth Century and After,* CXV (March, 1934), 281-90.

Nadolny, R. *Mein Beitrag.* Wiesbaden, 1955.

Namier, L. B. *Diplomatic Prelude, 1938-1939.* London, 1948.

—— *Europe in Decay: A Study in Disintegration.* London, 1950.

—— *Facing East.* London, 1947.

Noël, L. *L'agression allemande contre la Pologne: Une ambassade à Varsovie, 1935-1939.* Paris, 1946.

Norwid-Neugebauer, M. *Kampania wrześniowa 1939 w Polsce* [The September Campaign of 1939 in Poland]. London, 1941.

Nowak, R. "Die Zukunft der Karpatenukraine," *Zeitschrift für Geopolitik,* XV (Nov., 1938), 889-99.

Odrowąż-Wysocki, S. *Międzynarodowe stosunki prawne Polski* [The Legal Basis of Poland's International Relations]. Kraków, 1939.

Onacewicz, W. "The Diplomatic and Military Preparation of the Aggression against Poland in 1939." Unpublished Ph.D. dissertation, Georgetown University, 1954.

Orhanizatsiia Ukrains'kykh Natsionalistiv, 1929-1954 [The Organization of Ukrainian Nationalists, 1929-1954]. N.p., 1955.

Paneyko, B. "Germany, Poland and the Ukraine," *The Nineteenth Century and After,* CXXV (Jan., 1939), 34-43.

Papoušek, J. *Czechoslovakia, Soviet Russia and Germany.* Prague, 1936.

Paprocki, S. J., ed. *Minority Affairs and Poland.* Warsaw, 1935.

Paul-Boncour, J. *Entre deux guerres: Souvenirs sur la III République.* Vols. II-III. Paris, 1945-46.

Piłsudska, A. *Wspomnienia* [Memoirs]. London, 1960.

Piwarski, K. *Monachium 1938* [Munich, 1938]. Warsaw, 1952.

—— *Polityka europejska w okresie pomonachijskim, X. 1938–III. 1939* [European Politics during the Post-Munich Period, October, 1938–March, 1939]. Warsaw, 1960.

—— "Układ monachijski 1938 r." [The Munich Agreement of 1938], *Sprawy Międzynarodowe,* II, No. 1/2 (Jan.-June, 1949), 134-201.

Pobóg-Malinowski, W. *Najnowsza historia polityczna Polski, 1864-1945*

[Recent Political History of Poland, 1864-1945]. Vols. II-III. London, 1956-60.

Poland. Polskie Siły Zbrojne. Komisja Historyczna. *Polskie Siły Zbrojne w drugiej wojnie światowej* [Polish Armed Forces in the Second World War]. Vol. I, Part I. London, 1951.

Polish Research Center, London. *Poland and the USSR, 1921-1941*. London, n.d.

Pologne, 1919-1939. 3 vols. Neuchâtel, 1946-47.

Pospelov, P. N., ed. *Istoriia Velikoi Otechestvennoi voiny Sovetskogo Soiuza, 1941-1945* [History of the Great Patriotic War of the Soviet Union, 1941-1945]. Vol. I. Moscow, 1960.

Potemkin, V. P., ed. *Istoriia diplomatii* [A History of Diplomacy]. Vol. III. Moscow, 1945.

Presseisen, E. L. *Germany and Japan: A Study in Totalitarian Diplomacy, 1933-1941*. The Hague, 1958.

Problèmes politiques de la Pologne contemporaine. 4 vols. Paris, 1931-33.

Prokoptschuk, G. *Der Metropolit*. Munich, 1955.

Puacz, E. *Stosunki polsko-sowieckie* [Polish-Soviet Relations]. London, 1943.

Pushas, I. O. *Sovremennaia Pol'sha i SSSR* [Contemporary Poland and the USSR]. Moscow, 1928.

Raczyński, E. *W sojuszniczym Londynie* [In Allied London]. London, 1960.

Rauschning, H. *Hitler Speaks*. London, 1939.

Reddaway, W. F. *Marshal Piłsudski*. London, 1939.

Reeburg, S. "The Antecedents of the Polish Defeat," *Journal of Central European Affairs*, IX (April, 1949), 373-99.

Reguła, J. A. *Historia Komunistycznej Partii Polski w świetle faktów i dokumentów* [History of the Communist Party of Poland in the Light of Facts and Documents]. 2d ed. revised. Warsaw, 1934.

Reynaud, P. *Au coeur de la mêlée, 1930-1945*. Paris, 1951.

—— *La France a sauvé l'Europe*. 2 vols. Paris, 1947.

Rhode, G. "Aussenminister Josef Beck und Staatssekretär Graf Szembek," *Vierteljahrshefte für Zeitgeschichte*, II (Jan., 1954), 86-94.

Ribbentrop, J. *Memoirs*. London, 1954.

Ripka, H. *Munich: Before and After*. London, 1939.

Roberts, H. L. "The Diplomacy of Colonel Beck," in G. A. Craig and F. Gilbert, eds., *The Diplomats, 1919-1939*. Princeton, 1953. Pp. 579-614.

—— "International Relations between the Wars," in C. E. Black, ed., *Challenge in Eastern Europe*. New Brunswick, N.J., 1954. Pp. 179-95.

—— "Maxim Litvinov," in G. A. Craig and F. Gilbert, eds., *The Diplomats, 1919-1939*. Princeton, 1953. Pp. 344-77.

Rómmel, J. *Za Honor i Ojczyznę* [For Honor and Fatherland]. Warsaw, 1958.

Roos, H. *Geschichte der polnischen Nation, 1916-1960*. Stuttgart, 1961.

—— *Polen und Europa: Studien zur polnischen Aussenpolitik, 1931-1939*. Tübingen, 1957.

Rosé, A. C. *La politique polonaise entre les deux guerres*. Neuchâtel, 1944.

Rossi, A. *Le pacte germano-soviétique, l'histoire et le mythe*. Paris, 1954.

—— *The Russo-German Alliance*. London, 1950.

Rozek, E. J. *Allied Wartime Diplomacy: A Pattern in Poland*. New York, 1958.

Schmidt, P. *Hitler's Interpreter*. London, 1951.

Schmitt, B. E., ed. *Poland*. Berkeley, 1945.

Schuman, F. L. *Europe on the Eve: The Crisis of Diplomacy, 1933-1939*. New York, 1939.

—— *Night over Europe: The Diplomacy of Nemesis, 1939-1940*. New York, 1941.

Senn, A. E. "The Polish-Lithuanian War Scare, 1927," *Journal of Central European Affairs*, XXI, No. 3 (Oct., 1961), 267-84.

Seraphim, P. H. *Die Handelspolitik Polens*. Berlin, 1935.

Seton-Watson, H. *Eastern Europe between the Wars, 1918-1941*. Cambridge, 1946.

Seton-Watson, R. W. *From Munich to Danzig*. London, 1939.

Shandor, V. "Carpatho-Ukraine in the International Bargaining of 1918-1939," *The Ukrainian Quarterly*, X (1954), 235-46.

Shandruk, P. *Arms of Valor*. New York, 1959.

Sharp, S. *Poland, White Eagle on a Red Field*. Cambridge, Mass., 1953.

Shotwell, J. T. *The Curzon Line: The Polish-Soviet Dispute*. New York, 1945.

Shotwell, J. T., and M. M. Laserson. *Poland and Russia, 1919-1945*. New York, 1945.

Sieburg, F. *Polen—Legende und Wirklichkeit*. Frankfurt, 1934.

Sikorski, W. *Le problème de la paix: Le jeu des forces politiques en*

Europe orientale et l'alliance franco-polonaise. Paris, 1931.
—— "Poland's Defenses," *The Slavonic and East European Review,* XVII (Jan., 1939), 343-55.
Singer, B. *Od Witosa do Sławka* [From Witos to Sławek]. Paris, 1962.
Skrzyński, A. *Poland and Peace.* London, 1923.
Skrzypek, S. *The Problem of Eastern Galicia.* London, 1948.
Skrzypek, S. T. "The Soviet Elections in Eastern Poland, October 1939." Unpublished Ph.D. dissertation, Fordham University, 1955.
Sławoj-Składkowski, F. *Strzępy meldunków* [Scraps of Reports]. Warsaw, 1936.
Smogorzewski, K. *About the Curzon Line and Other Lines.* London, 1944.
—— "Między zachodem i wschodem: Uwagi o polskiej polityce zagranicznej" [Between West and East: Comments on Polish Foreign Policy], *Przegląd Współczesny* [The Contemporary Review], XVII (1938), 74-94.
—— "Poland and Her Neighbors," *The Slavonic and East European Review,* XVII (July, 1938), 105-20.
—— "Poland: Free, Peaceful, Strong," *Foreign Affairs,* XIII (July, 1935), 647-65.
—— "Polen zwischen Ost und West," *Europäische Revue,* XI (1935), 73-83.
—— "Polish Foreign Policy," *The Contemporary Review,* CLIV (July, 1938), 16-25.
—— "La Pologne entre l'est et l'ouest," *L'Esprit International,* VIII (1934), 351-76.
—— "La Pologne entre l'orient et l'occident," *La Pologne,* XV (1934), 142-51.
—— "La Pologne et l'Union soviétique," *La Pologne,* XV (1934), 321-29.
Sokolow, F. "Poland's Policy," *The Nineteenth Century and After,* CXXV (May, 1939), 534-41.
Staar, R. F. "The Polish Communist Party, 1918-1948," *The Polish Review,* I, No. 2/3 (Spring-Summer, 1956), 41-58.
Stahl, Z. *Polityka polska po śmierci Piłsudskiego* [Polish Policy after Piłsudski's Death]. Lwów, 1936.
Staniewicz, W. *Klęska wrześniowa na tle stosunków międzynarodowych* [The September Defeat in the Setting of International Relations]. Warsaw, 1952.
—— *Wrzesień 1939* [September, 1939]. Warsaw, 1949.
Stanisławska, S. "Stosunek opozycji polskiej do polityki Becka wobec

Czechosłowacji wiosną 1938 roku" [The Attitude of the Polish Op-
position toward Beck's Czechoslovak Policy in the Spring of 1938],
Sprawy Międzynarodowe, XII, No. 11/12 (Nov.-Dec., 1959), 30-67.
Stercho, P. G. "Carpatho-Ukraine in International Affairs, 1938-1939."
Unpublished Ph.D. dissertation, University of Notre Dame, 1959.
Strapiński, A. *Wywrotowe partie polityczne* [The Subversive Political
Parties]. Warsaw, 1933.
Stroński, S. *Polska polityka zagraniczna, 1934-1935* [Polish Foreign
Policy, 1934-1935]. Poznań, 1935.
Strzetelski, S. *Goering poluje na rysie* [Göring Is Hunting Lynxes].
London, 1942.
—— *Where the Storm Broke: Poland from Yesterday to Tomorrow.*
New York, 1942.
Studnicki, W. *Irrwege in Polen: Ein Kampf um die polnisch-deutsche
Annäherung.* Göttingen, 1951.
—— *Kwestia Czechosłowacji a racja stanu Polski* [The Czechoslovak
Question and the Polish *Raison d'État*]. 2d ed. revised. Warsaw,
1938.
—— *System polityczny Europy a Polska* [The Political System of
Europe and Poland]. Warsaw, 1934.
—— *Wobec nadchodzącej drugiej wojny światowej* [Before the Ap-
proach of the Second World War]. Warsaw, 1939.
—— "Die polnisch-sowjetrussischen Beziehungen," *Volk und Reich,*
XII (1936), 829-58.
Survey of International Affairs. 1920-46. London, 1925-58.
Symmons-Symonolewicz, K. "Polish Political Thought and the Prob-
lem of the Eastern Borderlands of Poland (1918-1939)," *The Polish
Review,* IV, No. 1/2 (Winter-Spring, 1959), 65-81.
Szembek, J. *Journal, 1933-1939.* Paris, 1951.
Szymański, A. *Zły sąsiad* [A Bad Neighbor]. London, 1959.
Taracouzio, T. A. *The Soviet Union and International Law.* New
York, 1935.
—— *War and Peace in Soviet Diplomacy.* New York, 1940.
Tarnowski, A. "Poland's Foreign Policy," *The Contemporary Review,*
CXLV (March, 1934), 296-305.
Tarulis, A. N. *Soviet Policy toward the Baltic States, 1918-1940.* Notre
Dame, Ind., 1959.
Taylor, A. J. P. *The Origins of the Second World War.* London, 1961.
Tikhomirov, M. N. *Vneshniaia politika Sovetskogo Soiuza* [Foreign
Policy of the Soviet Union]. Moscow, 1940.
Trukhanovskii, V. G., ed. *Istoriia mezhdunarodnykh otnoshenii i*

vneshnei politiki SSSR, 1917-1960 gg. [History of International Relations and Foreign Policy of the USSR, 1917-1960]. Vol. I. Moscow, 1961.

Umiastowski, R. *Russia and the Polish Republic, 1918-1941.* London, n.d.

Union of Soviet Socialist Republics. Sovetskoe Informatsionnoe Biuro. *Falsifiers of History.* Moscow, 1948.

Urbański, Z. *Mniejszości narodowe w Polsce* [The National Minorities in Poland]. Warsaw, 1932.

Vakar, N. P. *Belorussia: The Making of a Nation.* Cambridge, Mass., 1956.

Vashchenko, H. " 'Vyzvolennia' Zakhidn'oi Ukrainy bol'shevykamy: Ofitsiini dokumenty i diisnist' " [The Bolshevik "Liberation" of the Western Ukraine: Official Documents and Facts], *Ukrains'kyi Zbirnyk* [Ukrainian Review], Munich, I (Dec., 1954), 67-77.

Vietz, K. *Verrat an Europa.* Berlin, 1938.

Vnuk, F. "Munich and the Soviet Union," *Journal of Central European Affairs,* XXI, No. 3 (Oct., 1961), 285-304.

Voigt, F. A. *Poland's Position in Central Europe.* Birkenhead, 1943.

Vondracek, F. J. *The Foreign Policy of Czechoslovakia, 1918-1935.* New York, 1937.

Wahl, G. E. *Zwei Gegner im Osten: Polen als Widersacher Russlands.* Dortmund, 1939.

Walckiers, J. *L'U.R.S.S. et la Pologne.* Brussels, 1945.

Wandycz, P. S. *France and Her Eastern Allies, 1919-1925: French-Czechoslovak-Polish Relations from the Paris Peace Conference to Locarno.* Minneapolis, 1962.

Wanklyn, H. G. *The Eastern Marchlands of Europe.* London, 1941.

Wasilewski, L. *Kwestia ukraińska jako zagadnienie międzynarodowe* [The Ukrainian Question as an International Problem]. Warsaw, 1934.

Wasiutyński, W. *Między III Rzeszą i III Rusią* [Between the Third Reich and the Third Russia]. Warsaw, 1939.

Weinberg, G. L. *Germany and the Soviet Union, 1939-1941.* Leiden, 1954.

—— "Die geheimen Abkommen zum Antikominternpakt," *Vierteljahrshefte für Zeitgeschichte,* II (April, 1954), 193-201.

Weizsäcker, E. *Memoirs.* Chicago, 1951.

Weyers, J. *Poland and Russia.* 2d ed. London, 1944.

Wheeler-Bennett, J. W. *Munich: Prologue to Tragedy.* London, 1948.

—— "From Brest-Litovsk to Brest-Litovsk," *Foreign Affairs,* XVIII (Jan., 1940), 196-210.

—— "Twenty Years of Russo-German Relations, 1919-1939," *Foreign Affairs,* XXV (Oct., 1946), 23-43.

White, D. F. *The Growth of the Red Army.* Princeton, 1944.

Wielhorski, W. *The Importance of the Polish Eastern Provinces for the Polish Republic.* Glasgow, 1943.

—— *Polska a Litwa* [Poland and Lithuania]. London, 1947.

Winiewicz, J. "Doświadczenie polsko-niemieckie w latach 1918-1939" [The Experience of Polish-German Relations, 1918-1939], *Sprawy Międzynarodowe,* XII, No. 7/8 (July-Aug., 1959), 3-22.

Wojciechowski, Z. *Droga Niemiec do Rosji* [Germany's Way to Russia]. Warsaw, 1937.

—— *Między Niemcami i Rosją* [Between Germany and Russia]. Poznań, 1938.

—— *Niemiecka polityka wschodnia* [German Eastern Policy]. Warsaw, 1937.

Wojciechowski, Z., ed. *Poland's Place in Europe.* Poznań, 1946.

Wojtecki, A. *Sprawa Europy środkowej* [The Question of Central Europe]. Warsaw, 1939.

Wolski, A. "Pakt polsko-niemiecki z 1934 r." [The Polish-German Pact of 1934], *Sprawy Międzynarodowe,* VI, No. 6 (Nov.-Dec., 1953), 64-77.

Wraga, R. *Geopolityka, strategia i granice* [Geopolitics, Strategy, and Frontiers]. Tel Aviv, 1943.

Yakemtchouk, R. *La Ligne Curzon et la IIe guerre mondiale.* Louvain, 1957.

Yakhontoff, V. A. *USSR Foreign Policy.* New York, 1945.

Załuski, Z. *Przepustka do historii* [A Pass to History]. Warsaw, 1961.

Zawadzki, F., and Z. Klimpel. *Z problemów współczesnej polityki zagranicznej* [Some Problems of Contemporary Foreign Policy]. Warsaw, 1939.

Zay, J. *Carnets secrets: De Munich à la guerre.* Paris, 1942.

Zbierański, C. *Granice Polski a imperializm Rosji* [Poland's Frontiers and Russian Imperialism]. Toronto, 1944.

Zimmermann, L. *Deutsche Aussenpolitik in der Ära der Weimarer Republik.* Göttingen, 1958.

Żółtowski, A. *Border of Europe: A Study of the Polish Eastern Provinces.* London, 1950.

—— *Germany, Russia and Central Europe.* London, 1942.

Zweig, F. *Poland between Two Wars: A Critical Study of Social and Economic Changes.* London, 1944.

III. NEWSPAPERS AND PERIODICALS

Bil'shovyk Ukrainy [The Bolshevik of the Ukraine]. Kharkov-Kiev, 1930-39.

Bol'shevik [The Bolshevik]. Moscow, 1932-39.

Bulletin of International News. London, 1928-39.

The Central European Observer. Prague, 1931-38.

The Communist International. London and New York, 1930-39.

Czas [Time]. Kraków, Oct., 1936–Aug., 1939.

International Press Correspondence. Berlin-London, 1930-38.

Izvestiia [News]. Moscow, 1931-39.

Keesing's Contemporary Archives. London, 1931-39.

Kommunisticheskii Internatsional [The Communist International]. Petrograd-Moscow, 1919-39.

Kultura [Culture]. Rome-Paris, 1947-61.

Kurjer Warszawski [The Warsaw Courier]. Jan., 1931–Jan., 1938.

Mirovoe khoziaistvo i mirovaia politika [World Economy and World Politics]. Moscow, 1931-39.

Le Monde Slave. Paris, 1924-38.

Moscow News. 1932-39.

News Digest. London, 1934-39.

The New York Times. 1930-39.

Niepodległość [Independence]. London, 1950-58.

Osteuropa. Königsberg, 1925-39.

Pravda [Truth]. Moscow, 1931-39.

Prométhée. Paris, 1926-38.

Przegląd Wschodni [The Eastern Review]. Warsaw, 1932-35.

Les Questions Minoritaires. Warsaw, 1928-37.

Le Revue de Prométhée. Paris, 1938-39.

Sprawy Narodowościowe [Problems of National Minorities]. Warsaw, 1927-39.

Sprawy Obce [Foreign Affairs]. Warsaw, 1929-31.

The Times. London, 1931-39.

Tryzub [The Trident]. Paris, 1931-39.

Wiadomości [News]. London, 1948-61.

World News and Views. London, 1938-39.

Wschód-Orient. Warsaw, 1935-39.

Index